Postelection Conflict Management in Nigeria

The Challenges of National Unity

John N. Paden

WITHDRAWN
UTSA LIBRARIES

Monograph Series
School for Conflict Analysis and Resolution
George Mason University

GEORGE
MASON
UNIVERSITY | School for Conflict Analysis
and Resolution

This is School for Conflict Analysis and Resolution Monograph Series, Volume 1.

The views expressed in this report are those of the author alone. They do not necessarily reflect views of the School for Conflict Analysis and Resolution, George Mason University.

School for Conflict Analysis and Resolution
George Mason University
3330 Washington Boulevard
Arlington, Virginia 22201
USA

First published in 2012.

Printed in the United States of America.

The paper used in this publication meets the minimum requirements of American National Standards for Information Science—Permanence of Paper for Printed Library Materials, ANSI Z39.48-1984.

ISBN 978-0-9850966-0-1 (pbk.: alk. paper), ISBN 978-0-9850966-1-8 (pdf)

Library of Congress Control Number: 2012932052

This monograph is dedicated to the unity of Nigeria

Contents

Foreword

Tijjani Muhammad-Bande
Acting Director-General
National Institute for Policy and Strategic Studies
Kuru, Nigeria

This timely monograph seeks to advance our appreciation of both the obstacles to and the promise of national unity in Nigeria. This study is written by Professor John Paden, one of the most highly regarded scholars of Nigeria in particular and Africa in general, and is published under the auspices of one of the world's leading academic institutions devoted to conflict resolution. It is a well-researched and superbly written piece, full of rare insights and wisdom. I doubt if any reader, Nigerian or other, can read it without marveling at both its fine scholarship and its judicious recommendations for strengthening Nigeria's unity during the current difficulties and into the future.

Unity has been Nigeria's major preoccupation since it gained independence in 1960. The search for a stronger and more enduring union has taken the Nigerian federation through several constitutions and inspired numerous political and administrative devices. Questions of unity and secession also provoked a brutal civil war that lasted from 1967 to 1970. Despite the success of the post–civil war process of reconciliation, reintegration, and reconstruction, the country has continued to experience moments of intense worry. Many analysts agree that the nauseating sight of inequality and poverty amid plenty, together with government incompetence and corruption, lies at the center of Nigeria's crises of unity and development. Tensions and misunderstandings over religion, regionalism, ethnicity, and other forms of identity are also heavily implicated in the various violent conflicts in contemporary Nigeria. The quality of leadership at all levels in the country is critical to how well the challenges are tackled.

While this monograph provides a general background to contemporary Nigerian politics and society, the author's main focus is on developments between January and December 2011, especially in northern Nigeria. This period witnessed postelection violence in Kaduna State, festering ethnoreligious violence in Jos (Plateau State), and the escalation of violence by the Boko Haram extremist group in northeast Nigeria.

Combined, these have led to the loss of several thousand lives, in addition to widespread destruction of properties and livelihoods. The potential for these conflicts spilling over into other parts of the country and neighboring countries is great. In reviewing and reflecting on these worrying developments, the author argues that strategic decisions by policymakers and implementers need to be made around a number of issues. These include granting substantial powers over policing and security to local levels of government; reviewing educational curricular policies; making massive improvements in youth education and employment; seeking judicial pronouncements in favor of national unity; raising the quality of leadership; implementing recommendations issued by panels, tribunals, and commissions of inquiry that have analyzed Nigeria's major conflicts; and mustering the necessary political will to do what is required, through democratic means, to strengthen national unity. The author's basic assumption is that there is neither the need to dismember the union nor a neat way of doing so. There is, however, a pressing need to build a more just, inclusive, and productive Nigeria able to cater to the needs of all its citizens. Some Nigerians and friends of Nigeria might disagree with some of the details of the author's comprehensive recommendations, but very few would criticize the general direction the author proposes or his emphases on policy issues.

I should mention that, in relation to the ongoing search for peace and development in Nigeria, I am one of the many beneficiaries of the author's generosity. I have learned from him (and others) the value of commitment to public service, broadly conceived. He has also facilitated my signing, at different times, memoranda of understanding between, on the one side, George Mason University (GMU) and, on the other side, both the Usmanu Danfodiyo University, Sokoto (UDUS), and the National Institute for Policy and Strategic Studies (NIPSS), Kuru. The understanding between GMU and UDUS gave the latter invaluable support in the establishment of its Centre for Peace Studies. At NIPSS, responding to the president of Nigeria's call for the Institute to work harder at finding solutions to the violent conflicts in Nigeria, I looked toward GMU's world-famous School for Conflict Analysis and Resolution for partnership. We signed a memorandum of understanding that involved mutual support and assistance in research, publication, and training and in the exchange of scholars and advocacy for peace. This partnership reflects the multifaceted nature of NIPSS, which is not only a government think tank but also a policy research center and a leadership training center. NIPSS, Nigeria's foremost institute, has advised the Nigerian government for more than thirty-three years on possible solutions to an array of Nigerian problems. Peace and development have been at the center of the goals of successive Nigerian governments, though progress toward those goals has varied from regime to regime.

It is appropriate for NIPSS to be associated with this publication. For me personally, it is a great honor and a privilege. The author is my teacher, mentor, and friend and, in the true Nigerian tradition, an "uncle." I am certain that many will profit from his astute analysis and wise recommendations.

Preface and Acknowledgments

Academic books often take years to produce and scholarly researchers may wait until a conflict is resolved before assessing its causes and consequences. By contrast, those engaged in conflict mediation and/or resolution must try to assess complex factors and possible solutions in the midst of extreme trauma. This requires reflexive interaction between theory and practice. With this in mind, George Mason University's School for Conflict Analysis and Resolution (S-CAR) has established a monograph series of case studies, each of which is essentially a work in progress—in other words, it can be updated at a later point and assessed for its contribution to constructive outcomes.

Well into the writing of this monograph, S-CAR entered into a working relationship with Nigeria's National Institute for Policy and Strategic Studies (NIPSS). In part, this relationship was based on our extensive relationship with the Center for Peace Studies at the Usmanu Danfodiyo University, Sokoto (UDUS), a relationship that began in 2008 under its then vice chancellor, Professor Tijjani Bande. NIPSS's mandate includes academic input into the long-term thinking about basic Nigerian challenges such as national unity. The NIPSS/S-CAR linkage is based solely on intellectual exchanges and does not involve any contracts or financial arrangements. (See appendix C for the abbreviated text of the agreement between GMU and NIPSS.) Any suggestions or recommendations contained in this monograph, however, are solely those of the author and not those of S-CAR or NIPSS.

This monograph is written as an extended essay, reflecting the views and opinions of the author. It draws on more than four decades of research on, teaching about, and engagement with Nigeria. Although the draft manuscript has been read by and discussed with many colleagues, both in the West and in Nigeria, they are in no way responsible for the content. Footnotes and extensive media references are intended to provide a sense of "voice" to the very lively debates in Nigeria on the issues under consideration. All sources are publicly accessible. The author does not have access to classified information, although the federal or state governments in Nigeria sometimes leak summaries of official documents to the Nigerian media.

I would like to thank several North American colleagues who have read portions of the manuscript and made useful suggestions, especially John Campbell (Council on Foreign Relations), David Smock (United States Institute of Peace), William Miles (Northeastern University), Paul Lubeck (University of California at Santa Cruz), Eric Guttschuss (Human Rights Watch), and Pauline Baker (formerly President, Fund for Peace). My colleagues at S/CAR—especially Andrea Bartoli, Kevin Avruch, and Terrence Lyons—have been most encouraging in the process of setting up this monograph series for use by our graduate students and others.

On the Nigerian side, numerous friends and colleagues have encouraged my research and teaching over the years. I am especially grateful to my many academic colleagues, including Ahmad Abubakar, Tijjani Bande, Muhammad Junaid, Tukur Baba, Paul Izah, Haruna Sanusi, Hamid Bobboyi, and Attahiru Jega. To them I give a heartfelt *Na gode!*

(In the interest of full disclosure, I should note that the chair of the Independent National Electoral Commission, Professor Attahiru Jega, was the author's doctoral student at Northwestern University and is a longtime friend and colleague. While every effort has been made by the author to be balanced in an assessment of the 2011 elections and their aftermath, the chairmanship of Professor Jega was clearly an outstanding contribution. The administration of the election set a new high level in Nigerian elections, despite the inevitable political cross-pressures, regulatory loopholes, and advantages of incumbency.)

On the home front, I could not have continued my writing over the years without the support of Denise Napoliello (Robinson Professor Coordinator) and my wife, Dr. Xiaohong Liu. I would also like to thank Provost Peter Stearns, who is a model of a scholar-cum-administrator, and who granted me a leave of absence during fall semester 2011 to complete this monograph. Finally, Nigel Quinney has served as a wonderful editor and adviser in the final stages of this project.

Postelection Conflict Management in Nigeria

Introduction

This monograph focuses on Nigeria in 2011, a year that may go down in history as a tipping point on issues of elections and national unity, as well as on the capacity of governments to deal with religious extremism and ethnoreligious violence. The question that lies at the heart of this study is whether or not various forms of conflict management, mitigation, and resolution can be put into place to avoid an existential challenge to the stability of Nigeria.

The Challenges: Election Violence, Extremism, and Ethnoreligious Crises

In January 2011, Nigeria's dominant political party violated its own charter by ignoring the regional "power shift" principle during the party's nominating convention. (According to this principle, the candidate selected by the party to run for president alternates between a person from the northern region of the country and a person from the southern region.) The nominating convention in January marked the beginning of the buildup to the April presidential election, which witnessed a southern Christian incumbent facing off against a northern Muslim challenger. The violence that occurred in the wake of the election was the worst seen in Nigeria since the civil war of 1967–70. The losing candidate contested the outcome via the courts, but an election appeals verdict in favor of the incumbent was rendered in early November. The final confirmation of the election results was given by the Supreme Court on December 28.

The backdrop to the Supreme Court's decision was provided by the extremist group Boko Haram, which undertook a series of Christmas Day bombings of Christian churches near the capital city of Abuja and in the city of Jos in Nigeria's Middle Belt. Meanwhile, confrontations between Boko Haram and the police in Yobe and Borno states in the northeast left dozens dead and hundreds wounded. Nigerian Muslim leaders ranging from the sultan of Sokoto to Sufi leaders condemned the bombings as "un-Islamic." "I want to assure all Nigerians," said the sultan, "that there is no conflict between Muslims and Christians, between Islam and Christianity."[1]

The de facto leader of the political opposition, Muhammadu Buhari, condemned the killings and decried the government of Goodluck Jonathan as "incompetent." Conspiracy theories began to abound as to who would benefit from a potential breakup of Nigeria. The country was on a knife's edge in terms of ethnoreligious tension. In the north, there was widespread fear, anger, and a sense of hopelessness. The year 2011 was ending in northern Nigeria not with a whimper but with a bang.

This year-end volatile mix was reinforced by the decision by the Nigerian Supreme Court to reject the appeal of the major opposition party, the Congress for Progressive Change (CPC), regarding irregularities in the presidential election of April. The CPC presidential contender, Buhari, concerned about the general breakdown of law and order, predicted chaos.[2]

The final political event of 2011 was the declaration of a state of emergency in parts of four northern states by President Jonathan on December 31, and the closing of sections of the borders with Niger, Chad, and Cameroon.[3] "Fellow Nigerians," said the president,

> it has become necessary to address you on recent events in some parts of the country that have threatened our collective security and shaken the foundations of our corporate existence as a nation. You are all aware of the security challenges which the activities of the Boko Haram sect have foisted on the country. What began as sectarian crises in the North Eastern parts of the country has gradually evolved into terrorist activities in different parts of the country with attendant negative conse-

---

1   "Christmas Day Bombings: Sultan, Jonathan Move to Douse Tension," *Daily Trust*, December 28, 2011.

2   "Buhari: Chaos Looms," *Daily Trust*, December 29, 2011: "Former head of state Muhammadu Buhari yesterday said the country is sliding into total breakdown of law and order because of injustice, bad governance and 'massive and mindless' stealing of public resources. In a bluntly worded statement he personally signed, in reaction to the Supreme Court judgment dismissing his party's petition against the presidential election, General Buhari said Nigeria was 'now a fractured society, corruption everywhere, violence everywhere, a sense of helplessness and hopelessness nearly everywhere.' He said unless the leaders of the country move fast to arrest the situation, chaos would set in and there would be breakdown of law and order. But he said it does not look like the leaders are concerned with the grave situation, as while 'the country is sliding into this chaotic state, PDP governments at the centre and in the states are engaged in massive and mindless plunder of the country's resources in total disregard of the suffering masses. The country is now in an emergency situation. Law and order can break down at any time.'"

3   "Boko Haram: Read Jonathan's Declaration of State of Emergency Address!" *Vanguard*, December 31, 2011.

quences on our national security. Government, in an effort to find a lasting solution to the security threats occasioned by the activities of the Boko Haram sect, constituted a Presidential Committee under the Chairmanship of Ambassador Usman Gaji Galtimari, to ascertain the immediate and remote causes of the crises. While efforts are being made to implement the recommendations of the Committee, the crises have assumed a terrorist dimension with vital institutions of government including the United Nations Building and places of worship becoming targets of terrorist attacks. While the search for lasting solutions is ongoing, it has become imperative to take some decisive measures necessary to restore normalcy in the country especially with the affected communities. Consequently, I have in the exercise of the powers conferred on me by the provisions of section 305 (1) of the Constitution, declared a state of emergency in the following parts of the federation, namely (i) Borno State . . . (ii) Yobe State . . . (iii) Plateau State . . . (iv) Niger State (Suleja LGA). . . .

Let me assure our neighbors, especially within the ECOWAS sub-region, of Nigeria's commitment to its international obligations as provided by the ECOWAS Protocol on Free Movement of Persons. The temporary closure of our borders in the affected areas is only an interim measure designed to address the current security challenges and will be reviewed as soon as normalcy is restored. I commend the efforts of our political leaders at various levels as well as our traditional and religious leaders for their support for the various conflict resolution mechanisms and peace building measures that have been initiated by this administration. We call on the citizenry to continue to provide useful information to our law enforcement agencies to enable us to arrest the situation. Terrorism is a war against all of us. I call on all Nigerians to join hands with government to fight these terrorists.

In addition, President Jonathan raised the issue of drawing on foreign resources in the war on terror.[4] On December 31, he also declared the removal of fuel subsidies, which immediately doubled the price of petroleum at the pump and sparked waves of demonstrations and riots throughout the country.

The presence of the military (rather than the police) was evident everywhere in the north, especially at the numerous roadblocks. National

---

4 "Presidency Weighs Foreign Intervention in Terror War," *Guardian*, December 30, 2011.

Security Adviser General (ret.) Andrew Azazi (and his antiterrorism team) was increasingly visible as the key adviser to the president.[5] The proposed 2012 national security budget increased by orders of magnitude and would consume a projected one-fifth of the entire national budget. The impending retirement of the inspector general of police, Hafiz Ringim, led to speculation as to his successor and raised issues concerning "federal character"—that is, the attempt to represent all parts of the country equally—and regional balance between north and south.[6]

None of this daunted Boro Hakam, however, which responded to the state of emergency by threatening all Christians in the north and giving those who were originally from the south three days to return to the south or face death. Bombings and killings continued throughout the northeast.[7]

If we look back on 2011, the perceived marginalization of the Muslim far north, the rise of extremist fringe movements,[8] and the continuing

---

5   Late in 2011, Azazi set up an antiterrorism unit, headed by Sarkin Yaki Bello, originally from Sokoto. Bello had served as defense attaché in Washington, D.C., and as the head of the Joint Task Force in the Niger Delta. Although Bello is generally recognized as competent, and certainly knows the north, it will probably take months, if not years, to set up an effective organization under the national security adviser.

6   "Boko Haram Fallout: Battle for Next IGP Hots Up," *Vanguard*, December 31, 2011: "Aftermath of the Xmas day Boko Haram bombings and signals emanating from Aso Rock indicate that security chiefs would be changed by early next year. With the impending retirement of the Inspector General of Police in February after 35 years in service, the Deputy Inspectors General of Police have embarked on fight to the finish moves towards getting the nod to succeed Mr. Hafiz Abubakar Ringim. Towards this end, Sunday Vanguard gathered that the DIGs and some AIGs have employed the services of Islamic marabouts from as far as Sudan and Niger for special sacrifices and prayers, while the non-Muslims among them have recruited prayer warriors to embark on fasting and continuous intercession on their behalf. Aside the resort to marabouts and prayer warriors towards getting the exalted position of the IGP when Mr. Ringim retires, many of the senior officers are said to have been trying to curry the favour of those perceived as power brokers including emirs and traditional rulers, some members of the economic team and politicians believed to be close to president Jonathan."

7   It is beyond the scope of this monograph to follow Boko Haram developments in 2012. Suffice it to say that the bombings and conflicts have continued. See "Nigeria: Militant Leader Pledges Bombing Campaign," *New York Times*, January 28, 2012: "The leader of a militant Islamist sect has rejected offers for a negotiated peace and promised to kidnap government officials' family members and bomb schools, according to an Internet audio message. The recording, believed to have been made by Abubakar Shekau, said the goal of the sect, Boko Haram, was the adoption of Islam across Nigeria, whose population is split roughly equally between Christians and Muslims. If Nigerian security forces attack any Muslim places of worship, he said, 'you have primary schools as well, you have secondary schools and universities and we will start bombing them,' he said. 'Touch us and see. That is what we will do.' The sect attacked the northern city of Kano last week, killing 185 people, and has killed hundreds of other Nigerians in the past year." "Abubakar Shekau" is obviously a nom de guerre, and although he has appeared on social media sites, fully armed, it is not clear if he is "the leader" of Boko Haram.

8   The number of persons killed in northern Nigeria on all sides of the Boko Haram clashes between 2009 and the end of 2011 is well over one thousand. The international dimensions of this extremist group have prompted some U.S. political bodies to define it as a threat to the United

festering of ethnoreligious killings in the Middle Belt[9] together under-mined the numerous efforts at economic development and political sta-bility. At issue was clearly the need for longer-term policy and strategy, both in Nigeria and in the international community.

Nigeria in the Larger Context

One of the major global challenges of the twenty-first century will be to establish a harmonious relationship between the Muslim world and the Western world. Nigeria is by far the largest country in the world that is about half Muslim and half Christian, and Nigeria will be an important bellwether of the sociocultural relationship between the two religions. (See maps 1 ["Islam in Africa"] and 2 ["The Sokoto Caliphate"] in appen-dix A.) In addition, Nigeria has one of the largest Sunni Muslim popula-tions in the world, a population that historically has been moderate and on friendly terms with the Western world.[10] Since 9/11, Nigeria has been fully cooperative in the war on extremism, primarily on matters concern-ing the African continent.

Nigeria is also of global interest because it has evolved the largest and one of the most vibrant democratic experiments in Africa.[11] Histori-cally, it has swung back and forth between civilian and military regimes, but since 1999 the Fourth Republic has been based on a U.S. presiden-tial model with democratic elections and a functioning federal system. Nigeria is also a major oil and gas producer, which has resulted in a sharp division between haves and have-nots and has created the potential for conflict and instability.

All told, it is little wonder that Nigeria is a top U.S. policy priority in Africa. It is also the key leader-by-example among the developing coun-tries of Africa on many fronts. The central political question for Nigeria since winning independence in 1960 has always been its "national unity," a phrase that has acquired mantric status in the country's political dis-

---

States. See U.S. House of Representatives Committee on Homeland Security, Subcommittee on Counterterrorism and Intelligence, *Boko Haram: Emerging Threat to U.S. Homeland,* a report issued on November 30, 2011. The group was described by the panel as "an emerging threat to U.S. interests and the U.S. homeland." The panel called for the United States to "work more closely with Nigerian security forces to develop greater intelligence collection and sharing with the U.S. intelligence community." (See chapter 2 for discussion of Boko Haram.)

9 The number of persons killed in ethnoreligious violence in Plateau State since 1999 is in the thousands. (See chapter 3.)

10 With tensions growing between (Shi'ite) Iran and the West, the profile of the broader Sunni world is clearly a matter of U.S. foreign policy concern.

11 With 160 million people, Nigeria is twice as populous as Egypt and has three times as many people as South Africa.

course.[12] Any attempt to break up Nigeria would have the most serious implications for Africa and the broader world.

Yet, the presidential election in Nigeria on April 16, 2011, split the country along religious and regional lines and produced a violent postelection rampage. (See maps 3 ["Unification of Nigeria, 1914"] and 4 ["Ethnic Distribution in Nigeria"] in appendix A.) A report issued by Human Rights Watch (HRW) in May 2011 estimates that at least eight hundred people were killed and thousands displaced, although the numbers are certainly higher.[13] The HRW report states bluntly: "The presidential election divided the country along ethnic and religious lines."[14]

This sectarian postelection violence did not appear out of the blue, although it was overwhelmingly spontaneous. The U.S. Commission on International Religious Freedom (USCIRF), in its *Annual Report 2011* (issued prior to the election), chronicles a long history of ethnoreligious violence, especially in the Middle Belt, and has designated Nigeria as a "country of particular concern"—a warning flag to the U.S. Congress and the international community.[15] (See map 5 ["Contemporary Nigeria"] in appendix A.)

After the election, the Catholic vicar general of Kaduna Archdiocese, Monsignor Mathew Kukah, one of the wisest contributors to national unity in Nigeria (and who has since become bishop of Sokoto), said that "the results of the April general elections indicated that the country was drifting towards regional politics to the detriment of national unity." The *Daily Trust*, an influential newspaper published in the north of the

---

12   The national unity issue has been a central concern of the author over the years. This monograph is dedicated to the unity of Nigeria. Likewise, two of the author's previous books have been dedicated to the unity of Nigeria. See *Ahmadu Bello, Sardauna of Sokoto: Values and Leadership in Nigeria* (London: Hodder and Stoughton, 1986); and *Faith and Politics in Nigeria: Nigeria as a Pivotal State in the Muslim World* (Washington, D.C.: United States Institute of Peace, 2008).

13   Human Rights Watch, *Nigeria: Post-election Violence Killed 800: Promptly Prosecute Offenders, Address Underlying Causes*, May 16, 2011. The Sheikh Lemu Presidential Commission on 2011 Election Violence and Civil Disturbances reported to the government in September 2011, but as of December, the report had not been made public. Nigerian press reports, based on interviews with Lemu panelists, put the number killed in Kaduna State alone in the "thousands." (See chapter 1.) This is almost certainly too high for Kaduna State, but all sources indicate that the number of deaths in all states is probably above eight hundred. The concern in this monograph is not with the precise numbers of killings but with the overall magnitude, which is astonishingly high.

14   Human Rights Watch, *Nigeria: Post-election Violence Killed 800*. Human Rights Watch photographs of postelection violence in northern Nigeria can be seen at http://www.hrw.org/en/features/post-election-violence-northern-nigeria.

15   U.S. Commission on International Religious Freedom, *Annual Report, 2011* (Washington, D.C., 2011).

country, reported that "he called on the political leaders to work towards redressing ethnic and religious issues before they degenerate into an unpleasant scenario."[16]

Could Nigeria be drifting toward the same situation found in Ivory Coast and pre-secession Sudan—northern Muslims vs. southern Christians?[17] Had the international community been fixated on the process of the elections rather than on the patterns of election results, missing the larger issue of national unity?

Postelection violence has plagued other African countries, often along ethnic and/or regional lines. The Democratic Republic of Congo, for instance, witnessed violence after its election of November 28, 2011, the second election held in the country since the end of a civil war that left millions dead.[18] The International Criminal Court (ICC) is involved in numerous instances.[19] The Kenya case is pending, and has drawn attention because of Kenya's delicate ethnic balance and the possible political consequences of ICC intervention.[20] Even Nigeria is under "preliminary investigation."[21]

The elections in Nigeria in 1964 and 1965 split the country along regional lines and plunged it into one of the worst civil wars in African history, with approximately two million dead (most from famine and resultant diseases.)[22] Much of the postwar effort in Nigeria was focused

---

16 *Daily Trust*, May 20, 2011.

17 For discussion of the "road to Juba" scenario for Nigeria, see Conclusion. Whatever positive benefits might accrue to South Sudan would not likely be duplicated in Nigeria, where it is more likely that a whole series of zonal fractures would occur.

18 "Congo's Election: That Sinking Feeling," *Economist*, November 26, 2011. See also "Two Self-Declared Leaders Help Keep Congo on Edge," *New York Times*, December 11, 2011: "The declaration of Mr. Kabila's victory has been rejected by the man who finished second, Etienne Tshisekedi, a veteran opposition leader. He has a strong hold on the streets of this teeming downtrodden capital of nearly 10 million people."

19 See "International Justice: Cosy Club or Sword of Righteousness?" *Economist*, November 26, 2011: "All 26 of the suspects publicly indicted by the court have been African; of those in the court's custody, four are Congolese and one a Rwandan wanted for crimes in Congo. . . . If the court is making a difference anywhere, it should be in the broad zone of conflict that straddles Congo, Rwanda, Uganda and the Central African Republic."

20 Ibid.: "The ICC has one notable chance to prove its worth—in Kenya. . . . The fighting broke out in the Rift Valley and across Kenya after a disputed election in 2007. . . . During the violence of 2007–08, most of the killing around Eldoret was Kalenjin on Kikuyu; in other parts of Kenya it was the other way around. In all, at least 1,100 people were slain and more than 300,000 displaced; the country was not far from all-out civil war."

21 Ibid.: "The list of places where the court says it is carrying out preliminary investigations [includes] Guinea and Nigeria." For details, see "ICC to Investigate Jos Killings," *Thisday*, December 17, 2011.

22 The author was witness to the elections of 1964–65 and the resultant civil war while undertak-

on devising mechanisms so that "never again" would such trauma occur. But has a younger generation of Nigerian leaders neglected the national unity lessons of their elders?

Organization of This Monograph

This monograph is divided into four chapters that focus on key matters of policy and strategy, both for Nigeria and for the international community.

The first chapter examines the impact of the presidential election of 2011 on conflict. It provides a brief overview of the Nigerian context and the lead-up to the election; it describes international and official Nigerian responses to the election and examines postelection issues and allegations; it discusses long-term consequences for elections and national unity and surveys conflict management in Nigeria; it assesses the aftermath to the election review process; and it distills lessons learned. (See maps 6 ["Nigerian States with Shari'a Law, 2000–Present"] and 7 ["Presidential Election Results, 2011"] in appendix A.)

The second chapter deals with strategic responses to the Boko Haram extremist movement in northern Nigeria, including suggested policy reforms. It begins by looking at Boko Haram and human security in Borno, and then discusses a variety of potential reforms, including reform of local government, of the role of traditional leaders of police services, of education, of national leadership, of military strategy, and of capacities for strategic planning. (See map 8 ["Lake Chad Basin"] in appendix A.)

The third chapter deals with the ethnoreligious crises in Plateau State. It examines the Plateau context; patterns of conflict from 1999 through 2011; Plateau governors and conflict mitigation in the same period; postelection violence in Plateau State in April 2011 and beyond; and possibilities for conflict management in Plateau State.

The fourth chapter explores postelection challenges to national unity. It focuses on the range of challenges; the range of responses; constitutional challenges and possible responses; the role of the police and military; and conflict management and resolution.

---

ing research in Kano. The death of the former secessionist (Biafran) leader, General Ojukwu, in November 2011, may be used by some adherents to strengthen renewed claims for secession, while others (especially in the north) use it to emphasize Ojukwu's later attempts to integrate the southeast area back into Nigeria.

The concluding chapter examines analytical factors in conflict management; confidence-building measures in conflict mitigation; longer-term policies and strategies for conflict mitigation; the challenges of implementation; and conflict resolution and national unity in Nigeria.

A Case Study in Conflict Analysis and Resolution

The monograph is intended for a variety of audiences, including policymakers and policy analysts in the United States and other concerned members of the international community, as well as practitioners of conflict resolution throughout Africa and beyond. Another main audience consists of colleagues and students in the field of conflict analysis and resolution, especially those engaged in reflexive practice. It may also be useful for those with a focus on democratic theory and practice, including the unintended consequences of elections. Others may also find it helpful: public policy specialists, both international and domestic, who often need reminding of the cultural contexts of policies and strategic visions; those interested in religion and politics; those focused on the interplay between international and domestic "global" issues; and the general Western reader interested in Africa and/or the Islamic world.

The monograph does not presume to intrude on Nigerian politics or on the efforts of Nigerian scholars and/or participants to deal with the challenges outlined in this case study. Many of the suggestions are meant to be illustrative of the need to "connect the dots" and "think outside the box" of current realities. I would like to believe that these modest efforts contribute to a wake-up call as to the seriousness of the issues, from the perspective of an academic who has taught generations of students in public policy both in Nigeria and in the United States.

This monograph attempts to provide a clear narrative of "the Nigeria project," past, present, and future, and the challenges it faces. The study concludes with the hope for Nigeria's destiny as a strong, unified, democratic country in the community of nations, capable of handling the inevitable challenges of political elections and religious diversity.

CHAPTER 1

The Nigerian Presidential Election of 2011 and Its Aftermath

The Nigerian Context

With an estimated 158–160 million people, Nigeria is the seventh-most-populous country in the world.[1] It is a major exporter of light sweet crude oil and natural gas, which puts it in the vital interests of many in the international community. More than four hundred ethnolinguistic groups are scattered in different regions of the country, and three of these groups are larger than the populations of many medium-sized African countries. Obviously, Nigeria is extremely complicated. Having joined northern and southern Nigeria together in 1914, the British later recognized their creation as one that would undertake a long journey if it were to develop a sense of national unity. Since independence in 1960, and especially after the civil war (1967–70), the country has struggled to find mechanisms to promote "unity with diversity." Many Nigerians feel that the problem started with the amalgamation, or "mistake," of 1914, which joined northern and southern Nigeria. (At that time, the south consisted of the Eastern Region and the Western Region. See the map entitled "Unification of Nigeria, 1914" in appendix A.)

The ethnoreligious realities of Nigeria are at the heart of this contemporary search for unity. With about 80 million Muslims, Nigeria has one of the largest Muslim populations in the world. As noted in the introductory chapter, it is by far the largest country in the world that is about half Muslim and half Christian. This pattern has led some pundits, ranging from Professor Samuel Huntington[2] to former Libyan leader Col. Muammar Gaddafi, to predict that Nigeria is a cleft country and destined to split along religious lines.

Since independence, Nigeria has swung between various types of civilian rule and a generally benign form of military rule. In 1999, this

---

1   In 2011, China had a population of 1.3 billion, India 1.2 billion, the United States 310 million, Indonesia 240 million, Brazil 195 million, and Pakistan 174 million.

2   Samuel P. Huntington, *The Clash of Civilizations and the Remaking of World Order* (New York: Simon & Schuster, 1996).

13

changed with the establishment of a civilian Fourth Republic, based in large part on the U.S. presidential model, including a Federal Capital Territory (FCT) in Abuja and a robust federal system of 36 states and 774 "local government areas."

As in the United States, in Nigeria the only nationwide election is the election for president. In the election of 1999, a wide-ranging national coalition put together a Peoples Democratic Party (PDP), which has since emerged as the dominant party in the country. The PDP's candidate, Olusegun Obasanjo, became president and was reelected in 2003.[3] The test of the power shift principle came in 2007, when a new president had to run for office, because a president can serve only two terms (of four years each). According to the charter of the PDP, the party's candidate for president should have shifted from a southern (Christian) candidate to a northern (Muslim) candidate. At the same time (albeit according to an *unwritten* requirement of the charter), the party's presidential ticket should have included a vice presidential running mate from the opposite regional (and hence religious) side of the political street.[4]

The election of 2007 shifted the PDP candidate for the president from a southerner, Obasanjo, to a northerner, Umaru Yar'Adua. During the 1999–2007 period, the vice president had been a northern Muslim, Atiku Abubakar, and in the 2007 election, the vice president was a southern Christian, Goodluck Jonathan. Complications arose in May 2010, however, when Yar'Adua died and Jonathan became president,[5] selecting as

---

3   In 1999, northern power brokers selected Olusegun Obasanjo, a military general they knew well, as the PDP candidate. He was a Christian from the southwest (Abeokuta) and had suffered under the hands of the northern military ruler Sani Abacha, who died in 1998, thus opening the door for a return to civilian rule. However, after a few months in office, Obasanjo began to "retire" northern military officers, and there was a widespread sentiment in the north that it was "payback time" by the south, after years of northern domination. In 2007, when Obasanjo made an unsuccessful bid for a "third term," the north insisted that a northern candidate be selected. Obasanjo relented and "selected" Umaru Yar'Adua, the governor of Katsina, as his choice for president, and Goodluck Jonathan, the governor of Bayelsa, as vice president, thereby preserving the PDP commitment to a "power shift." Obasanjo appeared to regard his selections as "weak" and hence able to be "controlled" by his strong personality. Russian president Putin's selection of Dmitry Medvedev as his successor in 2008 could be seen as a similar and contemporaneous political tactic.

4   For a north-south map of Nigeria, see appendix A, map 3. For the six geocultural zones, (i.e., northwest, northeast, north central, southwest, southeast, and south-south), see appendix B.

5   Goodluck Ebele Azikiwe Jonathan was born November 20, 1957, in Otueke, in Ogbia Local Government Area, in what is now Bayelsa State, to a family of canoe makers. He holds a bachelor's degree in zoology, a master's degree in hydrobiology and fisheries biology, and a doctoral degree in zoology from the University of Port Harcourt. He has worked as an education inspector, lecturer, and environmental protection officer. He entered politics in 1998 and served as governor of Bayelsa State from December 9, 2005, to May 28, 2007, when he became vice president. Upon President Umaru Yar'Adua's death on May 5, 2010, he became president.

his appointed vice president the (Muslim) governor of Kaduna State in the north, Namadi Sambo.[6]

The presidential election of April 2011 would be a test of whether the PDP would stick to its regional rotation policy or Jonathan would run in his own right. With much of the world's focus in spring 2011 on the democratic awakening of the "Arab Spring," the pre-election period in Nigeria attracted comparatively little notice. Part of the Arab Spring phenomenon was its demographic profile, especially the "youth bulge" in the region, which was seen as an impetus for the uprisings. Nigeria (larger in population that the Arab Spring countries combined—see table 1) has a similar profile, a fact that some saw as very ominous.

Table 1. Demographics: The Arab Spring Countries and Nigeria (2011)

Country	Population (in Millions)
Tunisia	10.4
Egypt	80.0
Libya	6.4
Bahrain	1.2
Yemen	24.0
Syria	22.5
Total	*144.5 million*
Nigeria	158–160 million

The general anti-incumbency electoral mood in many countries, ranging from Japan to the United Kingdom (not to mention the street protests in the Arab world), led some to speculate that Nigeria's PDP might be seriously challenged in the April elections. The appointment in July 2010 of Professor Attahiru Jega, the highly respected former vice chancellor of Bayero University in Kano, as the chairman of the Independent National Electoral Commission (INEC) prompted hopes that these elections would be free and fair.[7]

---

6   Mohammed Namadi Sambo was born in August 1954 in Zaria, Kaduna State. He studied architecture at Ahmadu Bello University, graduating in 1976, and then went on to earn a master's degree in architecture. In 1988, he was appointed commissioner for Works, Transport and Housing, Kaduna. In 1990, he went back to the private sector. In May 2007, he became governor of Kaduna State. In May 2010 he was selected by President Jonathan to serve as vice president, following the death of Yar'Adua.

7   Attahiru Jega obtained his bachelor's degree in political science from Ahmadu Bello University

A unique aspect of the Nigerian electoral code requires that in the first round of a presidential election the winner win not only a plurality of votes cast but also 25 percent of the votes in two-thirds of the thirty-six states. This requirement was designed to ensure that a successful candidate would have backing throughout the country. If no one reaches the 25 percent threshold, a run-off election between the two top candidates must be held within two weeks, and whoever gains the most votes wins, regardless of their regional spread.

Although there were sixty-three recognized political parties in Nigeria on the eve of the 2011 elections, most were calculated to produce support for "favorite sons" at the state and local levels rather than for national contenders. There were four major parties: the PDP; the CPC, led by Muhammadu Buhari;[8] the Action Congress, Nigeria (ACN), which selected Nuhu Ribadu as its presidential candidate; and the All Nigeria Peoples Party (ANPP), led by Ibrahim Shekarau.

The challenge for the opposition parties, which had strong regional bases, was to achieve a national coalition prior to the presidential election on April 16. The ACN had support in the southwest. The ANPP had limited support in Kano (in north central Nigeria), plus Yobe and Borno (in the northeast). The major opposition party, however, was clearly the CPC, which had a broad northern base of support. Unfortunately for the CPC, it could not persuade the other parties to join it in a national coalition. Volumes could be written about the efforts that went into trying,

---

and his doctoral degree from Northwestern University in the United States. He is a former director of the Center for Democratic Research and Training, Bayero University (2000–2004), and a former president of the Academic Staff Union of Universities (1988–94). Professor Jega is originally from Kebbi State.

8   Muhammadu Buhari was born December 17, 1942, and attended the Katsina Provincial Secondary School. On entering the military, he attended the Nigerian Military Training College, Kaduna (1962); the Mons Officer Cadet School, Aldershot, United Kingdom (1962–63); the Defense Services Staff College, Wellington, India (1973); and the U.S. Army War College (1979–80). He was platoon commander, 2nd Infantry Battalion, Abeokuta (1963), and served with the UN Peace-Keeping Force in Congo (in the early 1960s). During the Nigerian civil war, he was commander, 2nd Infantry Battalion. He served as the military governor of North-Eastern State (now Borno), 1975–76; as federal commissioner for Petroleum and Energy, 1976–78; and as chairman of the Nigerian National Petroleum Corporation, 1978–79. He was military secretary, Army Headquarters, and a member of the Supreme Military Council, 1978–79. Subsequently, he served as commanding general officer in Ibadan, and subsequently in Jos. He was appointed head of state and commander in chief of the Nigerian Armed Forces, on January 1, 1984; on August 27, 1985, he was ousted in a putsch led by General Babangida. He was in political detention from August 27, 1985, until December 14, 1988. Later, under the Abacha regime, he served as director of the Petroleum Trust Fund between 1996 and 1999. He contested the 2003, 2007, and 2011 presidential elections. Currently, he serves as the de facto leader of the opposition in Nigeria. His "democratic" credentials during the Fourth Republic are widely seen to be above reproach.

especially with parties in the southwest, but a coalition was not to be, with sour grapes all around.

Within the PDP, the drama came during the primary convention in January, when the incumbent, Goodluck Jonathan, was challenged by a northern "consensus" candidate, Atiku Abubakar. Jonathan won the nomination, although the question of northern support (or lack thereof) continued to be argued in the background.

Although presidential election day passed with little violence, when the national results were announced (or hinted at via the grapevine), ethnoreligious violence erupted in the north. HRW observers labeled this election and its aftermath as the most violent in Nigeria's history.[9]

The official results of the presidential election are shown in table 2.

Table 2. Official Results of the Presidential Election Held on April 16, 2011

Official Figures	
Registered voters	73,528,040
Total number of voters	38,305,084
Votes for the PDP	22,925,275 (57%)
Votes for the CPC	12,395,774 (31%)
Votes for the ACN and ANPP	2,984,035
Combined votes for the CPC, ACN, and ANPP	15,379,809

Patterns

- Buhari (CPC) won in the twelve shari'a states (far north)
- Jonathan (PDP) won in all others, except Osun (where the ACN won)
- National turnout was 53%
- Lowest turnout was in the southwest
- States with highest voter turnout (all in the south-south and southeast):

Abia	78%	Edo	74%
Imo	83%	Akwa Ibom	76%
Rivers	76%	Bayelsa	85%

Source: ElectionMonitor, www.electionmonitor.com.ng, April 18, 2011.

---

9   HRW, *Nigeria: Post-election Violence Killed 800.*

The CPC did not accept the outcome in eighteen states and the FCT and decided to challenge the results in the courts. More ominous was the pattern of presidential voting, with the twelve states in the far north—the so-called shari'a states because of their use of shari'a law in the criminal domain—all voting for Buhari. The so-called Christian states in the south-south and southeast all voted (by improbable margins) for Jonathan, and the religiously mixed states split, but clearly supported the incumbent PDP candidate. (See table 3 for patterns of religious-based voting.) The PDP governors in twenty-nine out of thirty-six states tilted the political and financial balance in favor of the PDP presidential candidate.

After the election, the CPC chairmen in the south-south and southeast disassociated themselves from the national leadership's decision to challenge the election. They were then expelled by the CPC National Executive Committee (NEC), which insisted that the presidential poll was rigged.[10] The regional implications were there for all to see.

This chapter will examine, briefly, the lead-up to the presidential election, the election itself, and the postelection reactions, including those of the international community and the Nigerian government. The major focus will be on postelection conflict management.

Table 3. Religious Balance of States and Share of Vote Won by Buhari or Jonathan

Muslim State	Buhari	Mixed State	Jonathan	Christian State	Jonathan
1. Bauchi*	82%	1. Adamawa*	57%	1. Abia*	99%
2. Borno	78%	2. Benue*	67%	2. Akwa Ibom*	95%
3. Gombe*	60%	3. Kogi*	72%	3. Anambra	99%
4. Jigawa*	60%	4. Kwara*	66%	4. Bayelsa*	99%
5. Kaduna*	52%	5. Nasarawa*	59%	5. Cross River*	98%
6. Kano	62%	6. Lagos	67%	6. Delta*	99%
7. Katsina*	72%	7. Ogun*	58%	7. Ebonyi*	97%
8. Kebbi*	56%	8. Osun	38%	8. Edo	95%
9. Niger*	65%	9. Oyo*	58%	9. Enugu*	99%
10. Sokoto*	62%	10. Plateau*	74%	10. Imo*	99%
11. Yobe	56%	11. Taraba*	35%	11. Ondo	81%
12. Zamfara*	67%	12. Ekiti	52%	12. Rivers*	98%
Averages	*64%*		*58%*		*97%*

* = PDP incumbent governor

Sources: Author's estimate of religious balance; voting percentages are from ElectionMonitor (electionmonitor.com.ng).

10   "CPC Expels 10 State Chairmen: Suspends Two Others," *Daily Trust*, May 20, 2011.

Lead-Up to the Election

The elections were originally scheduled to occur as follows: April 2, elections for the National Assembly; April 9, presidential election; April 16, elections for gubernatorial and state assemblies. If a run-off was needed for the presidential election, it would be held on April 30, because the election had to take place thirty days prior to the swearing in of the new president, on May 29.

Because of technical difficulties in getting the printed ballots from overseas (where they had been printed in an effort to prevent fraud), the April 2 elections were postponed until April 9, the presidential election postponed until April 16, and the gubernatorial elections postponed until April 26 (the Tuesday after the Easter weekend). This shifting of dates had an impact on the international short-term observers, many of whom had planned to come for the April 9 presidential election but who instead ended up observing the April 9 national legislative elections, which were largely uneventful. (Two of the state gubernatorial elections—Kaduna and Bauchi—were postponed until April 28, because of the extraordinary violence following the presidential election.)

The underlying story of the elections is found in the nominating processes of the major parties, and particularly the ways in which regional balance issues were salient. In the case of the PDP, the political and financial powers of incumbency predominated. In the case of the CPC, the personality of Buhari was central and may have inhibited the CPC's capacity to form a coalition with other regional and/or minor parties, especially as the PDP was making deals with some of the smaller parties.

The ACN in the southwest was dominated by the personality of former governor Bola Tinubu, who could make deals, even to the point of selecting the presidential candidate. The selection of Nuhu Ribadu[11] rather than Attahiru Bafarawa[12] to garner the northern vote for the ACN so alienated Bafarawa that he swung his support to Buhari.

At the time Tinubu was accused by the CPC of making a deal with Jonathan to suppress the vote in the southwest in return for immunity from prosecution by the Economic and Financial Crimes Commission

---

11   Nuhu Ribadu was born in 1960 in Adamawa. He studied law and later joined the police, before being tapped by President Obasanjo to head the Economic and Financial Crimes Commission.

12   Attahiru Bafarawa was born in 1954 in Sokoto. He was a two-term governor of Sokoto, 1999–2007. He was originally a member of the ANPP but subsequently set up the Democratic People's Party. After joining the ACN for the 2011 election—despite supporting Buhari for president—he resigned at the end of 2011 and sought to revive the ANPP to serve as a northern regional block, a role similar to that of the ACN in the southwest.

(EFCC) and the right to nominate the next attorney general and the minister of petroleum. The Nigerian media was full of speculation about the presidential jet arriving in Lagos for late-night meetings with Tinubu.

But apart from the primaries and efforts at coalition building, the subtext of the political season was the lack of attention to the growing pressures for interfaith conflict. The report issued by USCIRF prior to the election provided abundant evidence of such conflict for anyone who cared to read it. The report examined interfaith violence in Plateau State, Bauchi State, Kaduna State, and Kano State, as well as more generally in northern and southeastern Nigeria. The report commented on the issue of "indigenes" vs. "settlers." The report also noted the lack of a response to the violence by the Nigerian government and highlighted the problems of state vs. federal jurisdiction. The Boko Haram attacks on government officials and against Christians in the northeast were detailed. The shari'a controversy was put into context in the twelve far northern states, and issues such as *Hisbah* police and international concern over harsh punishments were discussed. Discrimination and extremism were analyzed. Interfaith efforts at conflict resolution were also examined, such as the work of the Nigerian Inter-Religious Council (NIREC), which is composed of twenty-five Muslim and twenty-five Christian leaders and is cochaired by the sultan of Sokoto and the president of the Christian Association of Nigeria (CAN).[13]

The parallel tracks of sectarian conflict pressures and the political campaigns seemed to exist in separate worlds, at least until the presidential election. To the extent that policymakers within the international community were paying attention to Nigeria, they were often so focused on the need for a clean election that the larger picture of regional balance and sectarian issues seemed to escape notice.

International and Official Nigerian Responses to the Election

In general, international observers felt the presidential election day voting was peaceful and credible. Some announced in their reports that this was the best election in Nigerian history. The Swift Count process (discussed below) of the U.S. National Democratic Institute produced sample results that were almost identical to the official tally announced by Professor Jega.

---

13   U.S. Commission on International Religious Freedom, *Annual Report 2011* (Washington, D.C., 2011).

U.S. president Barack Obama called Jonathan in early May to congratulate him and issued an official statement supporting democratic elections, condemning violence, and calling for election appeals and protests to be taken to the courts, not the streets. Former U.S. ambassador Howard Jetter is reported as saying in Abuja, "The level of success and credibility recorded by Nigeria in the just concluded elections could make the country the standard bearer for democracy."[14]

The Nigerian government accepted the results, although it then set up processes for the Court of Appeal to hear complaints as well as a presidential commission to investigate postelection violence.

The Court of Appeal, constituted as the Presidential Election Petitions Tribunal, was scheduled to sit in Abuja, starting May 17. The president of the Court of Appeal, Justice Ayo Salami, was asked to select five judges from the Court of Appeal to sit on the tribunal.[15] The CPC had petitioned to nullify the election of Jonathan on grounds of noncompliance with the Electoral Act, and called on INEC to organize new elections between Buhari and Jonathan. The CPC challenged the results in eighteen states: Kaduna, Sokoto, Nasarawa, Kwara, Adamawa, Abia, Akwa Ibom, Enugu, Cross River, Rivers, Ebonyi, Bayelsa, Delta, Imo, Anambra, Benue, Lagos, and Plateau, plus the FCT. Insiders estimated that this appeals process would last until September or October at the earliest.

Meanwhile, in May, the Nigerian government also set up a presidential panel on pre-election violence in Akwa Ibom State, as well as postelection violence in the north. The twenty-two–person panel was led by Sheikh Ahmed Lemu, a venerable (he was eighty-two) and well-respected retired grand khadi (i.e., senior shari'a judge) from Niger State. According to the Nigerian press:

> Jonathan, while inaugurating the presidential panel in the council chambers at the presidential villa, spelt out five terms of reference for them to carry out their job. He said: "The panel has the following terms of reference: To investigate the imme-

---

14   "Ex US Envoy: 2011 Polls Put Nigeria in Good Stead," *Daily Trust*, May 19, 2011.

15   The suspension of Justice Salami in August 2011 caused great concern. See "The Suspension of Justice Salami," *Guardian* (Lagos), September 4, 2011: "On Friday, August 19th, 2011, the discerning, even if impoverished and traumatised citizens of the Nigerian nation-space woke up to an early morning nightmare, the ugly news that the National Judicial Council (NJC) had sent the President of the Court of Appeal (PCA), Justice Ayo Isa Salami, on suspension with a note to the President and Commander-in-Chief of the Armed Forces of the Federation to remove him from office, ostensibly under the provisions of section 238 (4) and item 21 paragraph (b) of part 1 of the Third Schedule to the 1999 Constitution of the Federal Republic of Nigeria 1999 (as amended)."

diate and remote cause(s) of the pre-election violence in Akwa Ibom State as well as the tide of unrest in some states of the federation following the presidential election and make appropriate recommendations on how to prevent future occurrence; To ascertain the number of persons who lost their lives or sustained injuries during the violence; To identity the spread and extent of loss and damage to means of livelihood and assess the cost of damage to personal and public properties and places of worship and make appropriate recommendations; To investigate the sources of weapons used in the unrest and recommend how to stem the tide of illegal flow of such weapons to the country; To examine any other matter incidental or relevant to the unrest and advise government as appropriate."[16]

Sheikh Lemu insisted on personal security for the members of the panel and called for "effective measures to forestall interference by anybody from any quarters."[17] Some commentators, however, were skeptical of government panels and have observed that in Nigeria none of the reports issued by previous panels or commissions dealing with violence has ever been published. The final report was rendered in September, but not made public. Yet, the Lemu panel consisted of a distinguished and balanced cohort and hopes were high among knowledgeable observers that the panel's report would be taken seriously.[18]

The HRW report compiled in part by Eric Guttschuss, a longtime observer of Nigeria's electoral process, provided a quick snapshot based on HRW's many observers. In his presentation to a conference held in Washington, D.C., on May 10, 2011, Guttschuss described "the most violent election in 50 years of Nigerian history."[19] While recognizing that INEC had improved from past performances, as had the security forces, he described how the PDP had hijacked ballot boxes at gunpoint in Akwa Ibom, and how results from Akwa Ibom had nonetheless been reported

---

16   *Leadership*, May 12, 2011.

17   Ibid.

18   The Federal Panel of Investigation into the 2011 Election Violence and Civil Disturbances consisted of the following twenty-two persons: Sheikh Ahmed Lemu (chairman), Justice Samson O. Uwaifo (vice chairman), Bishop J. Idowu-Fearon, Alhaji Muhammad Danmadami, Chief Ajibola Ogunshola, Mrs. Lateefat M. Okunnu, M. B. Wali, Dr. Timiebi Koripamo-Agary, Comrade Peter Esele, Alhaji Mohammed Ibrahim, Professor Femi Odekunle, Ambassador Raph Uwechue, Alhaji Bukar Usman, Sheikh Adam Abdullah Idoko, Major General M. Said, Barrister, P. C. Okori, Shamsuna Ahmed, Major General L. P. Ngubane, Alhaji Sani Maikudi, Rear Admiral Itunu Hotonu, Idowu Damilola Ogungbemi, and F. F. Ogunshakin.

19   The author attended the conference, which was organized by Johns Hopkins School of Advanced International Studies, and made notes on the presentations. He is grateful for private discussions with INEC chair Professor Jega at that time, as well as previously.

at the collation center. The urban areas were more accessible to domestic and international observers, but the rural areas were where the vote rigging occurred. Ballot stuffing was widespread, as were payments of about $2 per vote to rural people. Money was paid even to the local opposition party observers to agree to the results. The HRW report called on INEC to release complete results, including the results for individual polling units, as a means of ensuring accountability and neutrality. In the north, the CAN reported to HRW that at least 350 churches were burned or destroyed. In South Kaduna, at least 500 people were killed, mainly Muslims, who were ethnically cleansed in some villages. The HRW report estimated the total number of dead since the election at 800. The report noted that in the six months before the election—from November 2010 through April 16, 2011—at least 165 people had been killed. According to HRW, since 1999 and the beginning of the Fourth Republic, at least 15,000 people have been killed in election and/or ethnoreligious violence in the country as a whole—yet no one has been held accountable.[20]

"Speaking truth to power" is not always welcomed by the authorities, but reliable data and a readiness to spotlight and acknowledge unpleasant realities are essential if conflict is to be managed in Nigeria. Many observers (including this author) hoped that the Sheikh Lemu panel would set a new standard for assessing election-related violence.[21] Meanwhile, Kaduna State set up its own commission of inquiry.[22]

---

20   HRW, *Nigeria: Post-election Violence Killed 800.*

21   Sheikh Ahmed Lemu and his British-born wife, Aisha, were students at the School of Oriental and African Studies in London. The author knew him at that time and has followed his subsequent career in shari'a law, and that of his wife, a founding member of the moderate/mainstream Federation of Muslim Women's Associations of Nigeria (FOMWAN).

22   See *An Executive Summary on the Report of the Judicial Commission of Inquiry into the Post-presidential Election Disturbances in Kaduna State, April 2011* (n.d.). The commission's report notes that estimates of the numbers killed range from 401 (the figure given by the police) to 957 (according to the Nigerian Security and Civil Defence Corps). Even so, this variation of numbers killed in Kaduna State of more than 100 percent does not account for the continued killings of rural Fulani, and hence the true figures are probably higher. The commission noted "the following as the remote causes of the crisis: i. The non-adherence of the People's Democratic Party Zoning system as enshrined in its constitution; ii. PDP Northern Political Leadership Forum; iii. division preaching by religious leaders; iv. large number of unemployed youths in Kaduna State; v. indiscipline in the society/moral decadence; vi. general anti-PDP feeling; vii. desperate politicians and winner-take-all syndrome; viii. deep-rooted animosity and suspicion as well as religious intolerance and disregard by both Muslims and Christians particularly in the Southern part; ix. the issue of indigene and settler syndrome; x. failure of the police to investigate and where necessary confiscate these dangerous weapons compounded the situation." The commission's recommendations to the government included focusing on the following: "a. vulnerable and flash points: some of these vulnerable and flash points are Kafanchan, Zonkwa, Zango Kataf, Gonin Gora, Rigarsa,Tudan Wada Kaduna, Mararaban Jos, and Zaria; b. religious tolerance; c. unemployment; d. responsibility of parents to their children; e. settlers/indigenes and other dichotomies; f. the role of traditional institutions; g. political conduct; h. orientation for good citizenship; i. grazing reserves and cattle routes; j. creation of a new

Various external NGOs have also made efforts to track postelection conflict in Nigeria.[23]

Postelection Issues and Allegations

Some observers hoped that the court challenges would shed light on the CPC's concerns and allegations (as well as highlight the extent to which the tribunals afforded due process). According to a report in the Nigerian media about the appeals tribunal, "At the inaugural sitting of the panel, preliminary issues, including the application by the Congress for Progressive Change (CPC) to inspect electoral materials, will be disposed of to pave the way for the hearing of the substantive petition."[24] In the event, however, this process itself would become the grist for court challenges, all of which were decided in favor of the government.

While the appeals panel began its work, Buhari withheld his endorsement of the election. His key supporters had insisted on taking the results to the tribunal and he wanted to respect the process. According to an account in the *Daily Trust,*

> General Muhammadu Buhari yesterday said he would not congratulate President Goodluck Jonathan until his demands of subjecting results of 11 states to forensic analysis is done. The states are: Abia, Imo, Ebonyi, Enugu and Anambra in the South-East and Akwa Ibom, Rivers, Cross River, Delta, Edo and Bayelsa in the South-South.
>
> Buhari, who spoke through his spokesman, Yinka Odumakin, also said that their demand for re-computation of the results done using the Excel application has to be met by the electoral body. He said the results of the presidential election can only be adjudged to be credible if the issues he raised are tackled. . . .
>
> Earlier, Buhari's running mate, Pastor Tunde Bakare, has said the CPC resolved to contest the election results in 11 states. . . . "The average turnout rate in the south-south and south-east

---

state out of the present Kaduna state; k. implementation of Reports of Commission of Inquiry; l. compensations; m. crisis management (security bodies; traditional institutions); n. stopping the unlawful possession and use of firearms."

23   See Council on Foreign Relations, Africa Program, *Nigeria Security Tracker,* which is based on content analysis of Nigerian newspapers and focuses mainly on the north. Also, see Fund for Peace, *UNLock Nigeria,* which focuses mainly on the Delta and is based on reports from observers in the field. These sources are available on the Council on Foreign Relations and Fund for Peace websites, respectively.

24   *Independent,* May 11, 2011.

zones (without Ebonyi and Edo States) at 78 percent is 50 percent above the national average of about 52 percent" He wondered how President Jonathan was able to get over 85 percent of the valid votes cast in all the 11 states in the two zones with 10 of the said states at 95 percent and above, including four of the states at 99 percent and one a near perfect 99.6 percent in his home state.[25]

What, then, were the initial types of allegations and/or sources of suspicion that arose from the presidential election? They seemed to fall into three categories: pre-election, election day, and postelection. In all cases, the allegations revolve around the incumbents improperly exploiting their access to government resources: for instance, drawing on the Excess Crude Account (i.e., petroleum funds) to finance incumbent party campaigns; deployment of security forces; the process of printing and distributing the ballots; controlling the hiring of powerful residential electoral commissioners; controlling the National Television Authority (NTA) on matters concerned with campaign ads; and controlling permits for rallies.

Regarding the actual day of the presidential elections, the immediate postelection concerns by the challengers seemed to be as follows:

- Vote buying and ballot stuffing at the polling units, especially in the rural areas.

- Security forces' passivity at the polling units when malfeasance was occurring. (Police commissioners were rotated away from their states just before the election to prevent bias, but the result was that police authorities did not really know their new assignment areas.)

- Collusion by officials at the collation centers.[26]

- Overreliance on Project 2011 Swift Count, which randomly sampled about 1,440 of the 120,000 polling stations, which were then monitored by a well-regarded coalition of the Federation of Muslim Women's Associations of Nigeria (FOMWAN), the Justice, Development and Peace/Caritas Nigeria (JDPC), the Nigerian Bar Association (NBA), and the Transition Monitoring Group (TMG). The concern was that if the monitored polling units were known to party authorities in advance or even after observers were deployed on election day, the nonsampled polling units could be the focus for rigging.

---

25 "Buhari: Why I Didn't Congratulate Jonathan," *Daily Trust*, May 2, 2011.

26 See John Campbell's blog entry "Nigerian Presidential Elections: The Devil Is in the Ballot Collating," posted on *Africa in Transition*, April 19, 2011. The blog can be found on the Council on Foreign Relations website.

- The overly close association of National Security Adviser Azazi with President Jonathan, both being from the same local government area in Bayelsa State. This may have resulted in the military, police, and other security forces overreacting or underreacting during and after the election.

- A variety of serious allegations—such as printing extra ballots (supposedly in China) and distributing them at night to party stalwarts—that were presumably investigated by INEC legal staff but that nonetheless formed the stuff of urban legends.

The most basic demand by the CPC in court was to have access to the original biometric data on the 73 million registered voters so a more detailed analysis could be done of voting patterns and irregularities. This was denied by the court, both initially and in the final verdict.

The fact that the CPC took these concerns to the court system was a positive step, although there was widespread cynicism because the judicial authorities were part of the political elite system that was being challenged.

Long-Term Consequences:
Elections and National Unity?

The most obvious lesson from the presidential election does not concern the actual mechanics of the modified open ballot system, which seems to have gone remarkably well. Rather, it is the fact that INEC had no control over campaign finances and that the chairman of INEC had no control over the hiring or firing of his resident electoral commissioners.

A presidential election that featured an incumbent president perceived to be a Christian/southerner versus a principal opposition party challenger perceived to be a northerner/Muslim was bound to run the risk of splitting the country along regional and religious lines. This danger was created when the PDP decided to abandon (temporarily, at least) the principle of zoning and power shift spelled out in its charter. In short, the seeds of postelection violence were sown at the PDP's nominating conference in January—if not earlier, when Jonathan decided to contest his party's nomination.

This regionally based set of candidates created an election that Chairman Jega called a "crisis of expectation."[27] As reported in the widely read newspaper *Punch:*

> Professor Attahiru Jega, on Tuesday, blamed the post-presidential election violence in Nigeria on a "crisis of expectation" from "people who expected a particular outcome from the elections." Jega said this in a keynote address at a forum to assess Nigeria's April elections at the Paul H. Nitze School of Advanced International Studies, Johns Hopkins University, Washington D.C. "There were huge expectations on who wins and who loses and managing these expectations became a problem resulting in unfortunate circumstance," he said. Jega regretted that several members of the National Youth Service Corps, on election day, were targeted in the violence, which claimed hundreds of lives in some states in northern Nigeria. "A number of causes of this may be related to larger systemic issues rather than the actual conduct of the elections by INEC. Many people have talked about poverty, unemployment and what I consider crisis of expectation. Some analysts have pointed to what they perceive as ethno-religious dimension; it may be true, but frankly, I see less of this. I see larger systemic issue of unemployment, illiteracy and lack of proper education, poor political enlightenment and voter education," he said.

Many of these expectations were shared by poor northern citizens who were hoping for change and who had pinned their hopes on Buhari, whose nicknames in the northern press were "Mr. Integrity" (*Mai Mutuchi*)[28] and "Mr. Truth" (*Mai Gaskiya*). Buhari's critics seemed to expect him to control the full range of violence in the aftermath of the election. He did condemn it as "sad and unwarranted" and urged his supporters not to burn their voter cards, because the gubernatorial elections were coming up the following week. Yet, apart from the violence, a more fundamental casualty in the north may have been the reputations of many members of the traditional northern elites who sided with the PDP. With popular sentiment running so high in the north against the PDP, pro-PDP elites may have undercut their capacity to act in their traditional roles as conflict managers in future crises.

---

27   "Jega Blames Post-election Violence on 'Crisis of Expectation,'" *Punch*, May 12, 2011.

28   Buhari was also called "*Mai Kirki,*" which implies generous, sympathetic, goodness, and a range of other highly positive meanings.

One notable target for popular fury was Muhammad Sa'ad Abubakar III, the sultan of Sokoto,[29] who is also the president general of the Nigerian Supreme Council for Islamic Affairs (NSCIA) and cochairs the royal fathers' council with the Ooni of Ife (a traditional ruler in the Yoruba southwest). He was seen as a close confidant of President Jonathan, and his palace in Sokoto was attacked by street mobs after the election.[30] Subsequently, according to the press, "the Sultan . . . congratulated Jonathan on his victory at the presidential polls and pledged the solidarity of all royal fathers for the administration, saying, 'we are solidly behind you and your government, and we will continue to do all it takes *Insha Allah*, to assist this government achieve its programmes.'" Significantly, in response, "the President said his administration will continually engage the traditional institution and push for constitutional recognition of its functions."[31]

The north-south split and/or ethnoreligious split seems likely to endure for a long time, especially at the grassroots level. Northern anger is not likely to be assuaged by presidential panels, election tribunals, or statements by traditional rulers. Indeed, the election violence may prove to have been the precursor to an existential national crisis.

The Jonathan government is widely seen as walking on the Christian side of the political street. According to Charles Dickson, a well-known commentator and neither a Muslim nor a northerner: "Today, whether we like it or not, the president is Christian, the Senate president is Christian, head of judiciary is Christian, SGF is Christian, National Security Adviser is also one, the Chief of Army, the SSS Director, in fact welcome to the federal republic of Christians. I was privy to a recent heated discussion in which one of the participants blurted out, 'If we leave it to "them" the next Sultan will be Christian.'"[32]

---

29   The sultan of Sokoto, Sa'ad Abubakar III, was born August 24, 1956. He attended Barewa College, Zaria, before proceeding to the Nigerian Defence Academy, Kaduna, in 1975. He was commissioned in December 1977 as second lieutenant and posted to the Nigerian Armored Corps. He spent the next thirty-one years in the Nigerian Army, including in Sierra Leone (working for ECOWAS) and in Pakistan as Nigeria's defense adviser there, with concurrent accreditation to Iran, Iraq, Afghanistan, and Saudi Arabia, from February 2003 to February 2006. He returned to Nigeria after February 2006 to attend the senior-executive course at the National Institute for Policy and Strategic Studies, Kuru, where he wrote a research thesis titled, "Religious Extremism as a National Security Problem: Strategies for Sustainable Solutions." He was appointed the twentieth sultan of Sokoto on November 2, 2006 (and promoted to the rank of general).

30   The sultan's support for Jonathan may be seen in a positive light following the historic tradition of cross-ethnic alliances between the "north" and the "south-south" at the elite level. But the sacking of his palace indicates the growing gap between elites and grassroots constituencies.

31   "Sultan: We Support Lemu Panel on Election Riot," *Daily Trust*, May 20, 2011.

32   "In Nigeria, For or Against . . . You Must Belong," *Nigeria Plus*, June 9, 2011.

Conflict Management in Nigeria

The first rule in conflict management is to get all relevant parties to the table. In the case of Nigeria's disputed election, those parties must include legitimate representatives of the 15,379,809 who (officially) voted for the CPC, ACN, and ANPP.[33] Just any northerner, whether in the federal cabinet[34] or in a Track II capacity, will not suffice; to be seen as legitimate, the people at the table must be part of the "Buhari organization"— the inner core of his campaign—and the CPC. The complication in the aftermath of the election was that the CPC did not wish to be part of a government of national unity. Indeed, the CPC insisted on being treated as "the opposition" so as not to compromise its legitimacy with its grassroots supporters. It did not want to be part of the kind of elite bargain that the country has witnessed too many times in the past. The CPC has been committed to change and to fighting for a better deal for the tens of millions of Nigerians who have been excluded from the prosperity generated by the oil economy. The key to its program is education, jobs, and inclusion—very much in the spirit of Professor Jega's concerns voiced in an unofficial capacity at the forum in Washington in May 2011. To ignore this socioeconomic disparity in an OPEC state might be to invite unsanctioned violence in the North African mode.

The need to tackle—in Jega's words—"unemployment, illiteracy and lack of proper education" should be obvious to all. That need is all the greater when poverty exacerbates regional tensions. The Niger Delta—Jonathan's home base—has been the target of sporadic government efforts to address the problems of the poor, but little has been done to tackle the desperate poverty of the far north. Economic desperation fuels religious extremism, as any northern dignitary will readily admit.

Furthermore, the presidential electoral system can too easily produce a winner-take-all outcome, even without a second round of voting. Normally, the prospect of a second round of voting inspires several parties to form a coalition and assume the role of the official opposition prior to the first round of voting. In 2011, however, disarray among the opposition parties (produced in part by their diverse regional bases and in part by the lure of incentives by the incumbents) made it virtually impossible for them to build a coalition.

---

33   Supporters of Buhari claim that he actually won the 2003 and 2007 elections, and that his tally for the 2011 election was closer to 14 million than to the 12.4 million figure produced by the official count.

34   For a full list of northern federal cabinet members and other high-ranking northern officials appointed by President Jonathan in 2011, see appendix B.

If the international community is concerned that Nigeria not slide into a de facto single-party system or fall under military rule, dignity and respect must be accorded to the opposition party and its leader. Plus, the partition option, which is always lurking in the background, may step out from the shadows if major segments of the polity feel permanently politically dispossessed. This requirement of inclusion was the origin of the zoning and power shift mechanisms, because the north had the demographic weight to rule Nigeria in the early days of independence, and the post–civil war era required that new mechanisms be found to involve all regions of the polity.

Part of the difficulty for the Jonathan administration is to recognize that it caused much of the unhappiness—and the violence—in the north by breaking with the power shift principle. Furthermore, Jonathan himself is the quintessential "accidental president," having been plucked by the powers that be from his (nonelected) role as deputy governor to become a (nonelected) governor of Bayelsa, and then handpicked to be Yar'Adua's running mate in 2007. The PDP primary in January 2011 essentially came down to who had more money to buy votes—the billionaire former vice president with a business background or the incumbent president with a doctorate in zoology. It was an auction of historic proportions, even in a country without any real campaign finance regulations.

Unfortunately, the perception in much of the north—and perception so often becomes reality in this information-starved, rumor-rich country—is that Jonathan was the creature of former president Obasanjo, perhaps the most disliked politician in the north. If Jonathan had wanted to demonstrate his independence to skeptical northerners, he could have distanced himself from Obasanjo, and even held Obasanjo and other members of the "new wealth" families in Nigeria accountable for their corruption.[35] He did not do so.

The role of the international community also lent weight to the incumbent. The agreement establishing the U.S.-Nigeria Binational Commission had been signed on April 6, 2010.[36] In mid-April 2010, Jonathan

---

35   For background, see the book by former U.S. ambassador John Campbell, *Nigeria: Dancing on the Brink* (Boulder, CO: Rowman & Littlefield, 2011).

36   See U.S. Department of State, *Media Note*, April 2010: "On April 6, U.S. Secretary of State Hillary Clinton and Nigerian Secretary to the Government of the Federation Yayale Ahmed inaugurated the U.S.-Nigeria Binational Commission, a strategic dialogue designed to expand mutual cooperation across a broad range of shared interests. The Commission is a collaborative forum to build partnerships for tangible and measureable progress on issues critical to our shared future. The United States establishes such commissions with valued and strategic partners. Nigeria is Africa's most populous nation, its largest contributor of peacekeepers, its largest

made a visit to Washington as "acting president"—a designation he had been given because President Yar'Adua was terminally ill. Rumors of coups abounded at this time because of Yar'Adua's incapacity, and many in the international community wanted the power vacuum in Abuja filled. The United States in particular was impressed by the smart, young, modest acting president. At that time, Jonathan was not expected to run for president in 2011.

By fall 2010, however, it was clear that Jonathan would seek the nomination of the PDP for the presidency. The Binational Commission made it hard for U.S. officials to be neutral in a situation where they or their colleagues were working closely with Nigerian counterparts on common problems. In addition, it is always hard for Washington to step away from incumbent governments during an election cycle when U.S. policymakers fear that the stability and continuity provided by the incumbent administration may give way to a new, unknown government.

In the postelection environment, the United States would have to devise a way to put support for institutions—including the institution of multiparty democracy—above loyalty to friends. The United States would also have to recognize that the judicial appeals process is very much part of the election process, and that Washington would have to encourage a free, fair, and timely judicial process. In the end, the United States would need to be seen to be neutral, not a cheerleader for Jonathan as he ran a postelection victory lap, especially given its postelection blessings to the "best election ever in Nigeria."

It would be ironic if business interests within the international community—focusing on the problem of the insurgency in the Delta, the source of Nigeria's oil—ended up contributing to the destabilization of the north, thereby jeopardizing national unity. This international concern for the Delta would take on more serious dimensions with the postelection escalation of violence by Boko Haram and the question of why the Binational Commission shifted its focus on regional security from the Delta to also include the north. A closer link between the U.S. military and the Nigerian military could be seen as supporting a southern president against a grassroots insurgency in the north. (See chapter 4 for discussion of the role of the military.)

---

producer of oil and a significant trading partner for the United States. Secretaries Clinton and Ahmed are forming four working groups to address specific bilateral issues: Good Governance, Transparency, and Integrity; Energy and Investment; Food Security and Agriculture; and, Niger Delta and Regional Security Cooperation. They plan to launch the Good Governance, Transparency and Integrity working group first, in light of preparations and reforms necessary to ensure Nigeria's 2011 elections are free, fair, and transparent."

Aftermath of the Election Review Process

On October 1, 2011, Nigeria celebrated its fifty-first birthday. Because of terrorist threats, Abuja was almost a ghost town, locked down amid intense security. Details of the election appeals process were hidden on the back pages of most newspapers. Buhari, however, was in no mood to see election irregularities swept under the rug.

In a major speech at the end of September, Buhari warned that if the "judiciary is compromised, Nigeria is finished." As reported in the *Daily Trust:*

> Former head of State and presidential candidate of Congress for Progressive Change, General Muhammadu Buhari yesterday warned that any attempt to tamper with the impartiality of the judiciary portends grave danger for Nigeria's democratic experience. This is just as former Lagos State Governor and chieftain of the Action Congress of Nigeria (ACN) Bola Tinubu called for urgent dialogue on the rule of law, freedom from political oppression, electoral fairness, economic deprivation and national security.

> Speaking at the annual Conference and Awards Ceremony organized by Leadership Newspapers in Abuja where he was honoured as "Politician of the Year," Buhari charged the political class to be serious on issues concerning the independence of the judiciary. He underscored the need to stabilize the nation's democratic system in order to revitalize and make Nigeria great, stating that "We have got the riches. We have to stop being potential. We have to realize our potentialities."

> He said, "You know what happened to us in 2003, you know what happened up to December 12, 2008. For 50 months, we were in Court. And do you know what is happening now? When the Presidential Tribunal started under Salami, he was kicked out and new composition was put in place. I want you to please take note of three things about INEC. One, INEC asked for N87bn. Reliably, they were given about N100bn. They said they had registered 73.5m Nigerians. All these Nigerians from polling units to wards to local governments to states had their finger-prints recorded and their bio-metric data available. The first thing our legal team asked for was: let us have this because there were no elections in 20 states. And this was turned down. So how can INEC account for a hundred billion naira for doing nothing? Nigerians must insist on this because if we can donate a hundred billion naira to election officials and corrupt politicians and then we say it is against the security of the country to

bring evidence as agreed by the Electoral Act, then something is wrong."[37]

Buhari's speech was followed by a speech by Bola Tinubu, who received the "Person of the Year" award. "Through strict observance of the rule of law," Tinubu said,

> our courts are to be the guardian of fairness and justice. Without such a protector, democracy lies exposed to the ravages of power. This is the case in Nigeria today. The most glaring example of this has been the government's attempt to cut short the career of one of our illustrious jurists, Court of Appeal President Justice Isa Salami. What was his crime? Refusing to put his sense of justice on sale. For this, they tarnished his name and plotted to end his career. They rumoured that he was in the pockets of the ACN. This is a terrible lie against a good man. His verdicts were not for ACN. They were for justice. However, those in power could not tolerate his impartiality. They sacrificed one of Nigeria's finest jurists to send message to other jurists; go against our wishes and you shall lose those robes you hold so dear.[38]

The news report continues: "Earlier, the National Security Adviser General Andrew Owoye Azazi, who chaired the occasion, said the 2011 general elections were free and fair, adding that the violence that followed the presidential election had no link with the general elections but rather was caused by events before the election."

Clearly, a wide chasm separated the opposition leaders and the government on the matter of the election itself and on the legitimacy of the appeals process. (The question of limiting the length of time for an appeals process, which was a key recommendation of the earlier *Report of the Electoral Reform Committee*, is beyond the scope of this monograph.)[39]

Just over a month later, on November 1, the tribunal delivered its verdict on the legitimacy of the election held more than six months earlier. As reported in the press:

---

37 "Buhari: If Judiciary Is Compromised, Nigeria Is Finished," *Daily Trust*, September 30, 2011.

38 Ibid.

39 The so-called Uwais Committee submitted its report in December 2008. See *Report of the Electoral Reform Committee*, vol. 1, *Main Report*. The committee recommended that the appeals process be concluded prior to the May 29 swearing in of the president. The committee was chaired by Hon. Justice Muhammadu Lawal Uwais and included such well-respected figures as Ahmadu Kurfi, Bolaji Akinyemi, Godwin Ononiba, Musliu Smith, Olisa Agbakoba, Sheikh Ahmed Lemu, Attahiru Jega, Jibrin Ibrahim Aliyu Umar, Matthew Hassan Kukah, and others.

The Presidential Election Petition Tribunal yesterday in Abuja put a judicial seal on the victory of Dr. Goodluck Ebele Jonathan and his running mate, Namadi Sambo, at the April 16th, 2011 polls, declaring that they were validly elected as President and Vice President in that order. In a unanimous judgment delivered at the Court of Appeal amid heavy security, the five-man panel held that the April 16th Presidential election was conducted in substantial compliance with the 2010 Electoral Act and therefore declared it valid and unimpeachable. However, the petitioner, Congress for Progressive Change (CPC), through its national Chairman, Prince Tony Momoh, who condemned the judgment, said it would challenge it at the Supreme Court even as he said his party would be trusting to providence for justice. According to Momoh, "there are three judgments; the judgment of conscience, the judgment of the people and the judgment of God." Malam Nasir el-Rufai, a CPC chieftain and a former FCT Minister, said: "We were not surprised since the Tribunal had ruled that INEC cannot be compelled to bring its data base. More so, the judgment had since been decided with the removal of Justice Ayo Salami. We believe that posterity is the ultimate judge and one day God will give judgment on each and every one of us." But Jonathan who welcomed the judgment in a statement by his special Adviser (Media and Publicity), Dr. Reuben Abati, described it as a triumph for democracy and an affirmation of the sovereignty of the Nigerian people. He praised the CPC and its presidential candidate, General Muhammadu Buhari, for their respect for the rule of law and the Constitution, saying their recourse to judicial review of their grievances affirmed their faith in the nation's judiciary.[40]

The real question was how Buhari would react to the verdict, and what the national and even international implications would be. On November 2, the press reported that Buhari

yesterday said the dismissal of the party's petition that challenged the presidential election result did not come as a surprise. Speaking in the same vein, the National Publicity Secretary of the CPC, Mr. Rotimi Fashakin, described the judgment as a "miscarriage of justice." Buhari, who spoke through his spokesperson, Mr. Yinka Odumakin, said anyone who followed the judicial process that led to the tribunal's judgment would not be surprised that the outcome was against the CPC. "The judgment did not come to us as a surprise. Anyone who followed

---

40   "CPC Waits on God as Jonathan Wins in Court," *Guardian*, November 2, 2011.

the judicial process with regard to the handling of the presidential petition would not be surprised at the final outcome. First, it was the removal of the Appeal Court President, Justice Isa Ayo Salami, who was replaced by an Acting President, Justice Dalhatu Adamu, under controversial circumstances and then came the re-shuffling of the tribunal panel," he said. Odumakin said CPC practically lost hope in the entire process when the tribunal could not guarantee the party access to crucial electoral materials, let alone compelling the Chairman of the Independent National Electoral Commission (INEC), Prof. Attahiru Jega, to appear before it. He regretted that the refusal to allow CPC's legal team to conduct forensic investigation into the documents used to declare the presidential result had caused colossal damage to the case. He further lamented the futile efforts made by CPC to try to get Jega into the dock so as to enable the tribunal extract needed evidence to prove the rigging allegation. According to Odumakin, as far as the former head of state is concerned, it was obvious that the odds were against the CPC and there is no way it would have surmounted it under the circumstance. Fashakin said the party had decided to appeal against the tribunal's judgment. "Today's judgment was a miscarriage of justice; we shall appeal. We believe that there was evidence that INEC did not conduct election in South-east and the South-south. INEC could not tender the election materials used in conducting the election. The commission abandoned its pleadings by not being able to support its pleadings with evidence," he said.[41]

The readiness of the CPC to continue using the appeals process is notable given that the party responded to the November 1 verdict by challenging the integrity of the judicial process, By the end of November, Buhari was calling on his supporters not to give up hope and to prepare for the 2015 elections.[42]

---

41   "Buhari Not Surprised at 'Miscarriage of Justice,'" *Thisday,* November 2, 2011.

42   "Prepare for 2015 Elections, Buhari Tells Supporters," *Thisday,* November 28, 2011: "Former military Head of State and presidential candidate for the Congress for Progressive Change (CPC) in last April's presidential election, Maj-Gen. Muhammadu Buhari (rtd), Sunday called on his supporters to prepare for the 2015 general election. Speaking while inaugurating a poverty eradication project initiated by a CPC member of the Kaduna State House of Assembly representing Kawo, Buhari declared that he would not quit politics until good governance and sustainable democracy were entrenched in Nigeria. 'I won't quit politics until good governance and sustainable democracy is entrenched in this country. We should not be in any illusion that democracy dividends will ever come to us easily without making sacrifices and the time for proper change is 2015,' he said. He urged his supporters to shun acts of violence and enjoined them to ensure that they registered as voters with the Independent National Electoral Commission (INEC), to vote and to safeguard their votes during elections."

Buhari said the desired change Nigerians were yearning for could only be actualized if they vote for credible leaders and representatives at all levels of elections. He advised politicians and

As part of the CPC's preparations for the 2015 election, Buhari launched a "Renewal Committee" to "reposition for future electoral challenges."[43] The committee is to be led by Nasir el-Rufai, a young former member of the PDP who had decamped to the CPC after serving as minister of the FCT.[44] The previous director general of the Buhari campaign team since 2003, Sule Yahaya Hamma, stepped down and a basic reassessment of the 2011 campaign began.[45]

According to the media, Buhari was in "high spirits" in December.[46] Judging from the northern blogosphere, Buhari's grassroots popularity was still strong. Supporters posted messages addressed to "Father (*Baba*) Buhari," declaring, "We your followers will never give up until Nigeria is rescued from the cult PDP," "Buhari is still the only Nigerian past leader that has no corruption tag dangling on his neck," and "God may answer our prayers."[47] From the institutional perspective, the fact that the CPC pursued its election appeal to the Supreme Court and was also reevaluating its performance and preparing for a role in the next election bode well for the emergence of a vibrant opposition party. The question was whether the CPC could extend its appeal—based on its anti-corruption, anti-poverty, pro-education, pro-security programs—to other parts of the country besides the north.

While the election appeals process was thus unfolding, the presidential panel on post-election violence chaired by Sheikh Ahmed Lemu was also attracting attention In mid-summer, the panel had announced that

---

public officeholders to shun fraud and corruption and embrace discipline, hard work, justice, fairness and equity to get the country out of the woods. "I honoured this invitation as part of my consultations with stakeholders on the Nigerian project. I endorsed Muhammad Ali's empowerment initiative as our dear country is too rich to be poor," he said. He, however, promised to give full details of this political future and direction after the decision of the Supreme Court regarding his party's appeal against the judgment of the presidential election tribunal on the April 2011 presidential election which upheld the election of President Goodluck Jonathan."

43   "Buhari's Party Begins 'Renewal' Drive," *Daily Trust*, December 9, 2011.

44   Nasir el-Rufai was born February 16, 1960, in Katsina State. He went to Barewa College and then Ahmadu Bello University, where he earned a first-class bachelor's degree in quantity surveying. He attended courses at Harvard Business School and completed a law degree from the University of London. He set up a successful quantity surveying and project management consulting firm in 1982. From July 2003 to May 2007, he served as director general of the Bureau of Public Enterprises and then as minister of the FCT. He was a member of the PDP but broke with President Yar'Adua and became a vocal critic of the PDP before joining the CPC for the 2011 election.

45   Sule Hamma, originally from Kano, was a graduate student at the Institute of Administration, Ahmadu Bello University, and has been a longtime associate of Buhari.

46   "Buhari's Party Begins 'Renewal' Drive," *Daily Trust*, December 9, 2011.

47   Ibid.

"thousands" had been killed in Kaduna State. According to one press report from July:

> The Federal government investigation Panel on the 2011 post election violence and civil disturbances in Katsina state said Kaduna state has recorded the highest number of deaths and destruction during the unfortunate incident. Speaking to Sunday Trust shortly after a courtesy visit to the governor, Barrister Ibrahim Shehu Shema last Friday, Chairman of the panel, Sheikh Ahmed Lemu said findings have shown that thousands of people have been killed in Kaduna, two in Jigawa, and one person in Kano state. . . . "Thousands of innocent people were killed in Kaduna state and properties worth billions of naira have also been destroyed by the rioters. We have so far visited Kano, Kaduna, Katsina and Jigawa states," he noted. Sheikh Lemu assured Nigerians of the committee's readiness to be just to all parties involved saying, "we will give fair hearing to all and we will make useful recommendations to federal government to forestall future occurrences of such incidents. . . . The committee is expected to find out the number of deaths, number of injured persons, number of houses destroyed and other damages caused by the unfortunate violence. In the course of this, the committee is intended to hold an interaction session with security agents, traditional rulers, governors and other stakeholders," he said.[48]

In mid-September, the Lemu panel reported to the federal government. As of December, however, the report had not been made public. Given the seriousness of the mandate, many in the north were hoping that the panel would tackle the root causes of Nigeria's dysfunctional political culture, with its do-or-die imperatives, its divisive regional tensions, and its demographic youth bulge and resultant despair, plus its explosive ethnoreligious potential. Would the government prove itself capable of implementing fundamental recommendations?

Meanwhile, the positioning for the presidency in 2015 had already begun. In early November, the Senate president, David Mark, was endorsed by various Idoma ethnic societies in Benue State for the PDP presidential slot in the next election.[49] The April 2011 election seemed to be receding into the distance, as future calculations and coalitions began

---

48   "Post Election Violence: Kaduna Records More Deaths—Lemu," *Sunday Trust*, July 10, 2011.

49   David Mark is Senate president, which is the third-highest position in the federal government, after the president and vice president. He was born in 1948 in Benue State (in the northern Middle Belt), is Idoma by ethnicity, and is Christian. He was a high-ranking military officer before entering politics.

to emerge. President Jonathan continued to claim that "God made me a president."[50] Yet, violence in south Kaduna State persisted, with fingers of blame pointing in all directions.[51]

Lessons Learned

The approach in this chapter has been to focus on the macro level of politics and postelection violence, and wherever possible to avoid undue attention to individual actors. Yet, one of the lessons of the elections is that individual courage and integrity do matter. INEC chair Attahiru Jega did set a new standard of probity in Nigerian elections, despite enormous odds and subsequent court challenges. The work of reforming INEC will continue over the next several years—Jega's term is five years—and should be supported by Nigerians and the international community. It is to be hoped that the work of the Lemu panel has set a standard of honesty and effectiveness that others will emulate. Whether the panel has gone beyond looking for individual culprits to unearthing underlying causes remains to be seen.

The role of police, military, and security forces would normally be reviewed in the course of distilling lessons learned from postelection violence. The extent to which these forces overreacted or underreacted may have contributed significantly to levels and patterns of violence. The appointment of a chief security officer from the same ethnic and geographical area as the president may have been seen in the north as a violation of the "federal character" principle, in spirit if not in fact, and may thus have contributed to suspicions in the north of south-south favoritism. (See chapter 4 for a discussion of police, military, and security services.)

---

50   "God Made Me a President, Says Jonathan," *Next*, December 3, 2011: "President Goodluck Jonathan yesterday appealed to his political opponents to drop their petition against him, saying that God has made him the president of the country by the mandate given to him by Nigerians."

51   "Kaduna Fulani Blame Violence on Niger Republic," *Vanguard*, December 15, 2011: "Fulani community in Kaduna State has blamed the incessant attacks on minority Christians in the state on Fulani from Niger Republic. A representative of Fulani in Kamuru and former Executive Secretary of Kaduna State Emergency Management Agency, SEMA, Alhaji Abdulmalik Durunguw, said this at a peace and reconciliatory meeting between Ikulu communities made up of Bejju, Fulani and Hausa, at the Kamuru palace of Agwom Akulu, HRH Yohanna Kukah. . . . The area was among the places affected by the post-election violence, where some houses belonging to some Hausa/Fulani were torched by Ikulu natives, leading to the exodus of the non-natives to various refugee camps across Kaduna State. . . . He said Fulani from Niger Republic normally infiltrate the state to carry out violent attacks on innocent people in Kaduna, pointing out that in some cases their fellow Fulani's cattle were stolen by the invaders. . . . He said: 'As far as Fulani in Southern Kaduna are concerned, none of them can attack another ethnic group. We the Fulani in Southern Kaduna have no power to arrest these invading Fulani from the Niger Republic.'"

The transparency and legitimacy of the judicial process are crucial to the legitimacy of elections. Could the tribunals be both transparent and evenhanded? The need for campaign finance reform is obvious, as is the need for the EFCC to prosecute offenders without regard to political orientation. So, too, is the need to view the election cycle as permanent—that is, as an ongoing process, not one restricted to the month of April every four years. Another lesson of this presidential election is that fateful decisions were made well before the actual elections. Most important, the lack of attention by the government to the highly predictable postelection violence is shocking, to say the least.

Track II efforts at conflict resolution and post-traumatic healing should continue to be conducted off camera, so as to increase their effectiveness. In this process, universities (both in Nigeria and abroad) as well as NGOs have a role to play, with their conflict resolution centers and peace committees. (Chapter 4 offers further suggestions for reforms.)

If Nigeria is to repair the social and political damage wrought by the postelection violence, it needs wise and principled leaders, both at the national and at the state level. Unless leaders learn to manage the symbols of division and to provide positive reinforcement for policies of national reconciliation, the prospects for a unified, democratic Nigeria may remain elusive. There is no doubt that many of the postelection problems in the Middle Belt and elsewhere are exacerbated by governors who make local political calculations without attention to the national implications.

The international community in general and the United States in particular should also assess the role they have played. A realistic appraisal of how even the best-laid election observation plans in Nigeria can be undone by incumbents would be a worthy exercise and would enhance understanding of elections in Africa. The need for members of the international community to exercise judicious restraint while the appeals process was under way should be evident, which meant caution in embracing "winners" and dismissing "losers," at least until final appeal was exhausted at the end of December.

The larger issue of north-south relations in Nigeria is beyond the scope of this chapter, but clearly this is the enduring challenge for Nigerians of all political persuasions. Just as the insurgency in the oil-rich Delta is a "national unity" issue, so too are the results of an election in which northern Muslims supported one candidate and southern Christians unanimously supported another. It may take years to repair this damage, which may have consequences not only in Nigeria but throughout West Africa and beyond.

Unfortunately, the opportunity to learn lessons in the aftermath of the presidential election was largely overshadowed by two other challenges to national unity: the activities of Boko Haram, which originated in the northeast, calls for an Islamic state in Nigeria, and uses terrorist tactics; and the ethnoreligious crises in Plateau State in the Middle Belt that have turned Jos into an ethnically cleansed ghost town and resulted in thousands of killings throughout the state. Is Nigeria "a nation at war"?[52] Is there a threat to national unity?[53] We turn now to these challenges.

---

52   "A Nation at War," *Daily Trust,* November 16, 2011.

53   "Insecurity, Threat to Nigeria's Unity—Chief of Air Staff," *Tribune,* December 5, 2011: "The Chief of Air Staff, Air Marshall M.D. Umar, has stated that the state of insecurity in the country constitutes a great threat to the country's peace and unity."

CHAPTER 2

Strategic Responses to the Boko Haram Extremist Movement

The Movement for Sunnah and Jihad (Jama'atu Ahliss Sunnah Lidda-awati Wal Jihad), popularly known as Boko Haram (which means "Western Education Is Forbidden"), has claimed hundreds of lives in Nigeria since 2009, especially in the northeast states of Yobe and Borno. The movement emerged in northeast Nigeria in 2003 and has since spread to other areas of the north. The killing of its charismatic leader by police in 2009 only accelerated its growth. It appears intent on challenging the idea of a secular state in Nigeria and on setting up a shari'a-based system. Drive-by shootings and bombings by Boko Haram have confounded Nigerian state authorities at all levels, including in the national capital, Abuja. The apparent lack of contact between the Nigerian state and the grassroots communities in the north has limited information as to the exact nature and profile of this movement, complicating the task of devising effective responses.

Exacerbating this Boko Haram challenge, as noted in chapter 1, is northern disaffection at the outcome of the divisive presidential election in April 2011, in which a Christian incumbent candidate from the south officially beat a Muslim candidate widely popular in the north. The election was followed by widespread violence, including attacks on northern dignitaries perceived as supporting the incumbent. The tit-for-tat violence resulted in the destruction of Christian churches in the north and the ethnic cleansing of rural Muslims by Christian militias in places such as southern Kaduna. The Boko Haram movement is distinct from the more general sense of northern disaffection and anger following the elections. Whether these northern grassroots reactions will coalesce or otherwise reinforce one another remains to be seen.

This chapter focuses on the dilemma of responses by the Nigerian state to Boko Haram. Boko Haram has so far prompted a wide array of governmental reactions. These have ranged from local calls for amnesty and negotiations to the extrajudicial killing by police of the movement's charismatic leader, Muhammad Yusuf, and, since the national

41

elections in April 2011, the buildup of thousands of federal military and security forces in Maiduguri, the capital of Borno. There is an apparent disjunction between the military and security forces, who favor a hard-line response; political leaders, who seem to favor a hearts-and-minds approach plus negotiation and amnesty; and local elders, who are increasingly concerned that the heavy-handed response of the military is producing unexpected consequences. In addition, the bombing of the UN headquarters in Abuja on August 26, 2011, for which Boko Haram took credit, has underscored the possibility of international involvement in the increasingly sophisticated attacks.[1] As a consequence, international responses are also evolving.

During September, October, November, and December the attacks and counterattacks by police and military continued. (Weapons from Libya after the fall of Col. Muammar Gaddafi may have leaked from Niger Republic into northern Nigeria during this period.) On November 6, the international media reported that over one hundred people had been killed by Boko Haram in Damaturu (Yobe State) and Maiduguri. The targets were the police, the military, banks, churches, and an array of individuals. The U.S. embassy in Abuja issued a warning to U.S. citizens to stay away from upscale hotels in Abuja, because the embassy had information that such hotels would be targeted. (These warnings were later rescinded, but the damage to international confidence in Nigeria's security had been done—for instance, a major summit for potential investors that had been planned was canceled because of the warnings.)[2]

---

1   See "Muslim Sect Claims Bombing on Nigerian UN Building," Associated Press, August 26, 2011: "A spokesman for a radical Muslim sect in Nigeria known locally as Boko Haram has claimed responsibility for the car bombing at the United Nations' office that killed at least 16 people. The spokesman on Friday talked with the BBC's Hausa language service, which is widely trusted and listened to throughout Nigeria's Muslim north. They often make claims via that BBC service. . . . Gen. Carter Ham told AP on August 17 during a visit to Nigeria that 'multiple sources' indicate Boko Haram made contacts with al-Qaida in the Islamic Maghreb, which operates in northwest Africa, and with al-Shabab in Somalia." See also "Analysis: How the Nigeria Attack Shows Boko Haram Is Growing in Strength," *Daily Telegraph* (UK), August 26, 2011: "If the group has indeed established operational connections with AQIM across the border into Niger, kidnap of individuals for ransom and transfer into Niger or Mali would likely become a growing risk. The shared Hausa ethnicity and conservative form of Islam practiced on either side of the Niger/Nigeria border would facilitate movement by radical Islamists across this space. We had previously assessed that the failed Maiduguri suicide on August 15th represented no evolution in IED capability on the part of BH, and therefore likely no operational support from AQIM. [Yet] . . . the scale of the explosion at the UN building suggests a different method was used, for instance involving military grade explosive such as Semtex, or explosive made from ammonium nitrate. This would be clearer indication that training or supply lines have been opened between BH and AQIM." The subsequent death toll from the bombing of the UN building in Abuja was at least twenty-four.

2   Estimates for the death toll of the November 4–5 violence vary. The Chinese media reported 150 killed; *Al-Jazeera* placed the number at over one hundred. The *New York Times* figure was

In late November, Boko Haram announced that it regarded all existing politics as illegitimate and might target any and all political party
headquarters and any homes with partisan posters.[3] The Nigerian media
reported that security services had information about support of the
movement by some senior political leaders, but Boko Haram denied any
connection with the identified officials, and even threatened to kill them.
By late December, with the declaration of a state of emergency after the
Christmas bombings, Boko Haram had stepped up its attacks on churches
and threatened to kill Christians in the north if they did not flee to the
south of Nigeria.

Meanwhile, in July 2011, some national political leaders called for
"thought reform" or "re-programming" of the young men who have been
captured.[4] In early August 2011, the federal government set up a Presiden-

---

"at least 67": "On Friday, a car bomb exploded outside a three-story building used as a military
office and barracks in Damaturu, the capital of Yobe State, said Ibrahim Bulama, a Nigerian Red
Cross official. Gunmen then went through the town, blowing up a bank branch and attacking
at least three police stations and some churches, leaving them in rubble, he said. Gunfire continued through the night and gunmen raided the village of Potiskum, witnesses said, leaving
at least two people dead there. . . . In addition to the attacks around Damaturu, several bombings struck Maiduguri on Friday, about 80 miles to the east. One blast detonated about noon
outside the El-Kanemi Theological College where parents had gathered. . . . Another bombing
alongside a road in Maiduguri killed four people. . . . A short time later, suicide bombers in a
black S.U.V. tried to enter a base for the military unit charged with protecting the city from Boko
Haram fighters, said a military spokesman, Lt. Col. Hassan Ifijey Mohammed. The S.U.V. could
not enter the gate and the explosives were detonated outside the base, Colonel Mohammed
said. He said there were blasts at three other places in Maiduguri that killed no one. However,
government officials routinely play down such attacks because of political considerations." See
"Nigeria Attacks Kill at Least 67," *New York Times*, November 6, 2011.

3   "Nigeria: Boko Haram Vows to Attack Jonathan, Mark," *allAfrica.com*, November 25, 2011:
"Members of the Jama'atul Ahlil Sunna Lidawati wal Jihad, otherwise known as Boko Haram,
warned that it would, in a few days, embark on massive bombings of political party offices
across the country to correct the impression that they are agents of politicians, even as they
warned ordinary civilians who do not have anything to do with politics to stay away. The sect
also stated that President Goodluck Jonathan, Senate President David Mark, Jerry Gana, and
ex-Governor Ali Modu Sheriff are on their hit list and that it would soon attack them. The sect
has also denied having any relationship with Senator Muhammad Ali Ndume currently in the
custody of the State Security Service (SSS) over alleged involvement in its activities." For further
details, see "Nigeria: Boko Haram Disowns Konduga . . . Says Ndume Also a Target," *Daily Trust*,
November 24, 2011.

4   According to the *VOA News*, July 12, 2011, "Nigerian officials recently announced the arrest of
100 suspected Boko Haram members for carrying out a series of bombings across the country's
north. They said the suspects would undergo 'deradicalization' and 'perception management'
programs so they can return back to society." Also, see "Boko Haram: Military Chiefs, Political
Leaders Disagree," *Vanguard*, July 7, 2011: "Service chiefs and political leaders have disagreed
over the best approach to deal with the security challenge thrown up by the Boko Haram terrorist threat in Abuja, the Federal Capital Territory, FCT, and some states in the northern part
of the country. The service chiefs had been summoned to the National Assembly for a meeting
with the leadership of the legislature. Sources told *Sunday Vanguard* that there were marked
differences in the disposition of the security chiefs at the meeting and that of political leaders
who are seeking a political solution to the Boko Haram's spate of deadly attacks on the security
personnel, institutions and infrastructure by the pro-Islamic militant group. . . . The source

tial Fact-Finding Committee "to discuss the best way out of the security challenges posed by the Boko Haram Islamic sect in the North-eastern part of the country."[5] The so-called Galtimari report was presented in September and urged negotiations with Boko Haram, to be led by the sultan of Sokoto and the emir of Bauchi. Some local elders also called for negotiations. Unfortunately, by October, Boko Haram had issued a statement declaring that it did not recognize the authority of the sultan or the emir and would not negotiate with them.[6]

The complex relationship between federal, state, and local government levels, plus the inevitable institutional tensions among security services, military, police, other government agencies, think tanks, civil society organizations, and academic entities, plus differing perspectives among elected politicians and traditional leaders, has meant that no coordinated response has emerged, at least not until the declaration of state of emergency on December 31st, which essentially militarized the federal strategy.

Whatever immediate or short-term policies are adopted to tackle Boko Haram, the fate of the challenge posed by the movement will be determined by the medium- and longer-term approaches taken by the state. This chapter argues that the major issue to be resolved is the *apparent disconnect between grassroots citizens and the Nigerian state* in the northeast and elsewhere in the north.[7] The state may be looking for *cul-*

---

close to the National Assembly parley with the service chiefs said the top military officials did not buy the carrot and stick policy of the Jonathan administration." Some of the thought reform was to be sourced to local imams and religious leaders.

5   See "Boko Haram: FG Inaugurates Fact-Finding Panel," *Thisday*, August 3, 2011: "The committee headed by Alhaji Usman Galtimari, a senior civil servant from Borno State who headed a committee which produced a report following the 2009 Boko Haram uprising in which hundreds of people were killed, is to create a forum for a pool of suggestions what will guide the Federal Government on whether to negotiate with Boko Haram or not. . . . The members of the committee include Senator Mohammad Ali Ndume; Mr. Joe Kyari Gadzama (SAN); Col. Musa Shehu (rtd); the Minister of FCT, Senator Bala Mohammed; Minister of Defence, Dr. Bello Haliru Mohammed; and Minister of Labour and Productivity, Mr. Emeka Wogu as members, while Mr. Abdullahi Shehu from the Office of the SGF is the Secretary."

6   As of December, the debate continued regarding the efficacy of "dialogue." See "'Dialogue,' Most Viable Option to Tackle Boko Haram," *Tribune*, December 5, 2011: "National coordinator, Nigeria Inter-Religious Council (NIREC), Professor Is-Haq Oloyede, has said dialogue remains the most viable option in addressing the menace posed by the dreaded religious sect, Boko Haram."

7   The disconnect is apparent to most observers and even participants. See "Anxiety Mounts over Insecurity, Poverty, Others," *Guardian*, December 5, 2011: "Jigawa State governor, Sule Lamido, in an interview with The Guardian, put it succinctly, 'there is a disconnection between the people and the leadership, hence the leaders have no capacity to motivate or to inspire the people or restore confidence. Because of this disconnection, our institutions have collapsed. I thought it was bad enough that our public institutions alone were collapsing, but with the story of the failure of banks making the rounds, I am now alarmed.'" See also blog commentary, such as that of Mustapha Mamadu, "MEND, MASSOB, Boko Haram, et al: Why Current Peace Efforts

prits, but its chief goal should be to identify *causes* of the disaffection in the north of the country and then take concrete steps to address those.

Suggestions are made in this chapter for undertaking reforms that would enhance mass-elite linkages in several domains over the longer term, including

*   Enhancing human security in Borno

*   Strengthening the capacity of local governments to function as a robust third tier of government, including with direct federal-local funding

*   Recognizing the potential for traditional leaders to serve as conflict resolvers at the grassroots level

*   Reforming the capacity of the police to serve and protect at the state and local levels by reassessing nonfederal options, plus training and deployment issues

*   Providing enhanced resources for mass education at the basic levels, especially through teacher training, and directly engaging the Islamic educational facilities at grassroots levels

*   Enhancing national leadership capabilities to focus on conflict prevention and mitigation, especially through attention to "symbol management" in the Office of the President, via the media and other actors

*   Clarifying the role and accountability of the military forces in domestic disturbances, including a reassessment of the importance of identity politics in the allocation of such forces

*   Moving beyond ad hoc commissions to assess the policy and strategic implications of grassroots extremism, and better utilizing such resources as the National Institute for Policy and Strategic Studies for longer-term planning, drawing on lessons learned from the initial confrontations

---

Will Fail," December 17, 2011, http://www.gamji.com/article9000/NEWS9554.htm: "The Arewa Consultative Forum (ACF) apparently responding to the blackmail that the Northern elite has remained silent in the face of the 'unstoppable' Boko Haram attacks, held a peace conference last week. As expected, it was the very set of people that created our collective insecurity that came to speak. The real victims, the ordinary northerner and others that live in the north did not get to speak! And there lies the reason why no solutions would be found. From the Senate President who succumbed to the blackmail theory to the Sultan who believes the Traditional institution should have a role (presumably constitutional) in resolving the insecurity, it is difficult to miss the irony that the people's fury is targeted more towards the institutions these two represent (politicians and traditional rulers). The ordinary Northerner today seriously distrusts these two groups. What they should be working on is regaining their respectability since the last elections."

The main concern of this chapter is for the national unity of Nigeria and the kinds of policies and strategic approaches that might help build unity.[8] The threats to national unity come not just from extremist groups in the north but also from the south-south oil-producing areas, which are beyond the scope of this monograph. Thus, the example of Boko Haram is important and needs to be contextualized. The impact of the Boko Haram movement on the fears of Muslim extremism in other parts of Nigeria has been powerful and will likely increase. Hence, it is useful to summarize what is known, and what is not known, about the movement.

Boko Haram and Human Security in Borno

Earlier manifestations of Boko Haram came into public view around 2003–4, when clashes erupted in Yobe between the precursors of the movement and the police. Many were killed on both sides and the group, sometimes called "the Black Taliban" by outsiders, was dispersed.[9] By 2006, the authorities had arrested the apparent leader of a successor movement in Maiduguri, Muhammad Yusuf, but he was released, in part because of high-level influence. Then, in summer 2009, came a major clash between some of Yusuf's group and the police over an issue of not wearing helmets on motorbikes. In the resultant crackdown, hundreds of supporters were rounded up and killed or jailed.

The popular name of Boko Haram is a misnomer, although the symbolism of "Western Education Is Forbidden" is clear: Islamic culture will not tolerate its marginalization by Western culture. (*Boko* is the Hausa neologism for "book" and refers in general to Western education and more specifically to the use of English in education.) Yet, unlike with the

---

8   For a brief background on the context of Nigerian political risk, see the report by Peter Lewis, "Nigeria: Assessing Risks to Stability" (Center for Strategic and International Studies, Washington, D.C., June 2011). See also the report by Richard Downie and Jennifer G. Cooke, "Assessing Risks to Stability in Sub-Saharan Africa" (Center for Strategic and International Studies, Washington, D.C., June 2011). For a fuller background, see John Campbell, *Nigeria: Dancing on the Brink* (Boulder, CO: Rowman & Littlefield, 2011).

9   The author has followed this movement since 2004, and especially since 2009, when the group's leader was killed in police custody and the group went underground. This chapter will draw only the most basic outline of the movement, because it is constantly evolving. This ambiguity and process of change are part of the policy challenge. As noted in the Introduction, the author has access only to open sources, including academic inquiries and the hundreds of newspaper articles on the group. In general, the northern press (e.g., the *Daily Trust*) is more reliable than the southern press, which sometimes tends to be alarmist. Even the international press has picked up on these fears. See "Fear of Islamic Militant Attacks in Nigeria Spreads to Lagos," *VOA News*, July 12, 2011. The State Security Services (SSS) of Nigeria are widely regarded as ineffective in the process of dealing with the grassroots nature of the Boko Haram challenge, in part because of poor relations with local communities. Without access to classified sources, however, this assessment is hard to confirm.

earlier Maitatsine movement in the north, Boko Haram followers do not shun Western technology; indeed, they make conspicuous use of motorbikes, automatic weapons, and information media. Also unlike with the Maitatsine movement, Boko Haram's basic theology is seen as recognizably orthodox (albeit extreme and fundamentalist) in the north. The use of Hausa language as the lingua franca in the north, even in Borno, where it is not indigenous, is central to the communication processes of Boko Haram.

Yet, the key ingredient in the movement is a strict adherence to the perceived fundamentals of Islam, especially the enforcement of shari'a law, the rejection of a secular state, and the espousal of an Islamic state. One of the key symbols of shari'a is the prohibition of alcohol, and many of the bombings and drive-by shootings perpetrated by the movement have targeted nightclubs and beer halls, frequented by non-Muslims as well as more secular "modern-sector" Muslims. Whether the group has significant external links is an open question.[10]

The secular state is epitomized by the police, which in Nigeria is entirely federal. The fact that many of the federal police are non-Muslims from other parts of Nigeria, and that police barracks are excluded from the ban on alcohol in the northern states, has led some observers to conclude that there is an anti-Christian bias in Boko Haram. The additional fact that for much of the period of the Fourth Republic—from 1999 to 2007, and in 2010 and 2011—the presidents of Nigeria have been southern Christians has led to the northern impression that Nigeria is controlled by non-Muslims. The FCT in Abuja has become a symbol of the secular (or even "Christian") state.

In short, Boko Haram followers do not accept the idea of a secular Nigerian state. Rather than espouse secession of the north from Nigeria, the movement has tended in the past to emphasize the need to Islamize Nigeria. However, as the movement evolves there are indications that the goal is no longer to Islamize Nigeria but to set up a separate Islamic state

---

10   See "Islamist Threat in Nigeria Grows with Qaeda Help: Alarm Shown by West," *New York Times*, August 18, 2011. The interpretation by many in the West of possible links to al Qaeda, especially al Qaeda in the Islamic Maghreb (AQIM), was not widely shared in Nigeria, at least up until the bombing of the UN building in Abuja. According to the *New York Times* article, "Gen. Carter F. Ham, the head of the United States Africa Command, told The Associated Press that there were also signs that Boko Haram and AQIM wanted to establish a 'loose partnership' with the Shabab, the militant group that controls much of southern Somalia. . . . Such a collaboration 'would be the most dangerous thing to happen not only to the Africans, but to us as well,' he said. Boko Haram, however, is rapidly evolving. It has a virulent Web site taunting the security services, promising 'more attacks on the way!!!' all 'in the name of Allah,' and inviting e-mails to 'nigjihadist,' additional signs of outside influence, analysts say."

in the north. Security reports leaked to the Nigerian press in the summer of 2011 suggest that there are three factions within the movement, each with its own agenda, but this is clearly speculation and it is difficult to know what the real intentions of the group may be.[11] The emergence of Boko Haram is a Fourth Republic "civilian-era" phenomenon—that is, it did not emerge during the previous military period.

Boko Haram is based in Borno, not just in Borno State but in the entire area of northeast Nigeria (including Yobe State, which broke away from Borno State in 1991).[12] This broad area is distinguished by its nineteenth-century rejection of the Sokoto Caliphate, which includes most of the rest of the far north. The precolonial polity of Borno is the oldest continuous Islamic state in sub-Saharan Africa, dating from the eleventh century.

Borno was ruled by the shehu of Borno, who even today is ranked as second only to the sultan of Sokoto in terms of protocol among northern traditional rulers. The current shehu was crowned ("turbaned") in 2009 and represents a younger generation of Western-educated administrators with a specialty in local government.[13] His predecessor was inaugurated in 1974 and represented a more traditional approach.[14] All male members of the royal extended family are eligible for selection to traditional positions, and the state governors make the final choice. (Both the current and previous governors of Borno State are members of the ANPP, and thus in opposition to the dominant PDP.)

---

11 See "Boko Haram's Divided House," *Nigerian Voice*, July 24, 2011. Two of the groups revolve around personalities. The third group is reported as consisting of young men from Niger and Chad, as well as Maiduguri Metropolis and Jere Local Government. Obviously, in the wake of the death of a charismatic leader, there is a vacuum.

12 The 2006 census put the population of Borno at 4,151,193, and the population of Yobe at 2,321,591. The annual population growth rate for Nigeria as a whole is 2.38 percent; the median age is 18.7 years. The most populous state in Nigeria, according to the 2006 census, is Kano, with a population of 9,383,682. Many in the northern establishment feared the Boko Haram movement would spread to Kano, which has the largest urban center in the north.

13 Abubakar ibn Umar Garbai el-Kanemi, born in May 1957, entered Borno State government service in 1976. Subsequently, he attended Kaduna Polytechnic (1978–82) and Ahmadu Bello University, Zaria (1986), gaining an advanced diploma in local government administration. He became a permanent secretary in the Ministry of Finance in 1993, and in both the Ministry of Works and Housing and the Ministry of Local Government and Chieftaincy Affairs in 2008. He was appointed shehu by Borno State governor Ali Modu Sheriff on March 2, 2009.

14 The author attended the inauguration of the shehu in 1974, which was accompanied by the full panoply of a horse-charge durbar. Shehu Mustapha Amin el-Kanemi had a long reign (1974–2009). He was born in Dikwa in 1924 and became secretary to the wali of Borno in 1945. In 1952, he attended Ahmadu Bello University, Zaria, where he studied public administration. He was elected to the Northern Regional House of Assembly in 1956 and was reelected in 1959. In 1970, he was made district head. He became shehu in 1974 and as such was vice president of the Nigerian Supreme Council for Islamic Affairs.

Although the Kanuri are the major ethnolinguistic group in Borno, there are numerous minority groups in the area. Collectively, the Hausa language outgroup identity designation for people from Borno is "Beri-beri." As noted, Hausa has become the lingua franca throughout the north, and hence ethnolinguistic identity designations have become increasingly blurred in Borno, especially given mixed-marriage patterns among the Muslim populations.

Other salient features of Borno include

- A general/historical orientation to the east (that is, Chad and Sudan) rather than the western Savannah zones

- A more recent locus of refugees and migrants from the east, as political disorder has come to characterize these neighboring failed states

- A serious desertification of the area, symbolized by the radical shrinking of the Lake Chad catchment area[15]

- A general rejection of Sufism (common throughout the Sokoto Caliphate), in favor of "basic Islam" as practiced over the centuries

- A lack of economic opportunities for the demographic "youth bulge"

- A wide range of anecdotal characteristics[16]

- Porous borders with neighboring states[17]

Despite the semblance of a modern sector in Maiduguri (for instance, the presence of a federal university, a teaching hospital, and a wealthy elite), the majority of people are poor and, given the overall recession, are likely to experience deteriorating living conditions, especially as farming options worsen and opportunities in the urban areas shrink. This three-class society—"rulers" (*sarauta*), "big men" (*manya-manya*), and "commoners" (*talakawa*)—can easily be tipped into violence by events (such

---

15 See Tijjani Muhammad Bande, "Multilateral Water Organizations and Nigeria's National Interest: Lake Chad Basin Commission and Niger Basin Authority," in Attahiru M. Jega and Jacqueline W. Farris, eds., *Nigeria at Fifty: Contributions to Peace, Democracy and Development* (Abuja: Shehu Musa Yar'Adua Foundation, 2011).

16 As early as the 1970s, if one were to ask a businessman in Kano what enterprise offered the most promising opportunities in Borno, the answer would likely have been "gun running." At the same time, many indigenous academics at the University of Maiduguri were taking great pride in the long history of the Borno/Kanem empire, and they have made enormous contributions to an understanding of the history of Sudanic Africa.

17 For discussion of Nigeria's border policy in West Africa, see Hamid Bobboyi, "Nigeria, ECO-WAS, and the Promotion of Regional Integration in West Africa," in Jega and Farris, eds., *Nigeria at Fifty*. Dr. Bobboyi is a former director of Arewa House, Ahmadu Bello University, Kaduna, and since 2011 has served as the director of the Centre for Regional Integration and Development, Abuja, Nigeria.

as elections) and/or the demonstration effects of socioeconomic polarization.[18]

In short, the human security situation in Borno is precarious, with desert encroachment, a youth bulge, and few opportunities for jobs. In addition, because of the porous borders, Borno has attracted youth from surrounding countries, who are in even worse straits. Historically, the Islamic networks in northern Nigeria have served to accommodate migrants from surrounding countries. But the human security system in Borno is clearly overloaded.

What is missing from this locational profile of Borno is an answer to the question, who are the Boko Haram followers? Of the hundreds of Nigerian newspaper articles on Boko Haram since 2009, few help us to answer this question. What is clear, however, is that most followers are young men from the grassroots levels, although there are indications that the movement has had links within the ruling and big-men strata of society, at least up until 2009. The "martyrdom" of Muhammad Yusuf—leading to the cult of Yusufiyya—and the crackdown by the police have pushed the movement underground, and it has spread to other parts of the north.

The jailbreak by hundreds of Yusufiyya incarcerated in Bauchi State turned Bauchi into a key node in the larger northern network. Boko Haram preachers are now evident in Kano urban areas, as well as in other parts of the north. In June 2011, bank robbers in Katsina took their inspiration from Boko Haram and distributed their loot to poor people who have remained mired in poverty while new oil-rich elites have prospered. In short, the movement has rapidly evolved, especially since the elections of 2011, into something much larger than its original incarnation.

The response of the federal authorities (to be discussed below), especially the military Joint Task Force (JTF), appears to have added fuel to the flames of this grassroots northern movement. Most notably, the rounding up by the federal authorities of young men in the proximity of each bomb attack or drive-by shooting in Borno and the burning of houses

---

18   The starkest example of wealth disparity in the north is the Kano-based businessman Aliko Dangote, a close associate of establishment politicians. See "The Sun Shines Bright," *Economist*, December 3, 2011: "Her $3 billion fortune makes Oprah Winfrey the wealthiest black person in America, a position she has held for years. But she is no longer the richest black person in the world. That honour now goes to Aliko Dangote, the Nigerian cement king. Critics grumble that he is too close to the country's soiled political class. Nonetheless his $10 billion fortune is money earned, not expropriated. The Dangote Group started as a small trading outfit in 1977. It has become a pan-African conglomerate with interests in sugar and logistics, as well as construction, and it is a real business, not a kleptocratic sham."

regarded as hideouts have alienated many innocent citizens. The community, it would appear, has closed its ears to pleas by the authorities for information as to who is (or who is not) a member of Boko Haram.[19]

According to press reports, since summer 2011 tens of thousands of ordinary citizens from Maiduguri have fled to the neighboring state of Yobe to avoid the chaos.[20] Damaturu (the capital of Yobe) has been swamped by refugees, including women and children, who have left everything behind and appear to be without food or means of support. The reaction of the security forces in Maiduguri and Damaturu has been to bemoan the lack of community cooperation.

The disconnect between federal authorities in Abuja—including police, security, military, and politicians—and the local grassroots communities in the north, plus the government's insensitivity to the ethnoreligious identity politics of the north, needs to be addressed if extremist movements are to have a harder time recruiting followers. One excellent place to start weaning away support for Boko Haram is at the local government level.

Reforming Local Government

The Nigerian Constitution of 1999 established a three-tier federal system, with 36 states and 774 local government areas (LGAs), which are comparable to counties or parishes in other federal systems. Unlike the U.S. Constitution, which is two tiered (with county boundaries subject to modification by state authorities), the Nigerian Constitution specifies LGA boundaries, which makes them difficult to adjust to changing demographic or political circumstances. Political representation at the state or local level has also been left more or less unchanged despite the govern-

---

19   The "who are they?" question is complicated by the out-group ascriptions and possible copy-cat activities of rival factions. For a cautionary view, see Jean Herskovits, "Boko Haram Not Problem," *Sahara Reporters*, January 3, 2012: "The news media and American policy makers are chasing an elusive and ill-defined threat; there is no proof that a well-organized, ideologically coherent terrorist group called Boko Haram even exists today. Evidence suggests instead that, while the original core of the group remains active, criminal gangs have adopted the name Boko Haram to claim responsibility for attacks when it suits them. . . . None of this excuses Boko Haram's killing of innocents. But it does raise questions about a rush to judgment that obscures Nigeria's complex reality." The article can be accessed at the *Sahara Reporters* website, http://saharareporters.com/article/boko-haram-not-problem-jean-herskovits.

20   *Sahara Reporters* has covered the Maiduguri situation in detail. See, for example, "Maiduguri Neighborhood in a Lockdown as JFT and Boko Haram Engage in a Firefight," July 23, 2011; "On Negotiations with Boko Haram," July 18, 2011; "Nigeria: Borno Governor Admits Army Boko Haram Excesses—BBC," July 17, 2011; "Boko Haram: Ineptitude, Double Standard Fuel Crises," July 20, 2011; and "'We Will Cease Fire for Ramadan,' Says Letter Received by *Desert Herald*," July 22, 2011.

ment having the data generated by the census of 2006. (The dominant political party likes things the way they are, or so it would seem.)

The challenge of strengthening Nigerian LGAs is deeply rooted, in that they depend for financing not on local taxes but on the trickle-down (or 10%) block grants given to the states according to a federal distribution pool formula; those grants are in turn allocated from the states to the LGAs. Thus, the democratic federalism of Nigeria is extremely centralized in practice, with federal oil revenues being the major source of funding for all three levels of government. This has resulted in the governors of the thirty-six states having enormous power to influence politics at the local level (including the power to influence the selection of LGA chairmen). It has also essentially disenfranchised local communities from being able to define their own needs, whether for security, education, economic infrastructure, or other public goods. (The federal government may be reassessing this arrangement at present.[21] If so, this move should be welcomed by local governments.)

As discussed below, the LGAs are also constrained by constitutional provisions requiring a "federal character" balance within the administrative units. Yet another complication is the distinction made between "indigenes" and "settlers" in the Constitution, which has become a constant source of friction and even violence in many of the northern states (see chapter 3).

Reforming the Role of Traditional Leaders

Significantly, there is nothing in the 1999 Constitution about the roles of emirs and chiefs. These traditional rulers are now called "royal fathers" and (aside from their private resources) are financially dependent on the goodwill of the state governors. Historically, the fact that emirs and chiefs were appointed for life (provided they behaved appropriately) meant that they had intimate contact with the grassroots elements of their domains. In practice, since the 1970s, when all powers of traditional rulers—includ-

---

21   See "Proposed Constitutional Amendment: Bill to Favour Devolution of Powers to States," *Guardian*, August 14, 2011: "Contrary to public perception, the proposed amendment to the 1999 Constitution by President Goodluck Jonathan is far beyond the single tenure for president and governors, and may result in the devolution of the functions currently under the exclusive federal list to the concurrent list, where they would be handed over to the states and local governments. . . . In addition, the proposal seeks to set the 774 local governments free from undue interference by governors, who have formed the habit of tampering with council funds in the name of a controversial joint Account system. That system will cease to exist and the third-tier of government will start getting direct funding from the Federation Account."

ing security and policing—were allocated to more centralized bodies, the best of the emirs and chiefs have tried to serve as conflict resolvers or informal mediators within their domains.[22]

Members of the current generation of royal fathers have tended to be selected, at least in part, because of their Western education and success as professionals or business leaders. A close connection has developed between such traditional leaders and the modern political elites, who control resources and appointment and deposition procedures. These modern royal fathers may have less contact than their predecessors enjoyed with their grassroots constituencies, but they nonetheless constitute an underutilized resource in terms of linkages with grassroots communities.[23]

The current sultan of Sokoto, Muhammad Sa'ad Abubakar III, is the first among equals among the northern emirs and chiefs. He has argued for clear constitutional or legal standing for the emirs and chiefs. His role as cochair of NIREC, along with the president of the CAN, would suggest that conflict resolution or Track II mediation would be one of the responsibilities or duties of this potential "fourth tier" of authority. This initiative for official recognition by the sultan should be welcomed by the strategic planners in Nigeria, because it serves as a connection with the grassroots. At the same time, the legitimacy of such offices must be seen to be coming from the local communities, and not from federal or state authorities. (The office of sultan still enjoys enormous popular respect, even after the controversies surrounding the presidential election of 2011.)[24]

The delicate balance of a three-tier federalism based on an oil economy, plus the underutilized capacity of traditional authorities, should be

---

22   For background, see William F. S. Miles, "Traditional Rulers and Development Administration: Chieftaincy in Niger, Nigeria, and Vanuatu," *Studies in Comparative International Development* 28, no. 3 (Fall 1993): 31–50. For an earlier assessment, see Michael Crowder and Obaro Ikime, eds., *West African Chiefs: Their Changing Status under Colonial Rule and Independence* (New York: Africana Publishing Corporation, 1970).

23   For an effort by the emirs to deal with the problems of "*almajiri*" (i.e., children begging to support their Koranic school studies), see Haruna Manu Isah, "Almajiri Headaches: Emirs Declare War," *Gamji.com,* December 3, 2011, http://www.gamji.com/article9000/NEWS9543.htm.

24   The sultan has become very outspoken on issues of corruption, which he relates to the malaise of the country. For his remarks at his installation as chancellor of Ahmadu Bello University in November, 2011, see "Nigeria in State of Fear and Anxiety—Sultan," *Daily Trust*, November 25, 2011. For an indication of the key role of the sultan in northern leadership circles, see "Arewa Peace Conference Starts Today," *Daily Trust*, December 5, 2011: "Kaduna State Governor Patrick Ibrahim Yakowa and Sultan of Sokoto Muhammad Sa'ad Abubakar would serve as host and father of the day respectively." The article continues: "This two day Arewa Consultative Forum/ ACF event drew most of the traditional and political leaders of the north to discuss "causes of conflict in the region and the way forward under the theme 'Peace and Unity for development.'"

a subject of strategic and policy planning in Nigeria at the highest levels. Many of the constitutional constraints on the local levels can be interpreted legally in such a way as to avoid the extremely cumbersome process for amending the Constitution and allow for a more robust capacity to evolve to meet the community need at the grassroots levels. The pendulum swing since the 1970s toward extreme centralization should be allowed to recalibrate toward an appropriate and flexible balance between the various levels of government, and between the traditional and modern elements in a society under the extreme pressures of rapid change.

Nowhere is this more urgent than in the domain of police services. The 1999 Constitution places *all* police capacities in the federal exclusive list. With over 300,000 personnel, the police constitute the single-largest security resource. Police commissioners are rotated among the states and are responsible to the inspector general of police in Abuja. The question is how well they serve and protect the people at the local levels. (See chapter 4 for more discussion of this.)

Reforming Police Services

For historical reasons, three types of legal systems have evolved in Nigeria: national criminal and civil codes; shari'a law, in both criminal and civil domains in the twelve far northern states; and traditional civil codes for indigenous cultures, especially on matters of marriage, divorce, and inheritance. It is the duty of the police to enforce the national criminal and civil codes, but not the other two legal systems. This has left a vacuum in the shari'a states that has been filled by the state-sanctioned *Hisbah* police and other forces.[25]

During the colonial period in northern Nigeria, the British encapsulated the Maliki system of shari'a law in both criminal and civil domains.

---

25 The *Hisbah* can also get involved in politics. See "Gov Kwankwaso Floats Private Army, Relegates Hisbah Guard," *Vanguard*, August 22, 2011: "Governor Rabiu Musa Kwankwaso of Kano State has floated a new security outfit, known in local parlance as *Askarawan Kwankwaso* [Kwankwaso's police] to rival the activities of the Hisbah guard in the state. The private army, believed to be in the range of 7,000 men, made its first public appearance during the May 29th swearing-in of Kwankwaso and had since consolidated its presence in the streets, neighbourhoods, and government functions. *Vanguard* learned that the 'private army' that has Kwankwaso as the commander-in-chief is made up of people suspected to have played a major role in the governor's comeback bid during the 2011 election. Members of *Askarawan Kwankwaso*, kitted in white upon green uniform with a red cap to match, carry out similar functions as the Sharia implementation guards which the governor established in his first tenure for the enforcement of the Sharia legal system in the state. *Vanguard* learnt that Kwankwaso's decision to float a new security outfit followed alleged partisanship of the Hisbah Guard on or before the 2011 general election, having withdrawn from the streets after he was announced winner of the gubernatorial election."

At the time of the First Republic (1960–66), the emirs retained legal powers in the civil domains, but all criminal matters became part of a national code. The Native Authority (NA) system, inherited from the Indirect Rule policy of the British, allowed the emirs to retain judicial rights, as well as their own police forces (*dogarai*). Over time, the NA system was replaced by a regional system, including police and shari'a courts of appeal. With the collapse of the First Republic, following the assassination of key northern leaders, and the subsequent civil war, the periods of military rule were characterized by martial law. Police were put directly under the military, and the local government aspect of policing was eclipsed completely.

When civilian rule returned in 1999 and a new constitution was adopted, the twelve far northern states interpreted that constitution as allowing for shari'a law in the criminal domains. Each of the twelve states[26] enacted legislation in 2000 that established shari'a penal codes deemed appropriate to their states. Shari'a courts of appeal were set up. There was no shari'a supreme court, but there was an agreement that justices well versed in shari'a would be appointed to the national Supreme Court, in case some appeals went to that level. (As of 2011, this had not yet happened. The issue of *Hisbah* police was taken to the Supreme Court but, for political reasons, never decided.)

Meanwhile, as mentioned, the entire police force was federalized, and centralized in Abuja. For reasons of federal character and because of persistent fears that too close an association between security officers and politicians in certain localities could set the stage for coups d'état, key police officials have been rotated to different states. The police, like the military officer corps, are recruited from each of the thirty-six states, and their deployment and careers are determined at the central level. This means that in some cases, officers may not even speak the local languages of the communities they serve. (English is the official language of the police.)

This pattern of federalized police is a major difference between the Nigerian Constitution and the document on which it was modeled, the U.S. Constitution. Not having a state and local (including metropolitan) police force may have made sense during the military periods in Nigeria, but it is hardly a recipe for effectively handling the increasing volume of grassroots crime and security issues that have arisen since 1999. Indeed,

---

26   Sokoto, Kebbi, Zamfara, Katsina, Kaduna, Niger, Kano, Jigawa, Bauchi, Gombe, Yobe, and Borno.

until well into the Fourth Republic, the motto on the side of all police vehicles in Nigeria was "Fire for Fire"—in other words, "you attack us, and we will attack you." This motto has changed in recent years to more of a serve-and-protect model, but echoes of the military top-down approach to local crime are still apparent, especially in the case of the dreaded mobile police units, which can swiftly put down local disturbances during elections and other potential flashpoints.

At this point, the Economic and Financial Crimes Commission (EFCC) should be mentioned. The EFCC is a specialized police unit set up by President Obasanjo to gather evidence of corruption and malfeasance, especially at the senior levels of government. "Persons of interest" identified by the EFCC are referred to the regular court system. Initially under Chairman Nuhu Ribadu,[27] the EFCC made significant inroads into high-level corruption (plus other financial crimes, such as the infamous "419 scams"). Subsequently, the inquiries appear to have been politically biased, and in recent years the EFCC has been hamstrung by the politics of an oil-driven political economy.[28]

Given the international nature of many financial crimes, the London Metropolitan Police (in cooperation with Interpol) has launched its own investigations into money laundering, and several high-level Nigerian political figures have been indicted. But the pervasive nature of economic corruption in Nigeria has led to a stalemate with the international community, whose members are caught on the horns of the dilemma: wishing for a stable Nigeria and needing cooperation with Nigerian senior officials on antiterrorism and other weighty issues, while hoping for domestic reforms in Nigeria to tackle corruption.

Indeed, the lack of campaign finance regulations in Nigeria, and the advantage this gives to incumbents during elections, is one of the main sources of anger at the grassroots level. In April 2011, this anger exploded into a rampage of extraordinary violence, often targeted at incumbents

---

27   Nuhu Ribadu is a lawyer and policeman in his fifties, originally from Yola (Adamawa). During the 2011 presidential election, he ran on the platform of the Action Congress of Nigeria, based largely in the southwest. Clearly, his anticorruption agenda echoed that of Buhari, whom he respects.

28   See Human Rights Watch, *Nigeria: War on Corruption Hangs in the Balance: Urgent Need to Fix Key Anti-Corruption Agency*, August 25, 2011. The sixty-four-page report, *Corruption on Trial? The Record of Nigeria's Economic and Financial Crimes Commission*, which can be accessed at the HRW website, www.hrw.org, analyzes the record of the commission. In November 2011, the chair of the EFCC, Mrs. Farida Waziri, was removed by President Jonathan and replaced by her deputy, Ibrahim Lamurde.

from the dominant party, even those from the same ethnoreligious groups as the grassroots protesters.[29]

All of these problematic policies—highly centralized police, rotations of personnel that are intended to weaken links with local communities, heavy-handed control of local situations, inadequate mechanisms to deal with corruption and/or campaign finance abuses—have come into focus in the period since the elections in April 2011. The Boko Haram phenomenon is only one manifestation of this disconnect between the state and the people.

What, then, is to be done? The most obvious reform is to interpret the Constitution in such a way as to give operational police control over local communities to members from that community. Without the cooperation of local communities, the whole idea of community policing, common in the West, is undermined, as are hopes for civilian cooperation with the police. This constitutional reinterpretation is more than just a matter of police training, important as training may be; it is also a matter of accountability, especially given the history of extrajudicial killings by Nigerian police, who act with impunity in revenge for the killing of fellow police officers.

Another obvious reform would be a zero-tolerance policy for corruption by the police. Due process should be accorded to offenders, but adopting a policy of "one strike and you're out" would send a powerful message to the public that the era of impunity is over. (Clearly, political leadership would be necessary for this to occur.) Even high-level police commissioners and the inspector general of police should not be immune from investigation into accusations of corruption.

Finally, the role of the *Hisbah* should be clarified once and for all, by scholars who are familiar with the nuances of shari'a law, so as to dispel misconceived Christian fears about the powers of the *Hisbah* police. Non-Muslims are not subject to shari'a law in any state, and hence the *Hisbah* police can act only within the Muslim community. Alcohol bans and the prohibition of prostitution are matters for state law, not shari'a law. Each state should adopt a political process that tries to carve out reasonable accommodation between Muslims and Christians on sensitive issues such as alcohol, thereby denying extremists the opportunity to inflame tensions. It should be added that the current exemption of the police

---

29   See U.S. Commission on International Religious Freedom, *Annual Report, 2011*, for background. The report was published just prior to the elections. For more on postelection violence, see HRW, *Nigeria: Post-election Violence Killed 800.*

from alcohol bans is a sore point, and some political solution is needed here to lessen the direct confrontation with extremists, who see this as a cause célèbre.

Yet, as long as unemployment persists and income disparities increase, there will be a latent anger at the grassroots levels. What, then, are the solutions to the pain and despair of unemployment? Clearly, a major challenge will be reforming the education sectors.

Reforming Education

The answer that policymakers should give to the assertion "Western Education Is *Forbidden*" (i.e., Boko Haram) is "Western Education Is *Required* (or at least *Recommended*)."[30] "Western education," however, does not need to be conducted in the English language. Nor is it incompatible with religious and cultural values of the northern community. From the early days of the First Republic, policymakers in the north have struggled with the need to engage families and students at all levels of education, and with the need to engage the traditional advanced Islamic schools (*ilmi*) and the more basic Koranic schools, including in math and science.[31] Indeed, most of the northern leaders of the First Republic (1960–66) and Second Republic (1979–83) were teachers, and many were versed in religious learning.

The shift to military rulers and the adjustments to an oil economy have all but destroyed this early commitment to an educational system that is transformative. The early northern leaders believed that education was the foundation of all progress. They believed in cooperation with "People of the Book" (*Ahl al-Kitab*, a term for Jews, Christians, and Muslims, in contradistinction to "polytheists") and in the Koranic imperative that, if necessary, one should "go to China for knowledge."

In a globalized world, knowledge is the currency of power and prosperity, and knowledge comes through education. Those left behind in the global educational race present a policy challenge, but the Koranic imperative that "education is required" still stands. The challenge in northern Nigeria is how to implement this imperative, for men and women and for all strata of society. Obviously, education is not a short-term fix but a long-term investment.

---

30   In Islamic law, there are five categories of behavior: required, recommended, neutral, discouraged, and forbidden.

31   See John Paden, *Ahmadu Bello, Sardauna of Sokoto: Values and Leadership in Nigeria* (London: Hodder and Stoughton, 1986).

The colonial educational legacy in the north was very much in the British elitist mode, with sons of traditional rulers going first to Katsina College, and later to Barewa College in Zaria. With independence, a number of educational crash courses were set up in the north to allow northerners to catch up with the south, culminating in 1962 with the establishment of Ahmadu Bello University (in Zaria), which even today is probably the largest university in sub-Saharan Africa. Other universities in the far north followed quickly, in Kano (Bayero University, Kano), in Sokoto (Usmanu Danfodiyo University), in Maiduguri, and elsewhere in the Middle Belt.[32]

Since the establishment of the Fourth Republic, private university experiments have emerged in the north, ranging from the American (Abti) University in Yola—also called American University, Nigeria/AUN— with its emphasis on entrepreneurship and technology, to the Islamic University in Katsina, with its standard curricular offerings in Arabic as well as English. (Northern Muslim parents seem to prefer that their children learn Arabic in Nigeria than that they go to Yemen or other Middle Eastern university centers. The father of Umar Farouk Abdulmuttalab—"the Christmas bomber," who tried to blow up a plane over Detroit—has been one of the chief sponsors of the Islamic University in Katsina.)

The weakest link in the educational system is probably in the teacher training school system. These schools are often attached to established universities but suffer from a lack of financial and human resources. Most of their graduates go into primary school teaching, although some become secondary school teachers. (English-language skills are the critical variable determining who finds a job at the secondary level.) The national director of the teacher training schools programs in Abuja[33] has been hamstrung by the policy perception that teacher training is a second-class occupation, even though it is likely to have more impact on the quality of education at the grassroots level than teaching standard university graduates.

---

32   As noted previously, the author of this monograph served as Professor of Public Administration at Ahmadu Bello University and as the founding dean of the Faculty of Social and Management Sciences at Bayero University, Kano. At present he is active in creating and developing linkage relationships with Usmanu Danfodio University, Sokoto. He was invited to serve on the Board of Trustees of the American University, Yola, but declined because of his time commitment to the universities in Kano and Sokoto. In the 1980s, he worked closely with the vice chancellor of the University of Maiduguri. The second generation of universities, or "Seven Sisters," was founded during the same period in the 1970s in Kano, Sokoto, Maiduguri, Jos, Oyo, Calabar, and Port Harcourt.

33   Dr. Muhammad Junaid is one of the Western-educated sons of the late Waziri Junaid of Sokoto, who was perhaps the most revered Islamic scholar of the First Republic and the key adviser to the sultans of Sokoto.

Policy attention must be directed to the teacher training programs that will have the most impact on primary school educational capacities.[34] The recent commitment by international aid groups to fund primary school teaching in the north in the Hausa language should be encouraged and monitored for its educational impact. The question is whether there are vernacular-language textbooks available in math and science.

One controversial issue that requires resolution is how the compulsory Islamic Religious Knowledge (IRK) and/or Christian Religious Knowledge (CRK) courses should be taught in primary school. One proposal is to combine IRK and CRK so that students can have a better idea as to what their fellow citizens believe. This idea, however, raises sensitive issues and seems open to possible misinterpretations.

Just as some institutions provide university training and teacher training, vocational polytechnic schools in the north also need added support. These provide a pipeline from primary and secondary schools to practical, vocational opportunities.

Conflict resolution techniques should become part of the curriculum in military training and/or police training institutions.[35]

But the main policy question is how to fund the English-speaking Western (i.e., *boko*) schools in the north and how to link them with the Islamic primary and secondary schools. Funding tends to come from the center and percolate down to the state and local levels, constraining the capacity of local school systems to experiment and adjust to local realities. This arrangement invites criticism, from both mainstream and fringe groups, that the planners in Abuja do not understand local needs. If Nigeria is to evolve toward a true federalism, as a way of accommodating its diversity, local communities need to have greater control over many different areas of their own lives, including education. The pioneering efforts by Bayero University, Kano (BUK) to introduce some courses— especially in math and science—currently taught in the *boko* schools into the Islamic schools as well should be encouraged and results evaluated.

In part, the question of educational policy is a national political issue. Muhammadu Buhari has set investment in education as one of his three top priorities, along with security and anti-corruption. Many of the young

---

34 See "FG to Unveil 4-yr Plan for Education Sector," *New Nigerian*, July 26, 2011. Fortunately, the minister of education, Professor Ruqqyat Rufai, has announced that teacher training will be a priority.

35 Conflict resolution courses would be especially valuable at the Nigerian Defence Academy in Kaduna.

men who took to the streets to protest Buhari's loss of the presidential election in April 2011 had pinned their hopes on his election as a way to escape their educational dead ends. Whether the Jonathan administration will learn from the popularity of Buhari in the far north, especially with regard to educational reforms, remains to be seen.

This political issue raises the central question of how to reform national leadership capacities and structures with regard to strengthening national unity while still allowing for diversity.

Reforming National Leadership

A federation, if designed properly, resolves or at least manages conflicts at the state and local levels so they do not always rise to the national level. This is often achieved by drawing state boundaries that overlap the most likely sources of conflict, such as the plate tectonics of religion and ethnicity. Whether conflict does reach up to the national level depends, in part, on whether the conflicts spill over state boundaries, on how symbols of identity politics at the national level are handled, and whether "trigger events" such as elections are managed to minimize conflict.

The challenge in Nigeria—with approximately 80 million Muslims and 80 million Christians, and with over four hundred ethnolinguistic groups—is to manage the national leadership struggles so that they do not reinforce or exacerbate local-level conflicts. Since the civil war in Nigeria, a number of mechanisms have emerged in the country's political culture to mitigate the stresses of identity politics. At heart, they seek to balance national political and military leadership in terms of regional and/or ethnoreligious identities.

More specifically, these mechanisms have included

- Not asking questions of ethnicity or religion on the national census
- Achieving regional and religious balance on the presidential tickets
- Requiring political parties to avoid use of ethnic or religious designations
- Using geographic "zones" as surrogates for ethnicity and religion
- Requiring (in the Constitution) the federal character principle, by which each of the thirty-six states is entitled to representation at the national cabinet
- Encouraging a non-preferentialist religious balance in the federal capital, with a national mosque and a Christian ecumenical center

- Sharing the national budget, largely funded by oil revenues, in a transparent and balanced way among the states
- Encouraging conflict mediation centers at all levels, especially in mixed areas
- Promoting interfaith communication and cooperation, especially through NIREC
- Implementing the power shift principle.[36]

As explained in chapter 1, the presidential election is at the center of the Nigerian political system, because it is the only election conducted on a nationwide basis. Thus, when Jonathan's party ignored its power shift principle and decided to make him the party's presidential candidate for the election of 2011, the impact was bound to be felt throughout the country.

The presidential election results (detailed in chapter 1) may be summarized as follows. All twelve of the northern shari'a states gave Buhari the bulk (64 percent) of their votes. The south-south and southeast, largely Christian states, gave an extraordinary 97 percent of their votes to Jonathan. The religiously mixed states tilted toward Jonathan (58 percent), who had the incumbent's advantage, including the support of PDP governors in those states.

Given the patterns of the election and the postelection violence, what can the Jonathan administration do to mitigate the conflict triggered by the election and prevent violent extremist groups such as Boko Haram from taking advantage of the situation and extending their challenge to the unity of Nigeria?

To begin with, the credibility of the election tribunal appeals process should be strengthened by enhancing its impartiality. In addition, the Presidential Panel on Election Violence chaired by Sheikh Ahmed Lemu should be given a free hand to investigate the *causes* of violence and make appropriate recommendations. Furthermore, the reform of INEC should be encouraged, as should reform of campaign finance practices and the capacity of the chairman of INEC to hire and fire resident election commissioners.

More fundamentally, the *politics of national leadership* should be reviewed. The real challenge, in terms of policy and strategy, is at the national level.

---

36   See John Paden, *Faith and Politics in Nigeria: Nigeria as a Pivotal State in the Muslim World* (Washington, D.C.: United States Institute of Peace, 2008), 89.

In both the military hierarchy (to be discussed) and the civilian hierarchy, a balance in ethnoreligious/regional representation promotes stability. The federal cabinet is expected to reflect federal character. The key figures in the security, military, and police establishments are likewise supposed to reflect national balance, rather than spotlighting the president's favoritism.

With regard to the office of the presidency itself, symbol management is key, whether it involves the conspicuously evenhanded allocation of development projects or it features public statements about national problems and priorities. In terms of interreligious symbols, presidential "greetings" during religious holidays are always important, if seen to be heartfelt.

Effective leaders may be strong, or strategic, or adaptive (or all of those), but they must lead by example. Even their personal lives become objects of scrutiny, and "moral behavior"—with regard to drinking problems, extramarital sex, and personal or family money management—becomes part of their moral capital. In Nigeria, there is an expression to the effect "there are no secrets in Nigeria." Perceptions of moral hazard can set in and undermine legitimacy regardless of whether those perceptions are accurate or not. As in corporate culture, the tone at the top is crucial to the success of the whole enterprise.

Given the ubiquitous visual media, even something as simple as clothing can send a political signal. A southern president who dresses every day in the fashion associated with his ethnic group does not present the image of a neutral president who seeks to serve *all* the people. (The broad-rimmed black hat has become a sign of political loyalty to the president in the south, and is worn even by those are not from the same ethnic group!) During the military periods, one of the advantages of military dress was that it was ethnically neutral. The broader strategies of symbol management go to the heart of the national leadership challenge, especially in a country where perception inevitably becomes reality.[37]

For example, during the 2011 election campaign, billboards and posters showed Jonathan kneeling and being blessed by the Pentecostal president of CAN. (Other billboards showed Jonathan alongside President Obama and carried the caption "Yes, we can, Sir!" This visual assertion of

---

37 Jonathan's advisers have tried to transform his image, from that of a "humble," self-effacing person—a poor boy who walked barefoot to school—to that of a more decisive leader. See "The Re-invention of Goodluck Jonathan," *Daily Trust*, December 1, 2011.

links between Jonathan and the United States sent a message to northern Nigeria and may not serve U.S. interests in the broader Muslim world.)

Now that the election and the appeals process are over, it is imperative that the president reach out to his northern countrymen in every way possible. He should, for instance, reach out to those in the north who have obvious street credibility, including icons such as Buhari and Jega. The role of Vice President Namadi Sambo—an architect and Muslim—is complicated in that when he stepped down as governor to be Jonathan's running mate, his deputy governor, Patrick Yakowa, a South Kaduna Christian, took his place, and as incumbent won the governor's race in April 2011. After the elections, Kaduna has become a major site of backlash killings, including the ethnoreligious cleansing and killing of at least five hundred—and probably eight hundred—Muslims in rural areas in South Kaduna.[38]

The real dilemma for Jonathan's administration is that the street credibility of many northern elites, including traditional leaders, has been impaired by the election of 2011. How this can be rectified is not easy to say but should be a matter of policy and strategic concern. The federal character appointments by the president to the cabinet and other key posts (such as the chairmanship of the PDP) are crucial. While such northern appointments are *necessary*, whether they will be *sufficient* to defuse northern resentment remains to be seen. (See appendix B for details of the regional backgrounds of top federal officials. As that appendix shows, the least-well-represented geocultural zone is the northeast.)

The key to stability is not to overreact to the threats of religious extremists in the north by using disproportionate military power. The militarization of the response to Boko Haram may well provoke further violence. Boko Haram has taken responsibility for the killings of key officials in Borno and also for bombings in Abuja, including the suicide bombing of the national police headquarters. It has threatened to bring violence to Jos, Lagos, and even the presidential mansion ("Aso Rock"). What has been the police response?

Inspector General of Police Alhaji Hafiz Ringim promised to deal quickly and harshly with Boko Haram. In turn, the group declared him

---

38   Graphic photographs of the massacres in South Kaduna can be found on the Internet—which is accessible to all levels of society—and will no doubt help fuel cycles of revenge in the future. The figure of five hundred killings of Muslims comes from Human Rights Watch, *Nigeria: Postelection Violence Killed 800*. Meanwhile, Christian militias in Kaduna have threatened immediate retribution if harm should come to the (Christian) governor or his family.

a legitimate target for assassination.[39] The fact that Boko Haram would make such a threat even though Ringim is a northerner underscores the reality that the police are the enemy of Boko Haram, regardless of their origins.

Thus, the policy and strategic management of the military, police, and security forces may be the biggest challenge for the young Jonathan administration. The symbolism of identity politics permeates all aspects of military policy in the domestic context and requires a candid assessment.

Reforming Military Strategy

As noted at the outset of this study, the central political issue in Nigeria has always been the unity of the country. The military has been the guarantor of that unity since the days of the attempted Biafran secession and the resultant civil war. Senior officers with a strong commitment to the preservation and development of Nigeria ruled the country in 1966–79 and 1983–99 and formed one of the few national constituencies to offset regional and/or local identities. Major policy decisions have been made during periods of military rule, including the shift of the capital from Lagos to Abuja and the launch of major infrastructure projects, notably a national road system. But the central reality is that most senior officers have in their DNA a sense of responsibility to preserve unity.[40]

---

39   The name Ringim derives from a historic town in the Kano area. Jigawa State broke off from Kano State but is still seen in the north as part of "Greater Kano." In January 2012, Ringim stepped down as inspector general.

40   See, for example, the remarks of the chief of Army Staff, Lieutenant General Azubuike Ihejirika, in which he "warned politicians harbouring the idea of dismembering the country to discard such ideas as the Nigerian Army was prepared to pay the supreme price in defence of the unity of the country. 'It is wasted effort for anyone to think of dismembering this country.'" "Nigeria: Army Ready to Defend Unity of Country—Ihejirika," *Vanguard*, November 25, 2011. The death of General Odumegwu Ojukwu at age seventy-eight on November 25, 2011, is also a reminder that even the leader of the Biafran secession movement eventually returned to Nigeria from exile, in 1982, and "became a Lagos businessman and ran unsuccessfully for president several times." "Odumegwu Ojukwu, Breakaway Biafra Leader, Dies at 78," *New York Times*, November 27, 2011. Ojukwu was well known and respected in the north for saying, after returning from exile, that just as he once tried to lead the Igbos out of Nigeria, he was now prepared to lead the Igbos back into Nigeria. His *New York Times* obituary goes on to note: "The legacies of the war were terrible. Deaths from fighting, disease and starvation were estimated by international relief agencies at one million to three million. Besides widespread destruction of hospitals, schools, homes and businesses, Igbos faced discrimination in employment, housing and political rights. Nigeria reabsorbed Biafra, however, and the region was rebuilt over 20 years as its oil-based economy prospered anew." The fact that in 2011 Ihejirika, the chief of Army Staff and an Igbo from Abia, was "willing to pay the supreme price in defence of the unity of the country" (*Vanguard*, November 25, 2011) speaks volumes about the commitment of the senior officer corps.

During the Fourth Republic, Nigeria's unity has been threatened by south-south insurgents (as distinct from the strictly criminal entrepreneurs) who claim that the oil under the land is rightly theirs.[41] Military leaders have insisted that the insurgents be met with force, although political leaders devised an amnesty program that aims at rehabilitating armed youth and providing them with stipends if they renounce violence and turn in their weapons. (The long-term results of this amnesty program are not yet in.)

As in the Delta, in the north the police and military have been suffering casualties and have taken a hard line in response. National Security Adviser Azazi, who is from Bayelsa State, took a hard line even during the election period. The postelection deployment of three thousand troops (including Navy personnel!) to Maiduguri, and the announcement of plans to add another four thousand security personnel, creates the impression in the north that war has been declared. The question is whether this policy is perceived as the nation's government seeking to enforce national unity or as southern officers ganging up on the north at the behest of a southern president.

At this point, it is helpful to summarize some characteristics of the Nigerian military that are relevant to the issue of how best to respond to Boko Haram. Nigeria has one of the best-trained and best-equipped militaries in Africa and has been a central component of the West African commitment to peacekeeping in Liberia and Sierra Leone, as well as to African Union/UN missions in Darfur and elsewhere. On several occasions, the Nigerian Army has dealt with border clashes closer to home, notably in the Bakassi region of the southeast, which borders Cameroon, and in the north, along the border with Chad.

Yet, since the Nigerian civil war, which started when junior officers attempted to stage a coup, the structures and rotational processes of the military have been shaped by an abiding concern to forestall or defeat coups d'état. Periods of military rule have been punctuated by coups and attempted coups, often having a regional and/or ethnic component.

---

41 With the election of President Jonathan, who is from Bayelsa State in the Niger Delta, most of the leaders of the Movement for the Emancipation of the Niger Delta (MEND) have offered to defend his mandate "with their blood." Thus, the security focus has shifted in Nigeria to the issues of Boko Haram and other fringe groups in the north. For a description of the tensions between various factions in the Delta, see e-mails sent by MEND spokesman "Jomo Gbomo" (a nom de guerre) to the international community, (anewnigerdelta.mend@gmail.com), e.g., from August 24, 2011. He provides a critique of the Movement for a New Nigeria—a radical alternative to MEND—which wants to break up Nigeria.

One result has been an effort by the military to recruit officer candidates from each of the thirty-six states on an equal federal character basis, and to rotate officers outside of their home state bases so that they are not tempted to take sides in local political struggles. (Retired military officers, who have enormous influence, do tend to return to their home states or to set up second homes in places such as Kaduna or Abuja.)

In terms of defending the country from foreign aggression and participating in peacekeeping missions abroad, this system works well and has been much appreciated by the international community. However, because the Nigerian military in recent years has had to focus much of its attention on *domestic* disorder, a tension has developed between the military and the grassroots communities. If this sense of disconnection with local communities is to be overcome or at least reduced, military strategy needs to be reformed.

It is beyond the scope of this chapter to specify how the military and security forces can retool to deal with domestic and/or potentially secessionist disorder. But one thing is clear: the identity politics of the civilian domain grow more divisive when the military uses deadly force to deal with local uprisings. The danger that a local disturbance will metastasize into a national conflict is real. In the case of the military response to Boko Haram, the fact that many of the senior military and security officers deployed in the north have "southern names," including "Christian names," makes it hard for them to persuade local communities that they share similar interests.[42]

The introduction of foreign troops to maintain order in the north would not placate local animosity; to the contrary, it would exacerbate it—and provoke regionwide concern. This has been a major reason why the United States has regarded the Niger Delta conflict as a Nigerian matter, even when insurgents have kidnapped foreign citizens. Foreign intervention in the predominantly Muslim north would have even more serious consequences than intervention in the Christian south.[43]

42　In Nigeria, however, the appointment and rotation of senior military officers is fluid, especially as officers are retired, either after thirty-five years of service or at the age of fifty-six. See "Army Headquarters Effect Major Shake-Up," *Tribune*, August 25, 2011.

43　The entry of the Ethiopian (Christian) military into the Somali conflict in 2006 comes to mind. That event clearly had the effect of mobilizing a wide range of Somali clans (and even U.S. citizens of Somali extraction) to support al-Shabab. Whether the 2011 entry of Ethiopian troops into Somalia will have a similar impact, given the devastating drought and grassroots antipathy to the cruelty of al-Shabab, is widely debated.

Many of the families from which traditional leaders come also have family members in the military. One might suppose that this situation would give traditional leaders both an incentive and an opportunity to interact behind the scenes with the military on matters of local concern. The question arises as to the potential impact of traditional rulers with military ties on the Boko Haram situation. The complication is that most of the far northern emirs were part of the Sokoto Caliphate, and Borno has an extremely tenuous relationship with the northern emirate structures. Borno leaders at all levels certainly do not feel it necessary to "learn" from the Sokoto Caliphate in terms of religious matters. This sensitivity probably extends even to Buhari, who carried Borno State in the 2011 presidential elections, but who is originally from Daura in Katsina State.

The question remains as to who will drive the change in strategic thinking required to respond effectively to Boko Haram, and what kind of change that will be. While each of the issue areas and domains reviewed in this chapter—local government, traditional leaders, police, education, national leadership, and military—have their own analysts, the challenge of connecting the dots into a larger strategy must be met. This chapter now concludes by focusing on medium- and long-term capacities for strategic planning, and on lessons that policymakers should learn from the Boko Haram confrontation.

Reform Capacities for Strategic Planning and Lessons Learned

The standoff over approaches to Boko Haram among the chiefs of the military and security services, political leaders in the National Assembly, the northern governors,[44] and the Borno elders, as mentioned previously,

---

44   "Gov Aliyu to FG: Negotiate with Boko Haram," *Vanguard*, December 15, 2011: "Governor Babangida Aliyu of Niger State has called for discreet negotiations with the Islamic militant group, Boko Haram, who he claimed are inspired by misguided Islamic teachers. . . . Aliyu, who is also Chairman of the Northern Governors' Forum also bemoaned the north's failure to develop the region despite providing leadership for the country for most of its first decade of independence. . . . In calling for discreet negotiations with the group, he said: 'Negotiation with these people does not have to be a formal government negotiation.' Using the example of Borno, where the Boko Haram's violent campaign is fiercest, the governor said: 'We have religious leaders in Borno, we have the traditional rulers. They could be empowered to go into negotiation with these people.' . . . Faulting the promise of paradise given to lure potential suicide bombers, he said: 'Any good Muslim will tell you that suicide is not part of Islam. In fact, we have it that if you commit suicide you will not go into paradise no matter your reason. So for anybody to say he is a suicide bomber because he is extending Islamic tenets is not true. Nothing happens in the village or community without the knowledge of the traditional rulers. So any movement of foreign people in a village they will detect. But maybe because we are now in a modern age of the SSS [State Security Service] nobody places attention to them.'"

may be a short-term tactical encounter, but the larger issue is the strategic vision needed to deal with the increasing disconnect between the grassroots communities, especially those left behind in a rapidly changing oil-rich state, and those who are part of the larger political economy. Where will this longer-term strategic vision emerge? How will the considerable research capabilities of the university world be linked with the think tank capabilities of government or quasi-government entities? The central issue in all domains, of course, is leadership. One possibility is discussed below to illustrate the way in which strategic and policy concerns can be developed in an atmosphere outside the rush of day-to-day politics.

The National Institute for Policy and Strategic Studies (NIPSS) in Kuru, near the center of Nigeria, is intended as a midcareer training center for a cross section of military, security, and government officials. NIPSS seeks in particular to encourage strategic planning.[45] The director is Professor Tijjani Muhammad-Bande, the former vice chancellor of Usmanu Danfodiyo University, Sokoto.[46] He is familiar with the Sokoto caliphal system, with the North African political situation, and with the North American academic environment and has worked on policy and management issues in the Lake Chad/Borno area.[47] Most importantly, he is familiar with conflict resolution methods and literature and was instrumental in setting up the Center for Peace Studies at the Usmanu

---

45 NIPSS was founded in 1979 "as a policy formation center for bureaucrats, private sector leaders, army officers, and medium ranking and senior civil servants in Nigeria. Most policymakers in Nigeria have attended the NIPSS. . . . Notable graduates of the NIPSS are General Ibrahim Babangida, the former Nigerian Head of State . . . and Mallam Nuhu Ribadu, the anti-corruption campaigner." See *Wikipedia*, s.v. "National Institute of Policy and Strategic Studies," last modified February 4, 2011, http://en.wikipedia.org/wiki/National_Institute_of_Policy_and_Strategic_Studies. A Senior Executive "Course 33," with a focus on managing pluralism in Nigeria, was inaugurated on February 22, 2011, and concluded in late November 2011. This course is the premier senior training course, with an appropriate strategic focus each year. The director of NIPSS, drawn from the academic world, was appointed in April 2010 and clearly is putting his own stamp on the organization. See appendix C, "Addendum," regarding the legal mandate for NIPSS.

46 Professor Tijjani Muhammad Bande (BS, Ahmadu Bello University; MA, Boston University; PhD, University of Toronto) is a professor of political theory at Usmanu Danfodiyo University, Sokoto. He served as director-general of the African Training and Research Centre in Administration for Development, Tangier, Morocco (January 2000–February 2004), and was vice chancellor of Usmanu Danfodiyo University (February 2004–February 2009). He became acting director of NIPSS in April 2010 and serves directly under the Nigerian vice president, Namadi Sambo. He is originally from Kebbi State and is a cousin of Professor Attahiru Jega. Professor Bande was instrumental in creating a linkage agreement between his university in Sokoto and George Mason University (GMU) in northern Virginia. In September 2011 a linkage agreement was set up between the GMU School for Conflict Analysis and Resolution and NIPSS. See appendix C for an abbreviated version of the agreement.

47 Bande, "Multilateral Water Organizations and Nigeria's National Interest."

Danfodiyo University, Sokoto. His visit with a NIPSS delegation to Washington, D.C., in June 2011 explored some of the strategic challenges of a postelection Nigeria.

Whether NIPSS can encourage a comprehensive approach by the state to the challenge of grassroots-level engagement remains to be seen. While much of strategic thinking tends toward grand theory, the lessons of the Arab Spring in 2011 are a reminder that links with the local communities are crucial to the peace and prosperity of a nation and that higher-level officials ignore this challenge at their peril. The use of security forces to manage local aspirations, including dissent, is never an effective long-term solution. If a state is to tackle potential secessionist movements, especially in the highly pluralistic African context, it usually has to negotiate with them and/or try to win the hearts and minds of the communities from which they draw support; military force should be seen as a last-choice resort.[48]

Nigeria has been a leader in attempts to manage diversity, especially at the state and federal levels. An earlier generation of Nigerian leaders, both military and civilian, developed sociopolitical and economic mechanisms to mediate such potential conflict. Whether the current generation of midcareer technocrats (zoologists, architects, economists, and so forth) have the training or the experience to manage and prevent conflict remains to be seen.

Gaining this experience is not easy in a crisis situation. The governor of Borno State, elected in 2011, is an agricultural economist with an advanced degree in that field. But he is in a vulnerable position with regard to the religious and political turmoil in his state, especially when he is susceptible to assassination threats by local Boko Haram bombers and drive-by shooters.[49] The constitutional provision to allow for states of

---

48 Professor Bande reported to President Jonathan in late November 2011 on some of the issues mentioned in this chapter, especially the 2011 theme of "Course 33," dealing with management of diversity and pluralism. NIPSS has also been encouraged in the Nigerian press to take a more active role in major national challenges. See "Gov Elechi Tasks NIPSS on National Challenges," *New Nigerian*, July 26, 2011.

49 "Kashim Shettima was born September 2, 1966, in Maiduguri, Borno State. He attended Government Secondary School, Biu (1978-80), and then Government Secondary School, Potiskum (1980-83), and studied Agricultural Economics at the University of Maiduguri, finishing in 1989. He attended University of Ibadan (1990–91) and received a Masters Degree in Agricultural Economics. From 1991-93 he lectured on Agricultural Economics at the University of Maiduguri. He went into local government and became Commissioner in the Ministries of Local Government and Chieftaincy Affairs, Education, Agriculture, and later Health, under his predecessor as Borno Governor, Ali Modu Sheriff, who had confronted the Boko Haram and earned their enduring enmity. In January, 2011, in the ANPP primaries, Engineer Modu Gubio was selected as candidate for the governorship, but he was shot dead, presumably by members of the Boko

emergency—as happened for six months in Jos under President Obasanjo, when General Chris Alli took over from Governor Joshua Dariye—has not proven to be an effective means of dealing with longer-term issues. (The state of emergency declared by President Jonathan on December 31, 2011, similarly expires in six months.) Hence the need for strategic vision and the ability to manage and prevent domestic conflict.[50]

Of course, there are other alternatives to NIPSS's strategic initiatives. Some are within the military and security services, such as the National Defence Academy in Kaduna. In addition, the resource endowments of Nigeria have allowed for the creation of foundations similar to those that exist in the United States, which can fund research into issues of national and international concern. The Yar'Adua Foundation in Abuja is one example. (Several senior statesmen are currently in the process of setting up foundations, although one cannot tell yet what issues they will focus on.)

Other alternatives to NIPSS might include regionally focused institutions akin to the Ahmadu Bello Foundation, which was set up by the Northern Governors' Forum in October 2009. According to media reports, "It was a rare moment of soul-searching, sober reflection and eulogies yesterday when prominent leaders of the North gathered in Kaduna to launch the Sir Ahmadu Bello Foundation. On the occasion, there was a clear consensus that the late premier remained the region's greatest leader and a model to be emulated by the current crop of leaders."[51] Although billions of naira have been raised, the political discord among the northern governors has meant that the foundation may not have achieved all it could. The foundation has the potential to play a major role in encouraging the reform of education in the north, including engagement with the grassroots Islamic schools. This would certainly have been a major concern of the late premier, Ahmadu Bello.[52]

Haram. On April 26, 2011, Shettima won the governorship with 531,147 votes, while the Peoples' Democratic Party candidate, Muhammad Goni, received 450,140 votes." *Wikipedia* s.v. "Kashim Shettima," last modified July 2, 2011, http://en.wikipedia.org/wiki/Kashim_Shettima.

50   The test will be the impact of the state of emergency declared by President Jonathan on December 31 in parts of four northern states: Borno, Yobe, Plateau, and Niger. The latter focused on Suleja, which is the sister city to Abuja, and the alleged venue of some of the plots against Abuja.

51   See "Nigeria: Ahmadu Bello Foundation—North Honours Late Premier," *All Africa.com*, October 19, 2009. Also, see "Northern Govs Meet over Ahmadu Bello Foundation," *Nation*, October 1, 2009: "The Foundation, a non-governmental, non-profit making and non-political organization, was established to sustain the impressive legacies of the late Premier of Northern Nigeria, by engaging in charitable causes for the advancement of his values and development to humanity."

52   The author has written a comprehensive biography of Ahmadu Bello and is familiar with the historical sources pertaining to the late premier's educational values and policies. See Paden,

The real challenge in strategic planning is to get beyond the ad hoc commission reports that seem to pile up, yet either never see the light of day or deal only with the specifics of their charge, without reference to the broader context.

What, then, are the lessons learned from the Boko Haram movement about possible longer-term solutions? This chapter has argued that the evolving crisis with Boko Haram requires a more comprehensive analysis than the instant policy reactions ranging from "thought reform" to full-scale military crackdown. It has argued that the central issue is the disconnect between the grassroots and the political economy of the Nigerian state. A medium- or long-term solution to this disjunction would probably include the following steps.

- *Enhance capabilities to deal with human security issues.* This is crucial in the far northern fringes of the country, where desertification and lack of job opportunities prevail. The dilemma is also how to keep the policy of "open borders" (especially with fellow members of the Economic Community of West African States) while not serving as a magnet to migrants from neighboring failed states.

- *Reform local governments.* The LGAs need to be strengthened, both in their direct funding and in terms of their development functions. Encourage real engagement with the grassroots communities.

- *Reform the role of traditional leaders.* These historic institutions need to be clarified, strengthened, and officially recognized by the state, especially in light of the generational changes that have allowed distinguished professionals to take on these lifetime appointments. Again, links with the grassroots should be encouraged, especially in the areas of conflict prevention and mediation.

- *Reform the police.* The current constitutional requirement of a federal monopoly of police services will be hard to change, given the difficulties of amending the Constitution. Yet, through judicial review and/ or executive order some accommodation to the needs of local government needs to be made. The rotational system of officers should be reviewed, to ensure more links with grassroots communities.

- *Reform education.* Strengthen teacher training institutions and encourage the enhancement of the quality of primary and secondary school teachers. Allow local-language instruction at the primary level. Assess the issue of religious knowledge classes, given the cur-

---

Ahmadu Bello, Sardauna of Sokoto.

rent sharp disjunction between the Koranic schools and the primary schools. Explore ways of introducing Western knowledge (*boko*) into the *ilmi* and Koranic schools, recognizing that some international aid funders are restricted, at present, from assisting in this endeavor. Recognize that primary education can have short-term consequences, even at the symbolic political level (as in the former Western Region during the First Republic, where it was a central campaign issue), but its real impact is long term.

- *Reform national leadership functions.* The capacity for conflict prevention, mediation, settlement, and resolution should be central to leadership functions and protocol. While much of this capacity depends on personal style, there are mechanisms that should be encouraged in the emerging political culture of Nigeria, especially those of symbol management to avoid antagonisms and encourage a common sense of political destiny. The informal role of retired national leaders—"the wise men"—should be strengthened in terms of advising the upcoming generation of technocrats, who may be less familiar with the lessons (both good and bad) learned from the first fifty years of Nigerian political experience. The role of opposition leaders such as Buhari is especially important in this process.

- *Reform military strategy.* Assess the role of the military in *domestic* security situations, especially when the current rotational system often puts officers from different parts of the country into local situations that they may not have the cultural sensitivity to manage. Change the culture of the military in domestic matters to more of a local reserve guard capacity, so that the heavy hand of the federal government does not appear at every juncture. Simply pouring more money into the current structure may not solve the challenges.[53]

- *Reform capacities for strategic planning.* The need for an integrated, medium- or long-term approach is especially evident in the Boko Haram case. NIPSS would be one candidate for developing a think tank approach to the complex issues of grassroots disaffection and even secession. NIPSS would also provide a venue for midlevel military and security officers to be sensitized to professional conflict resolution approaches.

---

53 The proposed 2012 federal budget for security increased dramatically. See "As Jonathan Presents 2012 Budget . . . Security Beats 12 Ministries Combined," *Daily Trust,* December 14, 2011: "Explaining the huge security votes, Jonathan said government plans to invest massively 'including providing more support for the police, defence and counter-terrorism operations. . . . We can only achieve the developmental goals in a secure and peaceful environment.'"

While the above reforms will not happen overnight, the Boko Haram insurrection highlights the need for a comprehensive approach to religious and/or ethnic conflict. The challenges presented by northern Nigeria are many—ranging from demographic and climate change pressures, to the cross pressures of open borders in West Africa, to the needs for electric power and a better-managed petroleum system—but there is nothing more important than maintaining internal security and the unity of Nigeria.

As the sultan of Sokoto has said on numerous occasions, "without peace, there can be no development."[54] This quest for peace should engage the full attention of those who wish Nigeria well and those who are tasked with meeting the many challenges of enhancing the links between the grassroots populations, of whatever ethnoreligious identities, and those engaged in the fast-paced changes of an oil-driven political economy.

These challenges extend to those in the northern political opposition who have the crucial task of holding accountable those in power while reinforcing their own constituents' commitment to the unity and peaceful development of Nigeria.[55] Yet, until the Nigerian political class ceases to regard elections as do-or-die events, and until the positive trends of the 2011 elections are reinforced through continuing electoral reforms, there will remain a tension between democracy and security. This is the context in which the Boko Haram challenge will be remediated, or not.

---

54   In November 2007, the author accompanied the sultan for two weeks on his visit to New York and Washington, D.C., and listened to his many speeches on this subject. The author is aware that the sultan and Buhari were on opposite sides of the northern political divide during the 2011 elections.

55   As explained in earlier chapters, the role of Buhari, as the preeminent statesman from the north, is particularly important, since his main constituency has been the twelve far northern states, and especially the grassroots youth who pinned their hopes on him during the April 2011 election. (Note: the author is grateful to Buhari for serving as keynote speaker at the Brookings Institution launch of his *Muslim Civic Cultures* book in 2005, and his participation in the launch of his *Faith and Politics* book in Kaduna in January 2009.)

CHAPTER 3

Ethnoreligious Crises in Plateau State

Despite the crises in other northern states, such as Kaduna, Borno, Yobe, and the surrounding areas of Abuja, the situation in Plateau State is central to managing the challenges of national unity in Nigeria. This chapter focuses on ethnoreligious conflict in Plateau State in the Middle Belt of Nigeria. The chapter looks in turn at the historical and cultural context in Plateau State; patterns of ethnoreligious conflict from 1999 through 2011; Plateau State governors and conflict mitigation during the same period; postelection violence in Plateau State from April 2011 on; and possibilities for conflict management in Plateau State.

The Plateau Context

Plateau State, in Nigeria's Middle Belt, has always been part of the northern region in terms of politics and economics. Historically, it was the highland area that was inaccessible to the horse cultures of the Savannah and Sudanic zones, and hence remote from the Islamic reform movements of the nineteenth century. It is characterized by large numbers of minority ethnolinguistic groups, with no one group predominating. Because this was the non-Muslim area during the colonial era in the north (1903–60), the ban on Christian missionaries imposed by the British as part of their indirect rule policy did not apply to the Plateau highlands. Consequently, a large number of U.S. and Canadian missionaries, mainly of an evangelical orientation, settled on the Plateau, and Jos city developed as the headquarters for these groups.[1] Mission schools and hospitals, and the translation of the Bible into local languages, soon began to generate a cohort of educated men and women, many of whom went into the professions, especially the Army. During the First Republic, there was often tension between the far northern political leaders and those from the Middle Belt. During the subsequent military periods, all the mission schools were taken over by the state, and the early generation of Western missionaries began to retire, handing over leadership to indigenous church fathers. Middle Belt politicians came into their own on the national stage once the

---

1   The author has visited Jos on numerous occasions over the past forty years. He has also visited the Sudan Interior Mission archives in Toronto, Canada.

75

north was broken up in 1966. Middle Belt military officers emerged as a major factor in the military eras (1966–79 and 1984–99).

Meanwhile, throughout the colonial era the Jos environs attracted industries such as tin mining and drew worker migrants from all parts of the north. The Jos urban area began to attract (Muslim) Hausa petty traders from Kano, the major urban center in the north. During the First Republic, many of these Hausa migrants identified with the Northern Elements Progressive Union (NEPU) rather than the dominant Northern Peoples' Congress (NPC). They tended to settle in the Jos North district, while keeping close family and business connections in Kano.

The dominant ethnolinguistic group in Jos is the Berom, historically a stateless society with many small components.[2] In the late colonial era, the British decided to "create" a leader for the Berom, the so-called Gbong Gwom.[3] During the First Republic, the premier of the north (Ahmadu Bello), decided to recognize the Gbong Gwom as the traditional leader of Jos, because the alternative of a Hausa leader would mean empowering NEPU, his arch political rival.

This brief history of the Jos area is salient because during the Fourth Republic the issue of "settlers" versus "indigenes" has taken on deadly proportions. (Indigenes refers to those with historic ties to the area. Settlers are those who came later, in the twentieth century.) This clash has ethnic dimensions (Berom versus Hausa, or Jasawa as they are called in Jos) and religious overtones (Christian versus Muslim), and thus the struggle for constitutional recognition (or not) within a local government/political context has been at the heart of some deadly clashes. The constitutional interpretations of this "indigene" issue have been slanted locally to disenfranchise the Hausa/Muslim populations and even to deny settlers land use rights. There is, in other words, a dangerous mix of ethnic, religious, political, and land use factors in Plateau State that fuels tensions and conflicts. Elections can become triggers that propel that conflict into violence.[4]

---

2   See "Berom Chiefdom," Section 5.2.4 in Roger Blench et al., *The Role of Traditional Rulers in Conflict Prevention and Mediation in Nigeria* (London: Department for International Development, November 2006), 59–65.

3   Ibid., 62–65.

4   For an official Plateau State version of the conflicts, see the report written by the director-general of research and planning in the Governor's Office, G. N. S. Pwajok, "An Overview of the Jos Plateau Conflicts: January 2010–January 2011: Presented on occasion of the Nigeria Briefing on the Anniversary of the March 2010 Massacres in Jos Crisis, with the Theme: 'Jos-Plateau Conflict: Africa's New Sudan Crisis?' March 8, 2011, Capitol Hill, Washington, DC." This report presents a detailed account of violent conflicts in Plateau State during the years 2010–2011, and includes specific dates; the names and locations of pertinent local government areas, districts,

Meanwhile, in Plateau State as a whole, and especially in its rural areas, there are dozens of ethnolinguistic groups, often with settled family farming as the basis of the economy. In addition, there have been pastoralists, especially the Fulani, who historically moved their animals around depending on the season, seeking pasture and water. In the past, the pastoralist-farmer relationship was symbiotic, with the pastoralists providing manure for the fields, and farmers welcoming the annual transmigrations. In the colonial and postindependence eras, the farmers became associated with the Christian side of the religious street, while the pastoralists remained resolutely Muslim. In more recent times, with demographic pressures on land use exacerbated by climate change, the classical pastoralist-farmer relationship has become infused with tension. Farmers now claim that the herders are ruining their crops and fields, and

---

and villages; and descriptive remarks. More significant for purposes of this monograph, however, are the interpretations of the causes of the violence: "For the umpteenth time, Jos, which has not known peace since the inception of the country's democracy ten years ago, witnessed several attacks including multiple bomb blasts on Christmas Eve 2010 claiming many lives and properties. Christians and Muslims, indigenes and non-indigenes have become both perpetrators and victims. These have stretched the capacities of the people and the government of the State, Federal as well as agencies and stakeholders who have tried to intervene. Nigerians this time around are finding it difficult to reconcile a situation where the policy and the army, which are said to be involved in a joint operation as a panacea for averting further occurrences, are gradually drawn into the arena of conflict, which has not deescalated, attesting to the fact that the situation in Jos is more than what we can see on the surface. Using the Plateau experience, we need to take a close look at the dramatic changes in human organization, thought and behavior, which are taking place all over the world. The world is entering a new era in which the source of conflict will be based on cultural divisions rather than ideology or economic forces. Some Scholars maintain that conflict will occur along fault lines that divide civilizations. While others are of the view that the simultaneous forces of global disintegration and global homogenization constitute the primary sources of future conflict. In other words the forces of 'jihad and MacWorld' operate with equal strength in opposite directions. Jos Plateau State within this context became the fault line that divides civilization in the far North which is more Muslim and the south which is more Christian. This significantly affects the way the policies, actions or inactions of the State government, which is responsible for the daily discharge of public affairs are interpreted mostly with religious colourations. Prominent amongst these are the urban renewal policy of the present administration, popularly referred to as the 'Greater Jos Master Plan,' and the ban on the use of commercial motor cycles, which has variously been misinterpreted as part of an underhand attempt to drive out Muslims from Jos. Some critical issues: inaction by Security Forces in spite of civil authority efforts at providing intelligence, e.g. Dogo na Hawa (Sim Card), Maza killings, phone calls to the then GOC, Mohammed Aliyu Saga, etc.; rising culture in impunity as a result of centralized control of Security; inadequacies of Justice Administration in which demand for prosecution is often misinterpreted as persecution of suspects; usurpation of legislative, judicial and executive powers clothed in seemingly value free demands for a State of Emergency. (Further) issues: Instability in recruitment and deployment of security forces with perception issues. Within three years not less than 5 Commissioners of Police have been posted to Plateau State; issues of desert encroachment and porous borders, and infiltration by non-Nigerians especially from Niger and Chad; State-State relations as demonstrated by externalization of attacks with neighboring states like Bauchi serving as staging posts while encouraging legislation calling for dismemberment of Plateau; Federal-State relations, jurisdictional issues; State–non-State actors; Media management issues with emerging concepts such as 'ethnic cleansing' and 'genocide' escalating conflict, from riots to crisis and now bombings."

herders claim that farmers are stealing and/or killing their cattle. Violent clashes have broken out, at first sporadically during the military era of the 1990s, and more explosively since the return to civilian rule in 1999.

The ripple effect of these rural ethnoreligious-economic clashes is magnified in part because of the code of honor of the "cattle Fulani," which requires revenge for perceived wrongs.[5] In addition, the (Muslim) Fulani may well be the largest single ethnic group in Western and Sudanic Africa—stretching from Senegal to Sudan—although they are often identified by their clan names and have largely intermarried with Hausa or other groups in some areas. In Nigeria, they are generally divided into three categories: cattle Fulani (bororo), settled rural Fulani (Fulanin kauye), and urban/city Fulani (Fulanin birni). As noted above, the latter group has largely intermarried with the Hausa or other emirate ethnolinguistic groups, and hence the term "Hausa-Fulani" is common and describes approximately 30 percent of the overall Nigerian population, and the overwhelming proportion of the north.

For the most part, only the cattle Fulani and some settled Fulani still speak the Fulfulde language.[6] Yet, the identification of Fulani leadership with the nineteenth-century Islamic reform movement of Usman Dan Fodio and the establishment of the Sokoto Caliphate have meant that throughout the north the urban/emirate Fulani leaders have provided leadership in all spheres of government and economics. (In the northeast, especially Adamawa State and Taraba State, the emirate leaders still speak Fulfulde.) Hence, the recent pastoralist-farmer conflicts in Plateau State have much broader implications.[7]

In addition, since the 1990s, the type of Islamic orientation among many Muslim young people in Plateau State has tended toward a more strict constructionist variety, often called "Izala." The relative lack of Sufi brotherhoods in Plateau is in stark contrast to their presence in some of the far northern emirate states. Also, the lack of a traditional Muslim authority structure in Jos/Plateau has meant that a younger generation of Izala is not as constrained as in the emirate states. Indeed, the predomi-

---

5   Young cattle Fulani men go through an initiation rite called *Sharo* in which they whip each other with a wooden rod and remain expressionless. The ritual beatings cause welts and bleeding. The point is to endure pain without flinching. The author has witnessed such rites, usually accompanied by music and dance, in the Kano area while conducting research in the past.

6   Village Fulani increasingly use Hausa as a common language, and since Hausa women may marry Fulani men, the mother tongue of subsequent generations tends to be Hausa, even if the situational identity of "Fulani" remains.

7   For regional implications, see "The Fulani Question in West Africa," *Daily Trust*, December 5, 2011.

nant characteristics of Izala are its primary reference to the Koran and Hadith rather than subsequent legacies in West Africa. The Izala prefer to interpret the Koran (in both Hausa and Arabic) as they see fit, which means that there are many different interpretations and splits within the movement. Finally, there is a strong element of "conversion" (*da'wa*) activity among the Plateau Izala, often in direct competition with the evangelical efforts of Christian groups.[8]

Hence, the type of fervor often associated with the newly converted characterizes both the Christian and Muslim sides of the religious street. Given a strong "protestant" (antihierarchy) element among both Muslims and Christians, the question as to types of *authority* necessary to contain or mediate conflict becomes a challenge. The ethnic authority of the Gbong Gwom holds no real sway over the evangelical and/or Pentecostal Christians, and the vacuum of authority (or antiauthority predisposition) on the part of the Muslims complicates the matter of mediation. Thus, while the sultan of Sokoto is the nominal head of all Muslims in Nigeria, his real influence is among the historic emirate states, rather than in the "new towns" (the twentieth-century cities in the north).

The evangelical impetus on both sides leads to a religious competition on top of the already complicated ethnoreligious/political/economic landscape. In a winner-take-all civilian political system, it is not surprising that tensions often boil over. Without question, Plateau State has had the largest number of violent deaths from conflict of any state in Nigeria: many thousands have died since 1999. What are the more detailed patterns of such conflict?

Patterns of Conflict: 1999–2011

The ethnoreligious crises in Plateau State may be divided into two groups: those in and around Jos, and those in other parts of the state. For a summary of the Jos violence, see table 4. Other areas of Plateau State that experienced ethnoreligious violence are discussed below. The most serious violence occurred in Yelwa in May 2004, with well over a thousand people being killed. (This episode was a focus of the film *The Imam and the Pastor*.)[9]

---

8   See "Traditional Rulers and Islamic Sects" (p. 85) and "Traditional Rulers and Religious Disorder" (p. 91) in Blench et al., *The Role of Traditional Rulers*.

9   Alan Channer's *The Imam and the Pastor* illuminates the work of Imam Muhammad Ashafa and Pastor James Wuye, who together won the Chirac Foundation Prize for Conflict Prevention in 2009. The film came out in 2006 and was produced by Initiatives of Change, London. (See www.fltfilms.org.uk.) The film follows the clerics' efforts—under the auspices of the Inter-faith Me-

According to the northern media: "A non-governmental organisation (NGO), the Vindication of Rights Group (VRG) has called on the government of Plateau State to immediately investigate, identify, arrest and prosecute all persons identified with the destruction and murder of 723 citizens of Yelwa in Plateau State in May 2004. . . . VRG has discovered and identified the bodies of another eighty-three men, women and children slaughtered and thrown into two wells, while others were found in a grave beside a private clinic in Yelwa."[10] The Human Rights Watch report on this incident documents in great detail the massacres on both sides, including the revenge killings in Kano of Christians by Muslims, and makes recommendations to the government and security forces and to religious and community leaders.[11] The immediate result of this crisis was

---

diation Center, in Kaduna—in preventing interreligious conflict in Kaduna State and healing postconflict trauma after the Yelwa incident. The film is based on the book with a similar name, written by Ashafa and Wuye, and published in 1999 by the Muslim/Christian Youth Dialogue Forum in Kaduna. According to the Chirac Foundation website, the Prize for Conflict Prevention "aims to improve awareness and support for those who dedicate a part of their lives and resources to preventing conflicts."

10 "Nigeria: Group Wants Yelwa Killings Revisited," *Daily Trust,* June 17, 2005.

11 Human Rights Watch, *Revenge in the Name of Religion: The Cycle of Violence in Plateau and Kano States,* May 2005, vol. 17, no. 8 (A). The report covers the conflict in Yelwa, including the attacks of May 2–3, 2004, and the government's response to the attacks, the "Revenge and Retaliation in Kano," and the subsequent "brutal response of the police and the military." A year later (May 25, 2005), Human Rights Watch issued a follow-up statement: "One year after some 900 people were massacred in clashes between Muslims and Christians in northern and central Nigeria, the Nigerian Government has failed to prosecute those responsible for this cycle of violence. . . .

"In the central region that lies between the mainly Muslim north and the largely Christian south, armed Muslims on February 24, 2004 killed more than 75 Christians in the town of Yelwa, at least 48 of them inside a church compound. Then on May 2 and 3, hundreds of well-armed Christians surrounded the town from different directions and killed around 700 Muslims. They also abducted scores of women, some of whom were raped. Both attacks were well-organized, and in both instances, the victims were targeted on the basis of their religion.

"One week later, reacting to reports of the Yelwa attacks, Muslims in the northern city of Kano on May 11 and 12 turned against Christian residents of the city, killing more than 200. In addition, police and soldiers deployed to restore order in Kano carried out dozens of extrajudicial killings themselves. The victims included people who, according to eyewitnesses, were not even involved in the violence.

"'The Nigerian government bears a heavy responsibility for the massive loss of life in these eruptions of violence fuelled by religion,' said Peter Takirambudde, director of Human Rights Watch's Africa Division. 'The security forces were absent while hundreds of people were being massacred in Yelwa. Instead of protecting those at risk and trying to arrest the perpetrators, police and soldiers shot people on sight in Kano.'

"There have been numerous other incidents in Plateau state over the last four years, starting with the outbreak of violence in the city of Jos in September 2001, in which around 1,000 people were killed in less than a week. In 2002 and 2003, violence spread to other parts of the state. Human Rights Watch estimates that between 2,000 and 3,000 people have died in communal violence in Plateau state. . . .

"'The warning signs were there for a long time,' said Takirambudde. 'But the government chose to do nothing until the situation spiraled out of control.'

the announcement of "emergency rule" in Plateau for six months by the federal government, and the replacement of the elected governor (Joshua Dariye) by a military commander (Gen. Chris Alli).

Table 4. Large-Scale Communal Clashes in and around Jos, 2001–10

Year	Proximate Trigger and Extent of Violence
2001	Appointment of local administrator of welfare allowances leads to weeks of demonstrations. Tensions rise, resulting in violence.
	An estimated 1,000 to 3,000 killed. Violence expands across Plateau State. Attacks by youth groups in Muslim and Christian neighborhoods, on mosques and churches, and at the University of Jos. Sporadic attacks continue through 2002–3, killing hundreds and destroying 72 villages.
2004	National elections held but postponed in Plateau State.Local officials are appointed, resulting in disputes.
	More than 1,000 killed in attacks against Muslim and Christian villages from February to May, and 250,000 are displaced. Federal government removes state governor and appoints temporary replacement.
2008	Local government elections—the first in Jos since 2002—are scheduled, then delayed three times. Disputes emerge over party nominees and results.
	Nearly 800 killed in gang attacks and riots from November to December.
2010	A dispute over reconstruction of a home destroyed by clashes in 2008 leads to violence in January and reprisals in March and throughout the year.
	January: Up to 500 residents killed over 4 days. Many villages and homes destroyed. March: Up to 500 killed in an overnight attack.
	December: Nearly 80 killed following twin car bombs. Hundreds more die in frequent intermittent attacks.

Source: Chris Kwaja, *Nigeria's Pernicious Drivers of EthnoReligious Conflict,* Africa Security Brief, no. 14 (Africa Center for Strategic Studies, July 2011), 5.

The original table also includes an entry for 1994—during the military period—that provides a contrast with the Fourth Republic civilian period. "Appointments of local government leaders prompt protests and counterdemonstrations. Four killed. Several city markets, an Islamic school, and places of worship destroyed."

————————

"Some two weeks after the massacre in Yelwa, President Olusegun Obasanjo declared a state of emergency in Plateau state on May 18, 2004, and suspended the state governor. An interim administrator launched an ambitious peace program, and relative calm was restored.

"Six months later, in November, the state of emergency was lifted, but the peace program appears to have stalled." See also the Human Rights Watch report "Nigeria: Religious Violence Fueled by Impunity," at http://www.hrw.org/news/2005/05/22/nigeria-religious-violence-fueled -impunity.

According to Human Rights Watch, the outbreak of violence in Jos in December 2010 (the Christmas Eve bombings in Jos that sparked sectarian clashes) and January 2011 left more than 200 dead.[12]

Plateau State Governors and Conflict Mitigation, 1999–2011

The thirty-six state governors serve as chief executives in their respective states, and as such are the key intermediaries with the federal government on matters of internal security, police, and military interventions.[13] They have enormous influence over state budgets.

Plateau State is the only state under the Fourth Republic to have a federally declared state of emergency in which the governor, Joshua Dariye, was removed—for six months, from May to November 2004—and replaced by a presidential appointee, Major-General Chris Alli. It was declared that the ethnoreligious violence in the state had reached such a level as to warrant federal intervention.

Dariye came back into office on November 18, 2004, and remained until November 13, 2006, when he was impeached. He was replaced by his deputy, Michael Botmang, although on March 10, 2007, a Court of Appeals order put Dariye back as governor until May 29, 2007, when Governor Jonah Jang—like Dariye, a member of the PDP—replaced him. In April 2011, Jang was reelected, while Dariye was elected as senator for Plateau Central on a Labour Party ticket; he now serves in that federal capacity. Within the country as a whole, twenty-six state governors were elected in April 2011, while in ten other states elections were not held until governors had served their full four-year terms.[14]

---

12   See Human Rights Watch, "Nigeria: New Wave of Violence Leaves 200 Dead," January 27, 2011, http://www.hrw.org/news/2011/01/27/nigeria-new-wave-violence-leaves-200-dead.

13   For a brief summary of the national politics during this period, see John Paden, *Muslim Civic Cultures and Conflict Resolution: The Challenge of Democratic Federalism in Nigeria* (Washington, D.C.: Brookings Institution, 2005), 195–97.

14   After May 29, 2011, the breakdown by party of the 36 state governors was as follows: Action Congress of Nigeria, 6 (Edo, Ekiti, Lagos, Ogun, Osun, and Oyo); All Nigeria People's Party, 3 (Borno, Yobe, and Zamfara); All Progressives Grand Alliance, 2 (Anambra and Imo); Congress for Progressive Change, 1 (Nasarawa); Labour Party, 1 (Ondo); Peoples Democratic Party, 23 (Abia, Adamawa, Akwa Ibom, Bauchi, Bayelsa, Benue, Cross River, Delta, Ebonyi, Enugu, Gombe, Jigawa, Kaduna, Kano, Katsina, Kebbi, Kogi, Kwara, Niger, Plateau, Rivers, Sokoto, and Taraba). Elections in ten states will be held at different times in the future, based on the beginning date of the governor's term (Adamawa, Anambra, Bayelsa, Cross River, Edo, Ekiti, Kogi, Ondo, Osun, and Sokoto). Note: In January 2012, five governors whose tenure had elapsed were removed by the Supreme Court: Kogi, Adamawa, Sokoto, Cross River, and Bayelsa. All were members of the PDP.

Who are Joshua Dariye and Jonah Jang, and what role did Chris Alli play in the transition during the state of emergency? What have been their roles in the drama of ethnoreligious violence in Plateau State? What part have they played in mitigating conflict during their terms of office?[15]

Prior to his election, Dariye was an accountant and businessman, with interests in banking and real estate, and with expensive property in Abuja and London.[16] He was a strong supporter of President Obasanjo and had help from his initial political benefactor, Chief Solomon Lar. While governor, Dariye was arrested in London on January 20, 2004, and accused of stealing U.S. $9 million of public money and money laundering. He skipped bail in the United Kingdom in September 2004 and fled back to Nigeria. Back home, although governors are immune from criminal prosecution during their terms of office, in October 2006 he was impeached by the Plateau State Assembly, and in November had to step down to be replaced by his deputy. (As an elected senator from Plateau State, Dariye is no longer covered by immunity, but Dariye and other members of the National Assembly have thus far intimidated investigators and avoided prosecution.[17] One of Dariye's nicknames is "the cat with nine lives.")

According to a BBC profile of Dariye published in 2007:[18]

> Not known for his diplomatic finesse, Mr. Dariye once described the Hausa-Fulani as "unruly tenants," bent on evicting their own landlords. The statement provoked a torrent of criticism against Mr. Dariye, who issued a statement saying he was misquoted by "mischievous reporters." But his position had already further driven a wedge between Plateau's Christians and Muslims, leading to some sections of the state capital, Jos, being nicknamed Afghanistan and another section New Jerusalem. Suspecting that Mr. Dariye, who likes to say he is a born-again

---

15 For a discussion of Governors Dariye and Jang plus more detailed background on the Plateau State crisis, see Philip Ostien, *Jonah Jang and the Jasawa: Ethno-Religious Conflict in Jos, Nigeria* (research report, Muslim-Christian Relations in Africa Project, August 2009). This forty-two-page report, accessible at the Sharia in Africa website (www.sharia-in-africa.net), is probably the best introduction to the issues in this chapter. It discusses the indigene-settler problem; conflict in Plateau State, 1999–2007; peace talks, 1991–2007; Dariye and Jang; Jang and the Jasawa; and the crisis of November 2008. A full bibliography is included. Ostien, formerly a lecturer in law at the University of Jos, has been an independent scholar based in Madison, Wisconsin, since 2008.

16 Joshua Dariye was born July 27, 1957, in Horop, Mushere, Bokkos Local Government Area of Plateau State. He is from a minority ethnic group in that area.

17 Only the president, the vice president, state governors, and deputy state governors enjoy immunity from prosecution (see Section 308 of the Constitution).

18 See "Profile: Joshua Dariye," *BBC News*, July 24, 2007, at the BBC website, http://www.bbc.co.uk/news/.

Christian, had taken sides in the conflict, former President Obasanjo suspended him for six months and declared a state of emergency in the predominantly Christian central state. Mr. Obasanjo's action was quickly interpreted by Plateau's Christians as tacit support for Muslims, a situation that propped up Mr. Dariye as some kind of defender of the Christians. This was partly why he returned to a big welcome after his six-month suspension.[19]

Whether Governor Dariye used his position to favor the Christian side during the ethnoreligious crises in Plateau State remains a subject of partisan debate.[20]

Major-General Chris Alli, who was the emergency administrator of Plateau State from May to November 2004, is generally felt to be fair-minded and evenhanded. (His mother was Christian and his father was Muslim. He is regarded as Hausa-Igbirra.) He served as chief of staff of the Nigerian Army from November 1993 to August 1994.

Alli convened an official peace conference in 2004 to try to get to the root of some of the land controversies and determine the "rights" of different ethnic groups. In October 2004, the conference publicly laid to rest Hausa-Fulani claims to ownership of Jos, Yelwa, and Shendam.[21] Media accounts of the report included the following statement:

> Delegates to the peace conference declared the Birom, Anaguta and Afizere natives as owners of Jos. They also ruled that Yelwa and Yamini towns in the Shendam Local Government belong

---

19   "Profile: Joshua Dariye," *BBC News*, July 24, 2007.

20   For an international Christian perspective on the crisis, see "Recent Religious Violence in Central and Northern Nigeria" (pamphlet, Christian Solidarity Worldwide, Surrey, England, May 2004). This thirteen-page document discusses the roots of the crisis in Plateau State, violence in the lead-up to the attack on Yelwa, the Kano reprisals, the state of emergency, and the alleged bias in reporting by the international media: "There are two versions concerning the recent violence in northern and central Nigeria and the subsequent declaration of emergency in Plateau State. According to the version that has gained international currency, on Sunday 2 May at least 630 Muslims were murdered by Christian militiamen in the market town of Yelwa in southern Plateau State in the latest outbreak of chronic violence that has plagued the area due to competition between sedentary indigenous tribes in Plateau State and the pastoral Hausa-Fulani tribe over scarce resources. . . . The non-Muslims of Plateau State view the situation altogether differently. However, to their exasperation, their version of events has not been reported as widely. They point out that the Yelwa attack did not occur in isolation and was part of the ongoing violence that has plagued the area since 2002. They insist that the bulk of this violence has been perpetuated by Hausa-Fulanis accompanied by paid fighters from neighbouring Republics, and whose victims have overwhelmingly been Christians and traditional believers. They feel the constant presence of foreigners during these attacks indicates the international dimensions of the violence in Plateau State and northern Nigeria, linking the perpetrators of the violence with the global Islamist movement."

21   See Paden, *Muslim Civic Cultures*, 196.

to the Goemai natives. The administrator, Major-General Chris Alli (rtd), said . . . the issues pertaining to ownership of Jos and Yelwa towns were thoroughly debated at the peace conference before the conferees reached a consensus on the ownership of these towns based on historical facts and presentations at the conference. The administrator, who adopted 23 resolutions at the conference for immediate implementation . . . said resolution no. 1 of the conference considered the usage of the term "settler" in the state as offensive, discriminatory and against the collective quest for effective integration, assimilation and development.[22]

The Hausa-Fulani delegates to the peace conference did not agree with this conclusion, which seemed to convey "ownership" of land to indigenes at the expense of settlers. Indeed, the clash between indigenes and settlers was at the heart of the conflict and because this was interpreted to be a constitutional issue, it could not be sorted out at the state level. But what had been a state and local issue was now elevated to a national and constitutional issue.

Also, the official reification of indigenous ethnic groups at the peace conference, the number of which was set at fifty-four in Plateau State, seemed to convey rights of land usufruct to units that by their contemporary nature are dynamic, not static. These official indigenous groups did not include "other major Nigerian ethnic nationalities resident in the State, namely the Fulanis, Hausas, Igbos, people from the 'South-South' (Urhobos, Ijaws, etc) and Yorubas, [who] were allowed one representative each, although in the end the Fulanis and Hausas each had two."[23] In short, the real parties to the dispute (that is, the settlers) were given second-class status at the conference.

The election of Jonah Jang as governor launched the next phase of the drama. Jang was quite different in style and temperament from Dariye. According to a report for the Muslim-Christian Relations in Africa Project prepared by Philip Ostien:

> Jonah Jang, elected governor in 2007 as Dariye's successor, is a much soberer and more credible figure than Dariye. But he has been at least as uncompromising in his dealings with the Jasawa, perhaps more so. . . . Born in 1944, Jang is from Du, a town in Jos South LGA, in the heart of Beromland. He was

---

22   See *Daily Independent*, October 26, 2004. For the official report, see Ostien, *Jonah Jang and the Jasawa*, 16.

23   Ostien, *Jonah Jang and the Jasawa*, 15.

educated and made his career in the Nigerian Air Force, rising to the rank of Air Commodore. While in the Air Force he
served brief stints, under Babangida, as military governor of
Benue (1985-86) and Gongola (1986-87) States. Then, in 1990,
Babangida suddenly "kicked him out" of the military: involuntarily retired him, along with twenty or so other high-ranking
officers. Jang is said to believe that Babangida kicked him out—
discriminated against him—solely by reason that he is a Middle
Belt-Berom-Christian rather than a northern Hausa-speaking
Muslim of some description. Jang is said to hold his sacking by
Babangida as a grudge not only against Babangida but against
all northern Muslims jointly and for the most party severally.
There are holes in this story, but then it is speculation from the
newspapers. Jang is a serious Christian: he holds a Bachelor of
Divinity degree from the Theological College of Northern Nigeria, Bukuru, earned in 2002. He is evidently a believer in the
theory that Nigeria's northern Muslims, perhaps in coalition
with other Muslims inside and outside Nigeria (Yorubas, elements in Niger, Chad, Libya, Saudi Arabia, Iran, etc.)—various
as their several interests might be—nevertheless have the wish,
or determination, together to conspire to dominate Nigeria, to
claim its territory as much as they can for themselves and for
Greater Islam. In short, in this view, the Muslims want to take
over, implement sharia law, and plunder the country for themselves. At the moment they are particularly targeting Jos North
as a foothold in Plateau state. Most of what happens and has
happened in Nigeria is understood to support this view. Jang
wants to see Christians resist Muslim advances everywhere. Not
only to resist but fight back: infiltrate, absorb, disrupt, if necessary push them back, push them out. But above all do not let
their powers expand in any direction.[24]

This profile is sobering in terms of what it says about the potential
for Muslim-Christian relations to disrupt Nigerian unity. It is beyond the
scope of this chapter to chronicle all the ethnoreligious violence during
the period of Jang's administration (May 2007–present) or the various
attempts to use police and/or military forces to curb violence. Yet, Jang's
military background and his theological background put him in a unique
position in Middle Belt politics.[25]

---

24   Ibid., 18.

25   According to *Wikipedia*, in 1965 Jonah David Jang "enlisted as an Air Force Officer Cadet at the
      Military Training School in Kaduna. He was given flying training at Uetersen in West Germany
      (1965–1966) and further training at the Nigerian Defence Academy, Kaduna. He was commis-
      sioned 2nd Lieutenant in 1969 and promoted to Lieutenant in 1970. He attended a course on

Whatever the personal or political dynamics of the Jang administration, the larger question is whether Plateau State governors are part of the problem or part of the solution, and whether the legacy of military rule, with its coups and countercoups, is still getting played out in the civilian era of the Fourth Republic.[26] There had been ominous signs in the latter days of the Yar'Adua administration when the president was on his death bed, and also during the period of uncertainty that preceded the presidential election of April 2011.[27] Since the election, the question of a coup or "virtual coup" in which the NSA takes de facto control has received more attention within the north.

Postelection Violence in Plateau State: April 2011 and Beyond

As noted in chapter 1, President Jonathan won 74 percent of the presidential vote in Plateau State on April 16, 2011. Because of the Muslim vs. Christian undertones of the presidential election, serious postelection violence was anticipated in Plateau State, which has a history of conflict.

Supply Operations Training (Logistics) in Denver, Colorado, United States and promoted to Captain in 1972, Major in 1975 and Wing Commander in 1978, serving in most of the Nigerian air formations during this period. During the regime of General Ibrahim Babangida he served as Military Governor of Benue State from August 1985 to August 1986, then as Military Governor of Gongola State from August 1986 to December 1987. He voluntarily retired from the Nigerian Air Force in 1990." See *Wikipedia*, s.v. "Jonah David Jang," last modified October 12, 2011, http://en.wikipedia.org/wiki/Jonah_David_Jang. There is a discrepancy in accounts as to whether Jang was retired voluntarily or involuntarily. The author is grateful to Governor Jang for informal discussions in October 2011 at George Mason University's School for Conflict Analysis and Resolution.

26   In April 1990, there was an attempted coup against General Babangida in Lagos by junior officers from the Middle Belt. Part of the officers' platform was the excision of the far northern Muslim states from Nigeria. This event, which sent a chill through the political leadership in the north, impelled Babangida to fast-track the removal of the national capital from Lagos to Abuja. (His family was originally from the Gwari-speaking area that became the FCT.) The earlier assassination in Lagos of General Murtala Muhammad, the head of state who was originally from Kano, in February 1976 by Middle Belt officers with "Christian names" was one reason why senior officers and politicians feared junior officer assassinations within the military. The ultimate nightmare scenario among Nigerian senior military officers was to experience a split along religious lines. The old Protestant hymns popular in the Middle Belt, "Onward Christian Soldiers" ("marching as to war") and "A Mighty Fortress Is Our God" ("a bulwark never failing"), may have given the sense, when taken literally, that the Jos Plateau was an embattled Christian redoubt in a sea of hostile Muslims.

27   According to John Campbell's blog entry posted January 27, 2011: "The killings around Jos may be escalating. There have been accusations that the army stationed around Jos has favored the Muslim Hausa-Fulani 'settlers' over the Christian Berom 'indigenes,' and there are now recurring reports of civilians attacking soldiers, who respond by killing their antagonists. Previously, the army was seen as the ultimate guarantor of the Nigerian state and neutral in ethnic and religious disputes. In Plateau state, at least, that seems to be eroding rapidly." See "In Plateau, Nigerian Army Neutrality Questioned," *Africa in Transition*, January 27, 2011, http://blogs.cfr.org/campbell/2011/01/27/in-plateau-nigerian-army-neutrality-questioned/.

The Kaduna-based Interfaith Mediation Center (the Imam and the Pastor), which had been building up grassroots networks in Plateau State to serve as early-warning systems of potential conflict, and which had an impressive track record of post-traumatic healing efforts, concentrated on Plateau State during the election. Yet, perhaps because Jonathan was expected to win in Plateau State, and because many of the conflict issues in Plateau State were perceived to be at the state and local level, the immediate backlash was not as great as some feared. The military and mobile police were on full alert in Plateau State, and in the days after the election things appeared to be under control. (Ironically, it was Kaduna State that had the worst postelection violence.) But further violence was brewing.

By June 2011, the triple threat of postelection violence (see chapter 1), Boko Haram (see chapter 2), and the continuing legacy of violence in Jos began to have cumulative security implications. According to the Nigerian media:

> Gradually, but steadily, the security situation in Nigeria is assuming a frightening dimension, as the safety of the populace seems regularly imperiled by the spate of violence. . . . We are worried that the security apparatchik in the country seems incapable of tracing and tracking the perpetrators of this violence against the state. The perpetrators are neither fairies nor from outer space. The intelligence gathering ability of the Security services have collapsed, or so it seems. That explains why the perpetrators almost always succeed in wreaking their planned havoc. That is why we are concerned about the re-appointment of Gen. Andrew Azazi as the National Security Adviser (NSA). Whilst it is within the prerogative of Mr. President to appoint whom he deems fit, we believe that the task of securing the lives of Nigerians is a task that must be raised beyond primordial prisms. Gen. Azazi has not demonstrated his capability to tame the growing violence in Nigeria.[28]

By the end of June, panic had begun to set in, as the Boko Haram group seemed poised to attack Jos. According to the *Vanguard* newspaper:

> Fear gripped residents of Jos, Tuesday, following rumours of an impending attack by members of the Boko Haram sect. As early as 6 am, SMS messages started circulating that the sect would attack the state capital. The SMS advised receivers to be on the alert. The text message read: "Information received that Boko Haram members are entering Jos today. Do tell security men

---

28 "Gen Azazi and the Security Challenge," *Thisday*, June 8, 2011.

within your area please. This has just been received. Ensure you relay this to many people for everyone to be vigilant and be on the watch for seemingly lonely strangers loitering around buildings or gatherings. They may be carrying/hiding explosives, please." The text caused panic as parents did not send their children to school while many avoided markets and other places that could attract crowds. Security was beefed up at the state police head-quarters while visitors were subjected to thorough checks. . . . State police Commissioner, M. Abdulrahman Akano, described it as a "preventive measure." . . . Akano said, "We have put men out to gather intelligence. We have put policemen at strategic places in town. Above all, I will enjoin everybody to also pray, because when it comes to someone who is watching you, who is scheming for you, only God can protect."[29]

The invocation of divine protection in the Jos context was matched by the increasing reference to divine mission in the national discourse. In late June, President Jonathan was quoted in the press as saying: "I could not have attained this position without God, and God has a purpose for Nige-ria. I believe God wants me to make an impact in the lives of Nigerians."[30] At the same time, the ethnoreligious violence in Plateau State and the threats from Boko Haram were about to increase dramatically.

By August, during the month of Ramadan, there was a sharp increase in Plateau State in the violence between settled farmers and Fulani herd-ers, and also in the Jos North area.[31] According to the *Daily Trust:*

> *Miyette Allah Kautal Hore*, a Fulani socio-cultural group, has sent an appeal to President Goodluck Jonathan to probe "the gradual and brutal annihilation" of the Fulani ethnic group

29 "Panic in Jos over Rumour of Boko Haram Invasion," *Vanguard*, June 27, 2011.

30 "Jonathan: God Wants Me to Change Lives of Nigerians," *Daily Trust*, June 24, 2011: "President Goodluck Jonathan has said he will govern with the fear of God because he believes God has a purpose for his emergence as leader of Nigeria at this time. Jonathan was speaking to the Very Reverend Justin Welby, Special Envoy, who brought a message from the Archbishop of Canterbury, Most Reverend Rowan Williams to State House, Abuja. . . . Earlier, Welby had said the Archbishop of Canterbury was 'encouraged and delighted at the extraordinary leadership' which the President 'provided during the elections and the difficult post-election days.'"

31 "15 Killed in Fresh Hostility in Plateau," *Tribune*, August 16, 2011: "The relative peace in Pla-teau state was shattered on Monday with the invasion of Barakin-Ladi Local Government Area of the state by a group of people suspected to be Fulani herdsmen, leading to the death of 10 people, while another five were also killed in Jos North." See also "Fresh Jos Crisis Claims Family of Seven, Others," *Punch*, August 16, 2011: "Tension has gripped Jos and Bukuru metrop-olis following the murder of seven members of a family and three others in overnight attacks at Heipang and Foron villages, in Barakin-Ladi Local Government Area of Plateau State. . . . It was learnt that the latest attack might have been in connection with last Tuesday's attack in a Fulani settlement at Bisichi in Jos South Local Government council of the state. Two persons were reportedly killed and 400 cattle stolen in that attack."

from many parts of Nigeria. The National Chairman of the group, Alhaji Abdullahi Bello Badejo, complained in a letter to the President that Fulani people were being killed "on every slight provocation" especially in some parts of the North. "This is aside from other segregative attitudes of other Nigerians such as denial of grazing rights for their herds of cattle, attacks on their persons and their herds as well as discrimination in other forms that showed total hatred for the Fulani race," Badejo stated.[32]

The sultan of Sokoto, in his Ramadan speeches, related the ongoing violence to political manipulation. On August 14, the *Vanguard* quoted the sultan as saying that

> politicians in and out of power must resist the temptation of using religion as a means of gaining acceptability. . . . If you are playing politics you should not involve religion. Avoid the temptation. That easily leads to problems and violence most of the time. You should know that Nigeria belongs to all and not Muslims or Christians alone. We have other people from other religions. We should pay attention to the twin problems of poverty and illiteracy . . . and not use religion to divide them. We must pay attention to education and how to tackle poverty in the society which is the basic responsibility of every leader to give to his people and not to listen to rumours.[33]

Yet, the tit-for-tat killings in Plateau State had taken on a life of their own. On August 22, the *Tribune* reported that "following the killing of eight people last week in Barkin-Ladi Government Area of Plateau State, another six people were killed on Sunday in Jol and Kwi villages in Riyom Local Government Area of the State."[34] Each week, there were more killings on both sides of the ethnoreligious divide.

In response to this violence, Governor Jang called for the removal of soldiers from the state, arguing that they were being dragged into politics and exacerbating the violence. As the *Nation* reported on August 22:

> With yesterday's attack, the number of people killed in similar attacks in the last week has risen to 20. Disturbed by the spate of renewed killings in the state despite the peace efforts of the government, Governor Jonah Jang has called for the

32   "Probe Ethnic Hatred, Cleansing, Fulani Group Tells Jonathan," *Daily Trust*, August 21, 2011. This pattern of violence continued throughout November. See, for example, "12 Killed in Fresh Jos Violence," *Punch*, November 25, 2011; and "20 Killed in Plateau Fresh Attack: Scores of Houses Burnt—24 Hrs Curfew Imposed. NYSC Members Relocated," *Tribune*, November 25, 2011.

33   "Political Violence Will Continue Unless . . . Sultan," *Vanguard*, August 14, 2011.

34   "Renewed Hostility. Another 6 Killed in Jos," *Tribune*, August 22, 2011.

withdrawal of soldiers from the state. Jang said: "The Nigerian Armed Forces were being unnecessarily over-dragged into politics. . . . The involvement of the military in the internal affairs of this country in the name of security is high and by implication we are over-dragging the military into politics, they would be forced to eat 'the forbidden fruit.' . . . I am convinced that the armed forces are being polluted with this religious crisis in the country. Before now, the military personnel used to stay in the barracks, but today the Armed Forces have started taking sides in the religious crisis and if they are not called to order, it will be dangerous for the country. . . . Owing to the situation in Jos, soldiers have abandoned their primary duty posts and instead escort Fulani to the bush in search of cows. . . . I used to be against the establishment of State Police, but with the current situation, there are many dynamics into state security which have made me canvass for the creation of one."[35]

With the end of Ramadan, there was one major attack against the Muslims who were praying the Eid prayer:

> For many who trooped to the Rukuba Road Eid ground to observe the *Eid-el-Fitr* prayer following the completion of Ramadan fasting, thoughts of their encounter will forever be engraved in their minds. Over a dozen people who went to Rukuba Road Eid ground were killed when they were invaded by assailants armed with machetes, cutlasses and stones. Children were also said to have perished in the attack. . . . Even with about 20 armed soldiers and policemen within the vicinity, Alhaji Bala Musa said the youth, including women, kept throwing stones. At that time, the prayer was over and we were told to leave so that the security personnel would clean a way for us. But the number of attackers swelled. He continued, "They were in thousands, I can say. While we were waiting for the way to be cleared some of us who had reached their parked cars were attacked, windshields being broken and set on fire. It was horrific."[36]

At this point, both Christian and Muslim leaders called for calm, and the crisis in Plateau State began to attract international media coverage, which previously had been preoccupied with the Boko Haram attacks, especially the bombing on August 26 of the UN building in Abuja. According to the BBC:

---

35 "Six Killed in Plateau Attack," *Nation*, August 22, 2011.
36 "Thousands of People Attacked Us at Jos Eid Ground," *Daily Trust*, September 3, 2011.

Christian and Muslim leaders have appealed for calm in central Nigeria's Jos city after more than 40 people were reportedly killed in clashes on Thursday. Jos's Catholic archbishop Ignatius Kaigama told the BBC the two groups should hold talks to end hostility. Local Muslim leader Sheikh Sani Yahaya Jingir expressed a similar view. Over the past two years, more than 1,000 Muslims and Christians have been killed in violence in and around Jos. The BBC's Ishaq Khalid in Jos says the latest violence broke out when youths from the rival camps clashed in the area of Dusu Uku, with residents saying more than 40 people have been killed. Our reporter says the violence is widely seen as religious, but there are many other factors that trigger it—including political rivalry. In the Plateau state which surrounds Jos, Hausa-speaking Muslims are seen as supporters of the opposition, while ethnic Beroms, who are mostly Christian, are perceived to favour the governing People's Democratic Party. Nigeria's main Muslim body, *Jamatu Nasril Islam,* said 22 members of its community had been killed while the Christian Stefanos Foundation reported the deaths of 20 people. Our reporter says many residents allege the security forces were responsible for most of the deaths. They accuse the army of using excessive force to end the violence, our reporter says. An army spokesman denied the allegation.[37]

The question in Nigeria was whether Jos was, as one newspaper headline put the matter, "Sitting on a Time-Bomb."[38]

During September, the political blame game came into full swing. The Action Congress of Nigeria (ACN) blamed the PDP governor, Jang, for going abroad (for health reasons) in the midst of the crisis.[39] Jang in turn blamed the federal government for the recurring violence.[40] The national

---

37 "Jos Clashes: Nigerian Christians and Muslims Seek Calm," *BBC News Africa,* September 2, 2011, http://www.bbc.co.uk/news/world-africa-14763085.

38 "Jos: Sitting on a Time-Bomb," *Daily Trust,* September 2011.

39 "Violence: ACN Faults Jang's Absence," *Punch,* September 4, 2011: "ACN's publicity secretary, Mr. Sylvanus Namang . . . decried what he described as Jang's insensitivity to the plight of the people of the state. He said the governor's long trip abroad, when Jos was boiling, was embarrassing. He said, 'This is the high point of insensitivity, for a governor to abandon his people at the time they need him most.'"

40 "Jang Blames FG for Recurring Jos Violence," *Guardian,* September 10, 2011: "Plateau State Governor Jonah Jang says Federal Government's indecisiveness in dealing with perpetrators of the violence in Jos is responsible for the crisis in the state. . . . 'I want to task all the security agencies in the country to rise up to this embarrassing security challenge and put an end to this nonsense here in Nigeria. . . . I want to assure the people that the teamwork in our administration will drive away all enemies of Plateau out of the state, because we just won't allow this madness to continue. Never again! We are not driving anybody from Plateau, but if you don't want to live in peace, then go elsewhere. Peace we must have in Plateau, and this peace is non negotiable.'"

security adviser, General Azazi, "refuted the Plateau State Governor, Dr. Jonah Jang's claim that security agencies ignored him on the recent crisis in the state. Azazi has rather accused the governor of ignoring security advice on the situation in the state. Azazi said Jang should learn to act as leader with regard to the security situation in the state and not shift blame."[41] As the finger pointing continued, so did the killings.[42]

In such a situation, the larger question of federal-state security arrangements became painfully apparent. The governor even began to consider "self-help" or vigilante action:

> Against the backdrop of yet another 14 murders, among whom was a pregnant woman late Friday night, the Plateau State Government may have begun to consider self-help measures, including the use of armed vigilante groups, to defend the lives and property of its citizens. To this end, the governor, Dr. Jonah Jang, is scheduled to hold an emergency meeting with President Goodluck Jonathan Monday to discuss lasting solutions to the situation that has left the state in a permanent state of siege. A government official . . . said the latest round of killings has made it clear that the state government may have to resort to self-help as a lasting solution to the crisis plaguing the state, adding that the state is being compelled to organize vigilante groups among the people who would rise up to protect and challenge threats to their lives and property. The government official identified ethnic coloration as a major bane of the crisis, adding that the attacks had continued to follow a pattern, a development, he said, that had left the state confused. . . . Explaining that the security agencies have really not been of help as expected, the official added: "How do you explain a situation where the governor gives an instruction to the Commissioner of police on a tip off provided by the SSS and the next thing he tells him is that he takes instruction from the IGP."[43]

The spiraling violence was a concern for all northern governors, who convened an emergency meeting in early September in Jos.[44]

The next stage in the crisis began in September, when the federal government took over all security arrangements for Plateau State. The chief

---

41 "Azazi Counters Jang, Says He Ignored Advice on Jos Crisis," *Thisday*, September 10, 2011.

42 "Plateau: Trading Blame over Mindless Killings," *Punch*, September 15, 2011.

43 "14 More Killed in Jos, Jang Ponders Vigilante Response," *Thisday*, September 11, 2011.

44 "Northern Govs Call Emergency Meeting over Jos," *Thisday*, September 12, 2011.

of defence staff called out two Army brigades and flew them to Jos. The military, in essence, was now in charge of the emergency.[45]

Meanwhile, senior dignitaries were called in to try to mediate between the different factions in the crisis.[46] The Nigerian media pushed Governor Jang during a press conference to clarify what was going on. Exasperated, he is reported to have responded: "Am I God to end Jos Crisis? Is Plateau the only place that has security problem? Security situation is all over the country, so why are you so particular about Plateau State?"[47] Yet, there were editorial voices in society that felt the basic problem was contending elites and the lack of leadership.[48]

---

45   "Army, Air Force Move into Jos," *Vanguard*, September 14, 2011: "Following President Good-luck Jonathan's directive to the Chief of Defence Staff, Air Chief Marshall Oluseyi Petirin to take over the security of Jos and stop the sectarian killings, *Vanguard* gathered yesterday that the Nigerian Air Force has already been put on standby — a C-130 aircraft for the airlifting of troops from two Army Brigades, one from the South West and another from the North Central to complement soldiers on ground for the operation. The General Officer Commanding '3' Armoured division of the Nigerian Army, Major General Adamu Marwa, who only resumed duty last week has been summoned to Abuja for briefings concerning strategies to be employed towards implementing the presidential directive. Also, the Chief of Army Staff, Lt. General Onyeabor Azubuike Ihejirika, as well as the Chief of Air State, Air Marshall Mohammed Dikko Umar whose personnel and equipment would form the bulk of the deployments were said to be in marathon meetings for the better part of yesterday with their Principal Staff Officers, discussing operational implications of the President's order. *Vanguard* gathered that following the meetings, the army High Command has directed the deployment of some armoured vehicles used for reconnaissance activities, advanced communications and night vision equipment as well as light combat attack vehicles to Jos for the operation. Already, the Air Officer command-ing Tactical Command of the Nigerian Air Force, Makurdi, Air Vice Marshall Odesola was said to have deployed some of the air surveillance aircraft in the command for surveillance activities to cover the long expanse of land and valleys where most of the attackers on both sides of the divide pass through to perpetuate havoc."

46   "Obasanjo Meets Plateau Leaders over Violence," *Guardian*, September 16, 2011: "Former Presi-dent Olusegun Obasanjo yesterday met with some religious and traditional rulers in Jos, the Plateau state capital in what was believed to be a peace-brokering mission. The former presi-dent who arrived in Jos on Wednesday on a Presidential Jet was said to have met with selected representatives of various ethnic and religious persuasions considered key to the peace process in the state. . . . A source hinted that he (Obasanjo) would head for Maiduguri from Jos on a similar mission relating to the *Boko Haram* crisis there."

47   "Between God, Jonah Jang and the Plateau Crisis," *Vanguard*, September 22, 2011. The author of the article, Is'haq Modibbo Kawu, writes: "Frankly, I was not surprised by Governor Jonah Jang's response quoted at the head of this piece. Under his watch, crisis has turned beautiful Plateau State into an unparalleled killing field. Jos was the most cosmopolitan city in Northern Nigeria, drawing vibrancy from peoples from everywhere, to post success in different human endeavors; while its most reassuring geography made it a place to settle in or visit. . . . One of the most tragic expressions of leadership failure is refusal to rise above prejudices and mindset. Leadership obliges those at the helms to go beyond their own tunnel visions; appreciate the larger picture and work for the overall interest of society. Unfortunately in Plateau State, elites on the two broad sides of divide have been unable to rise above their entrenched positions. . . . In Plateau State, contending groups of elite have chosen to ruin their society, rather than build an inclusive peace or search for truth and reconciliation."

48   Ibid. See also editorial comments by Kawu.

Plateau State is in the center of the country, where the plate tectonics of ethnicity and religion interact, and where the symbolism of Muslim-Christian cooperation or conflict have enormous implications for the whole country. It is a state with strong ties to the international religious communities, both Muslim and Christian. It is also emblematic of the political struggles between political parties and elites. It is a state where the constitutional issues of state and federal relations, including the role of the federal police and military, are at a critical point.

News of the ongoing violence began to eat away at the confidence of the entire country. As the Christmas holiday season in December 2011 approached, specific and credible threats to churches were issued.[49] As noted previously, these were carried out with horrifying effect on Christmas Day. After the Christmas bombings, the Christian Association of Nigeria announced that all necessary self-defense measures would be taken by Christians. On December 31, the president declared a state of emergency, leaving everyone uncertain about what role the military might play in this new situation.

While fears and uncertainty thus escalated, there were also a few signs that a negotiated solution might be found to the crisis. In late December, for example, the Izala factions—including the Kaduna factions—apparently decided to join together under the leadership of Sheikh Sani Yahaya Jingir, the head of the Jos faction.[50] Although the Izala movement emerged in the "new" cities (e.g., Kaduna and Jos), where there were no traditional Muslim rulers, its main focus was to counter the widespread influence of Sufi brotherhoods by emphasizing "Koran and Hadith only" as a guide to belief and behavior.[51] The consolidation of the Izala move-

---

49   See "Fresh Threat in Jos; STF on 24-Hour Surveillance," *Tribune*, December 17, 2011: "A faceless group during the week dropped letters around the state capital. The letter reads, 'We, entire Muslims of Plateau state will never give up until we have our rights; we will use your boys to destroy you. Nothing can stop us from bombing these areas before December 26, 2011.' It was signed by one Idris Musa. It named targets as Archbishop Coyrt, ECWA churches, . . . Living Faith Church, Redeemed Christian Church of God, St. Murumba Church." The Special Task Force (STF) in Jos set up twenty-four-hour surveillance.

50   "Izala Factions Unite," *Daily Trust*, December 22, 2011: "Sheikh Sani Yahaya Jingir emerged as the national leader of the unified Izala movement, after days of consultations that culminated in the unification of the sect's two factions at a meeting in Kaduna. Until yesterday, Jinger was the leader of the Jos faction of the Jama'atu Izalatil Bidiah Wa Iqamatus Sunnah (JIBWIS), which had been split for about 20 years, with the other group headquartered in Kaduna. Announcing the decision to collapse the two groups, Chief Imam of the Abuja Central Mosque, Ustaz Musa Muhammad, said the unification was long overdue in view of the challenges facing the Muslim community in the country."

51   For the stated aims of the Izala, see ibid.: "The organization being the first of its kind in the history of Islamic propagation, scholarship and championing the cause of Islamic religion gained reputation of being fearless and unambiguous in attaining its targeted goals. The aims

ment, for the first time since the death in 1992 of its first "Grand Patron," Sheikh Abubakar Mahmud Gumi, presented new opportunities for leadership for negotiating conflict management.

But what kinds of conflict management might prove fruitful in this quintessential Middle Belt state?

Possibilities for Conflict Management in Plateau State

A number of questions for conflict management in Plateau State emerge from the previous narratives:

- How does the situation in Plateau State relate to theory and practice of conflict management elsewhere?

- What are the specific conflict issues in Plateau State?

- What are the root causes (e.g., identity symbolisms, human security issues, structural/constitutional issues) of the conflict in Plateau State?

- What are the roles of the military and security forces?

- What are the roles of the international community?

- How can transhumance herder protections be strengthened?

- What is the role of identity politics?

- How are federal envoys being dispatched to try to resolve the Plateau State crisis?

- What is the role of leadership, especially the role of state governors?

---

and objectives of the organization are: Eradicating and eliminating ignorance from society in general. Unity and brotherhood of the Muslim Ummah. Sensitizing and orienting Muslim Ummah on Islamic religion in relation to their developmental activities in their lives here and hereafter. Discarding, rejecting and throwing away of various unislamic beliefs in publications and in whatever form. Assuring, and affirming to the Muslim Ummah, that the holy prophet has accomplished and completed his mission fully, judiciously and diligently without leaving any matter unattended. Anybody claiming to be a prophet, or claiming that the prophet visits him, should be considered a great original liar. Propagating Islam in Nigeria, right from the grassroots (villages) level to the international level. Acting vigorously and actively towards acknowledging the saying of the holy prophet (PBUM) specifically where he says; 'whoever sees a negative thing, he has to change it with his hand, if he can't do that, then with his tongue, and if he can't do that, by his heart, and that is the weakest form of faith. Maintaining that a proof must be from the book of Allah and Hadith of the holy prophet and that proof should not be concealed under any circumstance." For background on the Sufi emphasis on intermediating saints, especially in the major northern brotherhoods (Tijaniyya and Qadiriyya), see John Paden, *Religion and Political Culture in Kano* (Berkeley: University of California Press, 1973).

- How do the Plateau State conflicts impact national unity issues and strategic capabilities?

The Theory and Practice of Conflict Management

Although a comprehensive description of the leading theories and practices within the conflict management field is obviously beyond the scope of this chapter, it is worth pointing out that conflict management is a recognized field of academic endeavor with an extensive literature.[52] In general, a distinction is made between conflict *management* (keeping conflict from reaching violent proportions), conflict *mitigation* (trying to lessen the consequences of violence), conflict *settlement* (temporarily resolving issues), and conflict *resolution* (achieving a more permanent solution to the sources of conflict). In all cases there is a *process* involved, ranging from determining a ripe moment for intervention, to identifying all the parties to the conflict, to introducing behind-the-scenes mediators, to conducting post-traumatic healing after the violence has ceased.

In practical terms, there are two important dimensions in the analysis of conflict: study of *values and identities* and analysis of the *structural conditions* that impact the genesis of and possible solution to a given conflict.[53] It is also useful to study the *narratives* that shape the participants' visions of the conflict.

The Specific Issues Fueling Conflict

In the case of Plateau State, the specific issues driving conflict include structural tensions between the federal, state, and local governments, especially with regard to security provisions; the indigene-settler issues as to who has land rights and rights of residency; the question of political representation at the grassroots level; the herder-farmer tensions; vari-

---

52   See Sandra Cheldelin, Larissa Fast, and Daniel Druckman, eds., *Conflict* (London: Continuum International, 2008). This volume reflects the depth of faculty resources at the George Mason University's School of Conflict Analysis and Resolution, which offered the first doctoral degree in this subject more than thirty years ago. See also Kevin Avruch, *Context and Pretext in Conflict Resolution: Culture, Identity, Power, and Practice* (Boulder, CO: Paradigm, 2012); and Susan Allen Nan, Zachariah Cherian Mampilly, and Andrea Bartoli, eds., *Peacemaking: From Practice to Theory* (Santa Barbara, CA: Praeger, 2011).

53   For an early set of doctoral research summaries of these issues, especially the empirics of "situational identities," see John Paden, ed., *Values, Identities, and National Integration: Empirical Research in Africa* (Evanston, IL: Northwestern University Press, 1980); and Paden, *Muslim Civic Cultures*. For Nigeria-related literature, see the writings of Darren Kew, executive director of the Center for Peace, Democracy, and Development, McCormack Graduate School, University of Massachusetts, Boston, especially his forthcoming book, *Democracy, Conflict Resolution, and Civil Society in Nigeria*, to be published by Syracuse University Press.

ous leadership visions of approaches to crisis management, especially the use of military force; and human security issues.

The structural problems are embedded in the Nigerian Constitution of 1999 and the ways in which it has been interpreted by the judiciary and/or the executive branch. The fact that all police are federal has advantages and disadvantages. The potential abuses by state governors in the control of police can be offset by more grassroots local knowledge by the police and contact in the serve-and-protect model. The other relevant constitutional issues are the matter of indigenes vs. settlers and the question of federal character at the local government level. All these issues need to be resolved before there is peace in Plateau State. The alternative to a cumbersome constitutional amendment process is to regard the Constitution—drawn up by the previous military regime—as an organic process, subject to reinterpretations by courts and executive orders.

Responding effectively to the specific challenge of improving herder-farmer relations requires leadership on all sides, but more importantly, it requires recognition of the fact that herders need rights of usufruct just as do farmers. (In Nigeria, as in the United Kingdom, all land is crown land and rights of usage may be conveyed in various ways.) To put it bluntly, herders need officially recognized trails on which to move their livestock during the different seasons of the year.

Leadership visions of crisis management may vary in numerous ways: by generation, by educational level, by ethnoreligious cultural background, by predisposition to use military force, and so forth. Whether the first recourse is to negotiations or to a law-and-order approach depends on many factors. Also, whether conflict is regarded as a state and local matter or as a federal (or even international) matter may depend on leaders. Some cultures prefer a wise-men mediation process, others prefer binding arbitration, and others favor adversarial litigation and/or apprehending of "culprits."

Finally, human security issues—including education, health, and job opportunities—are pervasive in every developing country. If wave after wave of young men find themselves with no prospects for marriage or employment, and if a demographic youth bulge is creating a tsunami of expectations, there will be conflict. This is especially true in an oil-producing country where the disparities of wealth are on constant display, and where the pressures of rapid urbanization create overwhelming obstacles to incorporation into mainstream society.

The Root Causes of Conflict

With regard to the deeper causes of conflict in Plateau State, the obvious ones are issues of *identity* and issues of *security*.

As regards identity, the official reification of fifty-four ethnic groups in the state (excluding the settler/migrant groups) is bound to cause conflict in the longer term, as intermarriage and other dynamics reinforce "situational ethnicity" (i.e., the in-group and out-group ascriptions of identity, depending on context). On a brighter note, in a situation of ethnoreligious diversity, the possibility, for example, of a Muslim-Berom identity or a Christian-Hausa identity emerging is a natural and positive development.

Yet, it is the religious identities that pose the real challenge in Plateau State. If the people living in the state embrace the legacies of evangelical Christianity, which sees Muslims as the "enemy," or strict constructionist versions of Islam, which see local Christians as stooges of the West, there is no hope for Plateau State—or for Nigeria. At this point, a solution would be to emphasize the points in common between the two world religions rather than the differences. This was the approach of the British during the colonial period and during the First Republic. The Muslim concept of "People of the Book" (*Ahl al-Kitab*) is likely to be the basis of cooperation, not only in Nigeria, but worldwide in the decades to come. The alternative is a prolonged period of religious wars, reminiscent of the sixteenth and seventeenth centuries in Europe, when Protestants and Catholics could not agree to disagree.

In many ways, the Muslim hierarchy in Nigeria and Nigeria's Roman Catholic and mainstream Protestant leaders have already reached this modus operandi. Also, Sufi Muslims, with their emphasis on "union" (*wusuli*) with God, and some of the Pentecostals probably have more in common in terms of religious experience than they may realize. In Jos, it may be the evangelicals and the anti-innovation legalists (e.g., the Izala) who have yet to cross this bridge of understanding. The challenge of situational identity is to see the People of the Book as having common identities and values, especially with regard to the pursuit of peace. NIREC, with its twenty-five Muslim leaders and twenty-five Christian leaders, is a model for such cooperation at the elite levels. At the grassroots levels, the example of The Imam and the Pastor is particularly relevant in Plateau State.

The issue of security is more complicated in some ways. Basic personal security involves the right to life, property, and freedom from fears of arbitrary governments and attacks on social groups. The national security forces of Nigeria are intended to guarantee these rights, in line with the country's Constitution. When the military, police, or security forces become part of the problem, rather than part of the solution, the violent conflicts they are intended to ameliorate are further intensified. Whether this is the case in Nigeria, under normal or state-of-emergency conditions, is beyond the scope of this chapter to assess, except to note that in Plateau State many of the participants in the conflicts, on all sides, seem to regard the security forces as part of the problem. Vigilante groups are hardly the answer, although they are symptomatic of the vacuum of security that currently exists. The answer is to arrange a police and security presence more responsive to the citizens at the grassroots levels.

The Role of the Military and Security Forces

This brings us to the role of the military in domestic-disorder situations. Declarations of states of emergency may bring some temporary respite from disorder, but in Plateau State the hiatus between May 2004 and November 2004 did little to solve the underlying issues and may have sown the seeds for later conflicts, especially on the settler-indigene issues. Yet, if citizens are killing each other, there may be few alternatives to having a professionally trained police force intervene. The training of police and military for domestic duties will require a long-term effort by both Nigerians and the international community. (It is beyond the scope of this chapter to offer detailed suggestions on this matter.)

The Role of the International Community

The role of the international community requires special scrutiny, not only because of its sensitivity in Nigeria, but also because of the increasing tendency internationally to hold national and local leaders accountable for crimes against humanity. The concept of Responsibility to Protect (R2P) is now widely acknowledged in the international community, of which Nigeria is a full member. The situation in Plateau State has already raised questions as to whether Nigeria can protect its citizens.[54]

---

54 See "Atrocities in Nigeria's Plateau State and the Responsibility to Protect" (policy brief, Global Centre for the Responsibility to Protect, New York, March, 2010). The Centre is part of the Ralph Bunche Institute for International Studies, the CUNY Graduate Center. According to the brief, "Nigeria has been a regional leader in putting R2P into practice through its engagement with ECOWAS. It now has an opportunity to show the same leadership through domestically upholding the responsibility to protect, making good on its statement to the 2009 General Assembly debate on R2P, with its constructive emphasis on prevention. This is imperative because the risk of a re-emergence of R2P crimes in Plateau state remains real. . . . In order to fulfill its responsibility to protect, Nigeria must critically assess its ability to prevent and halt R2P crimes and— with the assistance of international actors—develop the needed capacities and institutions."

The extreme option for the international community is to issue warrants for the arrest of state leaders through the International Criminal Court of Justice (ICC). While this has not yet happened in Nigeria, Plateau State may well be a test case.[55]

The full range of bilateral relations is beyond the scope of this chapter. Suffice it to say that binational commissions and military-to-military training programs are very much a part of twenty-first-century international relations.

The Need for Transhumance Herder Protections

The transhumance movement of livestock herders is part of a larger picture in West Africa. The ecological interdependence between the Savannah zone and the rain forest zone is such that large animal protein sources are raised in the interior and then moved quickly (to avoid sleeping sickness disease vectors) toward the coast. The interruption of the supply of such protein sources has had serious effects in the past, as during the Biafran war, when such sources were cut and large numbers of children died from protein deficiency. Seen in this light, the herders are not merely a throwback to earlier times but a key contributor to national food security.

Research has shown that the two major culture clusters in the Sudanic/Savannah zones of West Africa are made up not of diverse ethnic cultures but of cultures that have emerged from different ways of life: one culture consists of pastoral and migratory livestock cultures, the other of settled farming cultures.[56] Within the Nigerian context, it is imperative to conflict management efforts to take the migratory patterns of cattle Fulani seriously, including the impact of those patterns on the Fulani's access to educational and health services and to protection of life and limb. It is also vital to give legal recognition in Nigeria to transhumance trails, and

---

55 The author became aware, in September 2011, that certain Fulani ethnic organizations in Plateau State were trying to persuade the ICC to consider the case of Governor Jang, who, they insisted, had issued "shoot to kill" orders, which, they argued, was a form of genocide. While this one-sided approach may not have reached the threshold to attract ICC action, it did "concentrate the mind" of state officials in terms of the seriousness of the situation in Plateau State. Yet, in December 2011, the Nigerian media focused on the news *Thisday* wrote: "Following the incessant killings that have bedevilled Jos, Plateau State of recent, investigators from International Criminal Court, Hague (Netherlands) are billed to visit the state to look into the various crimes against humanity." See "ICC to Investigate Jos Killings," *Thisday*, December 17, 2011.

56 See Richard Hay, Jr., and John N. Paden, "A Culture Cluster Analysis of Six West African States," in Paden, ed., *Values, Identities and National Integration*, 25–51. In this study, the thirty major ethnic groups in Chad, Mali, Mauritania, Niger, Senegal, and Burkina Faso were coded on a variety of cultural variables and, using Q factor analysis, analyzed for larger cultural clusters.

to promote negotiations between the herders and a new generation of farmers to agree on a mutually acceptable set of trade-offs.

One suggestion (passed on to the author by a senior northern leader) as to how the international community could assist in this matter would be to use the existing technologies of satellite infrared photography to identify the subsoil trodden paths of cattle herders from the past. These patterns could then be used to help identify and negotiate future trails and grazing areas.

But whatever technical or political solutions are eventually adopted, the point is to recognize that the field of conflict resolution as a whole is familiar with the historic and contemporary issues of herder-farmer conflicts.[57] Indeed, the West African academic and policy literature is replete with serious studies of such clashes. The specialists in this area should be encouraged to make their research better known to policymakers.

It should also be noted that some of the traditional emirate leaders are familiar with and involved in the matter of cattle Fulani transhumance. The most senior leader in this regard is the Lamido of Adamawa, who presides over a significant Fulfulde-speaking population.

The Impact of Identity Politics

The identity politics of Plateau State are obvious to all who live in the area. The most serious clashes are between the cattle Fulani and a variety of ethnolinguistic farming villages, and between the Hausa and the Berom in the Jos area. Yet, it is the official recognition of ethnic groups as indigenous or not in Plateau State that is at the heart of the conflict challenge. Because ethnic groups are both dynamic and situational, the static approach to ethnic identities must be modified.

In many ways, the focus on identity politics at all levels (federal, state, local) in Nigeria is both part of the conflict problem and part of the solution. Considerations of federal character require efforts to include all groups, even while such groups are now identified, in most situations, by geocultural zones or even (informally) by religious categories (e.g., as in NIREC). Plateau State seems stuck in a time warp on this matter. The con-

---

57   For example, Professor Tukur Baba, the director of the Center for Peace Studies at Usmanu Danfodiyo University, Sokoto, originally from Taraba State, is a Fulfulde-speaking specialist on the challenges of integrating cattle Fulani into contemporary society; Professor Muhammad Junaid, originally from Sokoto, also at Usmanu Danfodiyo University, wrote his doctoral dissertation in Britain on the education of Fulani pastoralists; and Professor Tijjani Bande, the director of the National Institute of Policy and Strategic Studies (NIPSS), speaks Fulfulde as well as Arabic, French, Hausa, and English.

stant reference to ethnic groups—quite apart from the indigene-settler issue—certainly doomed the Chris Alli Commission in 2004, despite its good intentions.[58] (See below for suggestions on future commissions or conferences.) Yet, even geocultural "zoning" as a surrogate for ethnicity can have problems, as is likely to happen in the run-up to the 2015 presidential elections, because both the southeast and the north will feel that it is their turn, and the resultant perception may be one of winners and losers.

The Potential Role of Federal Envoys

President Jonathan has suggested that federal envoys might play a valuable role in mediating discussion in Plateau State or in otherwise facilitating conflict management there. The idea has already taken concrete form, with former president Obasanjo being dispatched to the north in 2011 to talk with the parties to the conflict. Unfortunately, the north tends to regard Obasanjo as extremely partisan on both the religious issue (he is a self-styled born-again Christian who, after his term in office, studied Christian theology in Lagos) and the regional issue (he is seen as the source of much neglect of the north during his terms of office, especially his early retirement of many senior military officers). The key to effective mediation would be a longer-term approach by persons, armed with a federal mandate, who are regarded as more evenhanded, if not entirely neutral, in their reputations.

Given the current climate of distrust in Nigeria on matters of religious and regional interests, the goal of federal (nonmilitary) intervention in Plateau should be *balance*. The Chris Alli Commission was both too large (with well over twenty members) and ethnically biased; a future commission—whether charged with investigating causes of conflict or mediating among the parties—should be smaller and balanced. The question is, what kind of balance?

The author's suggestion is to focus on achieving a balance between religious identities—that is, Christian and Muslim—and to use a NIREC model as an alternative to the ethnic model. While this approach carries some risks, it also carries promise of real conflict resolution. What would such a commission, or set of federal envoys, look like? It would be small

---

58   The official designation and conferral of entitlements on ethnic groups is reminiscent of the old Stalinist approach in the Soviet Union, or some practices in China, where ethnic autonomous regions, census-required identities, and even passport nationality IDs have been required. In Africa, the Bantustan era of Apartheid is well known with its "homeland" areas and resultant nationality identity passports. In Nigeria, every effort has been made since the civil war to use more-flexible identity categories, especially "state of origin" and "town/location of origin."

in size, with no more than six members; none of its members would be from Plateau State; it would be equally divided between Christians and Muslims; it would have the trust of both sides of the religious street; its members would have the stature and experience to be effective; and it would have the confidence of the federal government, to which it would report.

For purposes of illustration only by the author, such a commission (or set of mediating envoys) might include the sultan of Sokoto (or his representative);[59] the Lamido of Adamawa (or his representative);[60] Imam Muhammad Ashafa;[61] former head of state General Yakubu Gowon (ret.);[62] recent vice presidential candidate for the CPC Pastor Tunde Bakare;[63] and Pastor James Wuye.[64] Thus, we would have three distinguished Muslim leaders and three distinguished Christian leaders, each of whom has shown his willingness to work across the religious divide. The choice of Pentecostal Christian leaders, rather than some of the obvious Roman Catholic leaders who have contributed so much to interfaith dialogue in Nigeria (such as the archbishop of Abuja, John Onaiyekan, or the newly appointed bishop of Sokoto, Mathew Kukah) is meant to reflect the Christian realities of Plateau State. Four of the six envoys have extensive experience at the national political and economic level in Nigeria and are well known. Two of the envoys (Gowon and the sultan) are former military officers. The imam and the pastor represent a distinctively Middle Belt approach to grassroots conflict mediation and are known and trusted by the international community. There are obvious difficulties of such a commission influencing their coreligionists, given the larger context of tensions, but it might jump-start a process of conflict mitigation.

---

59 A suggestion by the author for the sultan's representative might be Ahmed Dasuki, the son of former sultan Ibrahim Dasuki; Ahmed has worked closely with the current sultan, especially in healing rifts between branches of the royal family. He is also one of the most distinguished entrepreneurs and businessmen in Nigeria.

60 A suggestion by the author for the Lamido's representative might be the newly appointed Wali of Adamawa, Muhammad Sanusi Barkindo, who has had a distinguished career in the Nigerian National Petroleum Corporation.

61 Imam Ashafa, one of the subjects of *The Imam and the Pastor*, and co-director of the Inter-faith Mediation Center in Kaduna, has worked extensively with his partner, Pastor James Wuye, in Plateau State.

62 Gowon grew up near Zaria but is of Angas (Middle Belt) ethnicity. Best known for his "No Victor, No Vanquished" policy after the civil war, he is a devout Christian in his personal life.

63 Pastor Tunde Bakare is a Pentecostal preacher from the Southwest who was Buhari's vice presidential partner in the race for the presidency in April 2011. Including the Buhari faction in mediating conflict in Plateau State is crucial to the chances of reaching a negotiated settlement.

64 Pastor Wuye, originally a Pentecostal preacher from Kaduna State, has worked extensively in Plateau State, including with Imam Ashafa.

Leadership, and the Role of State Governors

What role can and should the governors in Plateau State play in conflict management? More generally, what part should state-level leadership play?

The previous governor of Plateau State, Joshua Dariye, was basically a businessman with a checkered history in terms of his financial dealings. He has drawn the attention of the criminal justice system both in the United Kingdom and in Nigeria. The incumbent governor, Jonah Jang, is a former Air Force officer with a firm commitment to the unity of Nigeria, a serious Christian, and a staunch ethnic (Berom) defender.

The future role of Governor Jang may well be the key to conflict mediation and resolution in Plateau State. The fact of his military service is the crucial element in his potential to view the conflict problems in his state through the lens of national unity. This readiness to take a broad national perspective is counterbalanced by his pro-Berom history. But if his former colleagues in the military (or elsewhere) could intervene and persuade him that his state has become a national unity issue, he might opt to play the role of statesman. (He is not eligible to run again for governor in 2015, so a national role would be a natural next step, whether in office or as an elder statesman.) The fact that he is a devout Christian could well be an advantage in his future role as statesman, because the broader Muslim community in Nigeria still respects the People of the Book legacy of the First Republic.

The bombings and killings in Plateau State continued throughout 2011 and have persisted into 2012. At a local level, there have been tit-for-tat killings on a regular basis. At the same time, the bombers have become ever bolder, attacking television soccer-viewing centers in Jos North[65] and provoking the government to ban nighttime use of commercial motorcycles.[66] How leaders at all levels respond to these provocations may well determine whether Plateau State becomes the Achilles' heel of Nigerian unity.

National Unity Issues

What then are the national unity and/or strategic issues that are inherent in the Plateau State crisis? It may be too simplistic to say, "As Plateau State goes, so goes the nation." But the national implications are clear: if

---

65   "Jos Blasts Death Toll Rises to 4," *Thisday*, December 12, 2011.
66   "Okada Operations Banned beyond 7 pm in Jos," *Next*, December 12, 2011.

ethnoreligious conflict is allowed to fester in the middle of the country, it may eventually destabilize the entire "Nigerian project."[67]

The national unity implications for Nigeria of the crisis in Plateau State are so evident to most senior Nigerian officials that they do not need further elaboration. The question of what kind of strategic policy thinking is able to deal with this crisis and related problems, however, does bear closer inspection. The author has recommended in previous chapters that NIPSS, under the directorship of Professor Tijjani Bande, tackle some of the larger issues that drive destabilizing conflict. The recent visit to the United States by a NIPSS team focused on the theme of managing Nigeria's pluralism for peace and national development, and team members showed themselves interested in developing a long-term macro vision for their country.[68]

Another reason for NIPSS to take on the conflict resolution issues outlined in this chapter is that NIPSS is located in Kuru, right in the middle of Plateau State. The population of Kuru is mainly Berom, and although small in size (around four thousand people) Kuru is only about twenty kilometers from Jos and hence is fully aware of the turmoil in Jos. Kuru straddles the Jos-Abuja highway and is strategically located on the rail line connecting Port Harcourt and Enugu in the south-south and southeast, Kafanchan and Bauchi in the Middle Belt, and Maiduguri in the northeast.

If devising responses to the challenges of ethnoreligious conflict management discussed in this chapter could be made part of the ongoing mission of NIPSS (which reports directly to the vice president, and on occasion to the president), NIPSS could be a central part of a Manhattan Project–scale effort to address the challenges of national unity in Nigeria.

---

67   The indigene-settler issue, a key component of underlying intercommunal violence, is clearly a national challenge. Plateau State leaders feel that some indigenes face discrimination in other (northern) states. For more on this, see the 2006 Human Rights Watch report, "They Do Not Own This Place," available on the Human Rights Watch website at http://www.hrw.org/reports/2006/04/24/they-do-not-own-this-place-0.

68   The NIPSS delegation's research theme was divided into these subthemes: (1) United States of America in perspective; (2) dimensions of pluralism; (3) ethnoreligious diversity and challenges of nation building; (4) federalism and result management for development; (5) constitutionalism, citizenship, and national identity questions; (6) institutional framework for sustainable peace, security, and national integration; (7) pluralism, power, and party politics.

CHAPTER 4

Postelection Challenges of Violent Conflict and National Unity

Previous chapters have dealt with various sources of instability that require more effective conflict management than Nigeria has so far been able to muster. Each of these instances of instability—postelection violence, violent extremist groups with a religious agenda, ethnoreligious killings and crises in the Middle Belt—has the potential to destabilize Nigeria as a whole and to trigger further conflict elsewhere in the country. The question of how the government should respond to these challenges has raised numerous issues and prompted often conflicting suggestions: local engagement vs. military action, open vs. closed borders, short-term vs. longer-term policies, mechanisms of identity management (including ethnoreligious identities), constitutional constraints on policy options (including the role of police), and the human security aspects of demographic changes. One recurrent concern is how to handle the political fallout of security crises so as to strengthen rather than weaken the fabric of national unity. The overarching challenge for conflict managers is to step back from each of these specific issues and connect the dots between them, in the process creating a blueprint for a strategic approach that addresses all of them simultaneously.

The fundamental premise of this monograph is that Nigeria needs to strengthen its national unity, ideally using democratic rather than authoritarian means. In a time of tensions, turmoil, and growing insecurity, "the Nigeria project" is being questioned in many parts of the country. Hence, whatever policies emerge to deal with particular conflict issues, decision makers must not lose sight of unintended consequences. The use of the military to maintain order, for instance, although increasing, should be recognized by Nigeria's leaders as at best a short-term solution.

In many ways, the question of national unity has been an ongoing challenge since Nigeria achieved independence in 1960. Certainly, the presidential election of April 2011 has set in motion a chain reaction of events that echoes the north-south tensions of the past. These tensions, however, are no longer confined to the elite political class. Regional, political, religious, and ethnic polarization has spread to the grassroots. In many urban areas of the north, youth gangs reflect numerous societal and national fault lines: Muslim vs. Christian, PDP vs. CPC, newcomers vs. longtime residents, and poor vs. rich. The stark contrasts between local poverty and the beneficiaries of an oil economy cannot be wished away, nor can the usual resort to elite bargains be used to maintain stability today.

There is increasing chatter in the southern Nigerian blogosphere regarding "the mistake of 1914"—the original amalgamation of north and south. The calls for a national conference to discuss future options of autonomy and even independence for specific zones of the country are starkly reminiscent of the turmoil that followed the elections of 1964 and 1965[1] and the subsequent attempted coup staged by junior officers, which led to one of the bloodiest civil wars in African history.[2] Such web chatter ignores the reality that there is no clean way to break up Nigeria. There is no "north-south" or "Muslim-Christian" or "geocultural zone" solution. There is no "four-state" solution, and certainly no "thirty-six-state" solution. Proponents of a confederation of ethnic groups need to be aware of the negative international experience of such arrangements; moreover, with more than four hundred ethnolinguistic groups in Nigeria, the fracturing of the body politic along these lines would lead to endless conflict and chaos. Most thoughtful Nigerians recognize that they will hang together or hang separately. The senior officers of the Nigerian military recognize this reality and keep an eye on politicians who might undermine this premise.

This chapter analyzes the range of challenges to the Nigerian state during the 2011 period, especially in the north; the range of responses to those challenges; constitutional constraints and possible responses; the critical role of the police, military, and security forces in conflict management; and broader approaches to conflict management and resolution.

The Range of Challenges to the Nigerian State

The Challenge of Postelection Violence

Determining whether postelection violent conflict is political, regional, religious, economic, or ethnic is a fruitless pastime. It may well be all of

---

1   The author, while conducting research in Kano during 1964 and 1965, witnessed these elections and their aftermath.

2   For details of the attempted coup of January 1966, see John Paden, *Ahmadu Bello, Sardauna of Sokoto. Values and Leadership in Nigeria* (London: Hodder and Stoughton, 1966).

the above, with the proportions of each element differing depending on circumstances. The tendency in the northern establishment to cast post-election violence as *political* is partly a way of deflecting attention from its ethnoreligious and/or regional aspects, and hence in itself is a method of conflict management, because *religious* divisions are far more deep-rooted and enduring than disagreements provoked by cyclical elections. Thus, Katsina governor Ibrahim Shehu Shema, commenting to the Lemu panel, "described the violence as political, saying, 'we must tell ourselves the whole truth. The post election violence is political because it only happens during election period. Its causes are political. Whenever there is an election we must witness such kind of violence. Unless we resolve to work together, the unfortunate trend will continue. Katsina state has its own share in the last April post election violence,' he said."[3]

The political aspects may have predominated in Katsina, home state of Buhari, with its predominantly Muslim population. However, in Kaduna State, with its northern Muslim and southern Christian population split, the ethnoreligious aspect was painfully apparent. With hundreds killed in Kaduna, and with countless churches and mosques burned and some areas plagued by ethnic cleansing, the challenge of conflict management goes well beyond standard political negotiation.

The question as to whether elections trigger violence is important to answer if democratic norms are to be preserved and strengthened. The history of national elections and violence in Nigeria is mixed and troubling in many ways. The election of 1964 was boycotted in the southwest, and there was a re-run in that region in 1965. Because the party divide in that area was so deep—a divide not along ethnoreligious lines, but with regard to national alliances—the chaos that followed the elections of 1965 helped precipitate the attempted coup by junior officers, during which the northern political elite associated with the "winning" party in the southwest were assassinated. The civil war that followed has trauma-tized Nigeria ever since. All the living former military heads of state in Nigeria—Gowon, Babangida, Obasanjo, Buhari, and Abubakar—fought on the federal side in the civil war.

A review of the full range of civilian elections since the civil war helps to put the 2011 crises in perspective. The Second Republic presidential election of 1979 saw a split between the northern-based National Party of Nigeria (NPN) and the southwestern-based Unity Party of Nigeria (UPN),

---

3   See "Post Election Violence: Kaduna Records More Deaths—Lemu," *Sunday Trust*, July 10, 2011.

with the southern minorities supporting the north and the southeast running its own candidates. The election of the NPN candidate (Shehu Shagari) did not result in any significant postelection violence. Nor did his reelection in 1983,[4] again with the southwest (UPN) and southeast (Nigerian Peoples Party, NPP) running their own candidates, and the south-south supporting the north.[5]

The election of 1993, following a decade of military rule, saw the intentional breakup of the regional blocks by General Babangida, who insisted that two parties align "a little to the left" (Social Democratic Party) and "a little to the right" (National Republican Convention). This split the north and set up an alliance of the north-southwest and the south-south, leaving out portions of the north and southeast. The problem was that portions of the south-south (and southeast) boycotted the election, and Babangida annulled the whole process (and thus the Third Republic). When the presumed winner—M. K. O. Abiola, a wealthy Muslim businessman from the southwest—was later jailed by the military government of Sani Abacha, strong regional tensions developed, especially in the southwest, but they did not express themselves in violence.[6]

The elections of May 1999, which ushered in the Fourth Republic, were relatively trouble-free, because there was a widespread desire to get rid of military rule at any cost. The election of President Obasanjo in 1999 (and 2003) was with the explicit promise that power shift would occur in 2007 to the north. Again, there was little serious violence in 1999, 2003, or 2007, thanks in part to opposition leader General Buhari, who insisted on taking grievances to the courts and not to the streets. His role in 2011 may be controversial in terms of his inability to control postelection violence, but he did unequivocally condemn the violence as "sad and unwarranted" and has once again pursued his complaints through the courts.[7] His advice to his supporters to "defend their mandate" was precisely the slogan used by civil society organizations throughout Nigeria, and usually meant monitoring the election process from the polling stations up the chain of ballot custody. The problem was that the grassroots supporters

---

4   For a microstudy of the 1983 election in the north, see William F. S. Miles, *Elections in Nigeria: A Grassroots Perspective* (Boulder, CO: Lynne Rienner, 1988).

5   For details on these elections, see John Paden, *Muslim Civic Cultures and Conflict Resolution: The Challenge of Democratic Federalism in Nigeria* (Washington, D.C.: Brookings Institution, 2005), appendix A.

6   Ibid.

7   Prior to the election, Buhari made clear that he would not challenge the results in court. Following the election and the postelection violence, he stated that, even though he would not use the court, the CPC could.

had lost faith in both the election process and the judicial process. The result was a spontaneous explosion of postelection violence that has been the worst of any in Nigeria's history, excluding the run-up to the civil war.

Whether the far northern Buhari supporters will be assuaged by the Jonathan government and/or the judicial process remains to be seen. There is an ominous undercurrent of disaffection, which has been compounded by the apparent lack of transparency of the Lemu Panel, which is critical to interpreting the postelection violence. The skepticism about the appeals process, especially after the verdict of November 1 and the final verdict by the Supreme Court-issued on December 28, may also take on a political/regional undertone. The sacking of Justice Isa Salami as the head of the Presidential Election Petitions Tribunal sent a chill through the opposition parties. Whatever the merits of INEC under the leadership of Professor Jega, the challenges to the election process and results must be seen to have been dealt with fairly and swiftly by the appeals process. The culmination in November and December was overshadowed by the Boko Haram attacks, but the CPC disaffection with the judiciary is clear. The need for the international community to recognize the leadership of Buhari in this multiparty democratic process is imperative.

Why is the April 2011 postelection violence a challenge to national unity? There are several answers:

- The presidential election's splitting of the country along regional lines
- The far north's sense of being cheated out of "its turn" by Jonathan not respecting his own party's principle of power shift
- The backlash in the south against the ethnoreligious violence in the north
- The frustration with the slow process of the tribunals, and the sense that the cards are stacked in favor of the incumbents
- The increased militarization of the response to northern violence, often led by figures who are seen to personify Christian identity
- The undermining of the grassroots legitimacy of many traditional and modern northern leaders, which makes it more difficult for them to serve as conflict resolvers in the future

Meanwhile, the public discourse in the media and by governmental officials has shifted since April 2011 to challenges by a previously obscure group in northeast Nigeria, the Boko Haram, as discussed in chapter 2. Boko Haram's violent tactics are a challenge to the entire political system and to the socioeconomic class system that the oil-driven political economy has produced, with all of its perceived corruption. The call for a shari'a-based political system may not take a violent form in most cases, but when it does, it has ripple effects throughout the country.

The Challenge of Boko Haram

The violent attacks by Boko Haram challenge the unity of Nigeria in fundamental ways:

- They highlight the gap between the grassroots communities in the far north and the structures and influences of the state

- They shift the vision of Nigeria from a secular/constitutional framework to an explicitly religious set of principles, and reflect a vision that is unsustainable in a country that is half Muslim and half Christian

- They create a de facto security state in which democratic civilian control of the military is eroded to the point that a full-scale return to military rule is easy to imagine

- They create a palpable fear in the capital, which reduces its capacity to function as a seat of democratic federalism

- They invite the involvement of the international community, especially in matters of counterterrorism, which could provoke a political backlash if it is perceived to have a regional bias

- They target Christian migrant communities in the north, especially meeting places such as bars, nightclubs, and churches

- They encourage fringe groups in the non-Muslim south to demand a renegotiation of the "mistake of 1914"

One fear is that Boko Haram may try to assassinate key national leaders. Although this has not happened yet, the group has issued threats to security force leaders and to the president himself. Many of these national leaders are identified as Christian, and a successful assassination of one of them might set in motion the same nightmare scenario that resulted in the civil war of 1967–70.

Another challenge to the vision of Nigeria posed by the Boko Haram's violence is that the political and security reactions it provokes might include trying to close the northern borders with neighboring states, thus undermining Nigeria's capacity to be a leader in the Economic Community of West African States (ECOWAS). This is a dilemma for policymakers, because while there is evidence of foreign infiltration of persons across Nigeria's northern borders, attempts to close those borders exacerbate tensions in the far north, which has historic commercial, religious, and family ties across international borders.[8]

The Challenge of Ethnoreligious Crises in Plateau State

The Middle Belt contains a mixture of ethnic and religious groups. Whether the sparks that lead to violence are disputes over land, grazing rights, or political representation, they can ignite major conflagrations when they acquire ethnoreligious dimensions. The extreme forms of violence in Kaduna State after the election have been mentioned previously. The escalating ethnoreligious violence in Plateau State shows no sign of abating and has the capacity to ignite a national inferno.

The peculiar contexts of both Kaduna and Jos, neither of which possesses traditional leaders (other than those invented by the British), mean that the shock absorber role normally played by emirs and chiefs in the far north is absent. Also, the particular forms of evangelical Christianity in these two states, and on the Muslim side the fact that the strict constructionist Izala groups are strong in these two states, create a volatile mix of identity politics, without the authority structures to contain it.

The usual role of governors in these two states, in terms of how they fit into identity politics, means that these executive offices may be limited in what they can do to bridge the political and socioreligious gaps. More specifically, the Plateau State case is complicated by the grievances of pastoralists and farmers, which again could have national implications.

The Plateau State case also highlights the constitutional conundrum of settler vs. indigene populations. The reverberation in Kano State of violence in Plateau State, especially Jos, is a clear example of how violence in one state can spill over into another. Whether or not security forces evolve with a state mandate as well as a federal mandate, the challenge of containing state-level violence is one that will have ripple effects throughout the country. Social media and cell phones can help propel democratic movements, as seen in the Arab Spring, but they can just as easily be used to provoke violence when they communicate the horrors and violence meted out to ethnic and religious cohorts.

---

8   For a detailed study of cross-border relations between Nigeria and Niger Republic, see William F. S. Miles, *Hausaland Divided: Colonialism and Independence in Nigeria and Niger* (Ithaca, NY: Cornell University Press, 1994). Miles documents the legacy of a virtually open-range frontier and examines the various attempts at tightening the border. See also William F. S. Miles, "Development, Not Division: Local versus External Perceptions of the Niger-Nigeria Boundary," *Journal of Modern African Studies* 43, no. 2 (2005): 297–320. In *Elections in Nigeria* (see note 4), Miles describes human rights violations against ordinary borderlanders during the muscular attempts to enforce a border closing in 1984.

Other Postelection Challenges to National Unity

While this monograph has focused on challenges to national unity that have been manifest in the north, events in the north reverberate strongly in the south, where there exist forces and sentiments that may pose an even greater danger to the future unity of Nigeria. These include explicit threats in the Niger Delta to defend "our brother" Jonathan at all costs, even suggesting the setting up of local militias in case Boko Haram does harm to the president or to the oil and gas facilities in the Delta. There is evidence that the Biafran revival movement in the southeast has gained credibility since the election, posing a clear and present danger to a federal Nigeria. (This ethnic-based vision of Biafra is often amplified by diaspora elements in the United States, especially Igbo professionals who remember the trauma. The 2011 death of General Ojukwu, the Biafran leader, was a factor in the renewal of this particular form of subnationalism.) In addition, the official count gave 97 percent of the vote to Jonathan in the southeast (and south-south), and although this tally is probably inflated, it does indicate that the previous patterns of alliance voting in that area are a thing of the past. These results are interpreted in parts of the north as evidence of southerners ganging up on the north.

The call for a Sovereign National Conference (SNC) by many leading intellectuals in the south has taken on new meaning.[9] The idea of an SNC usually surfaces when there are extreme regional tensions in the country, and although SNC proponents often couch their ambitions in terms of "confederation," the word "sovereign" is widely interpreted to mean that *everything* is on the table, including the unity of the country.

It is beyond the scope of this monograph to elaborate further on these other challenges to national unity, except to note that the presidential election of April 2011 was clearly a tipping point, with alarms going off in parts of the country outside the north. Without a candid analysis of such developments by policy planners and/or conflict mitigators, it is hard to imagine strategic approaches to ameliorate the crisis of national unity. What, then, have been the responses to these challenges so far, and what might be done to counter them more effectively?

---

9   Nobel laureate Wole Soyinka is one of the best-known intellectuals to voice his opinion. The author served on an academic panel with Soyinka at Northwestern University in 2007 during which he called for the excision of the northern states that had opted for shari'a law in the criminal domain.

The Range of Responses

As noted above, the short-term federal response to postelection violence was to set up the Lemu Panel and the Presidential Election Petitions Tribunal. The depth of concerns expressed by opposition parties to the tribunal's personnel changes and interim decisions did not bode well for its verdicts of November 1 and December 28 to be accepted by the CPC faithful, although by the end of 2011 the state of emergency in parts of the north eclipsed many other expressions of discontent.

The short-term responses to the challenge posed by Boko Haram have been outlined in chapter 2. These have included setting up a presidential commission, the Galtimari Commission, which is looking for ways to negotiate with Boko Haram. That movement, however, has rejected the authority of the traditional leaders proposed as mediators and has said it will not negotiate until all of its followers have been released from jail (a highly unlikely eventuality given the seriousness of some of the charges those followers have been convicted of or are facing).

Apart from the presidential commission, the main responses to Boko Haram by the Nigerian federal government have been to increase personal security for leaders and key sites; to expand the use of the military and security forces to hunt for perpetrators; to internationalize the response by bringing in (since August 2011) counterterrorist training specialists and forensic experts from abroad; and to declare a state of emergency on December 31.

President Jonathan has engaged Israeli security experts to provide personal protection for himself and the Presidential Villa. (This may afford high-quality security but may also have the unintended consequence of importing Middle Eastern politics into Nigeria.) All major sites in Abuja—including foreign embassies—now have strict security provisions, and all major transportation networks have checkpoints manned by police and troops. (This has slowed traffic significantly; a journey in the capital now takes five times longer than it used to, according to observers familiar with Abuja.) During the National Day celebrations in Abuja on October 1, 2011, traffic was at a virtual standstill and many fearful residents left town.

The military has been posted at all strategic points. The military's rules of engagement, however, have not yet been revised to deal with domestic deployments, and consequently a heavy-handed approach still prevails. There is evidence that the military and security forces are closely assessing their organizational effectiveness. The negative impact of the current iron-fist approach on the public in the north is compounded by the perception that the leadership of those forces, lacking an appreciation of the region's identity politics, does not understand the dynamics of the north. This political disconnect was also evident in the government's efforts to enforce stricter border controls in the north and to deport foreigners back to Niger Republic and Chad.

The United States has been invited to train counterinsurgency resources in Nigeria, and, according to media reports, training specialists were in Nigeria as of September 2011. FBI specialists have participated fully in the analysis of explosive devices planted by Boko Haram, as have UN specialists, especially since the bombing of the UN building in Abuja on August 26. Many foreign embassies in Abuja initially put themselves on lock-down status and approved "voluntary departure" options for dependents. Subsequently, some of these measures were relaxed, although the pendulum might easily swing back toward tighter security measures as new dangers emerge, such as the threats issued in early November to bomb major hotels.[10] The concern about links with al Qaeda in the Islamic Maghreb and/or links with al Shabab training camps in Somalia has garnered the Boko Haram movement international attention.

On top of the Boko Haram challenge, the situation in Plateau State has added to the national tension and security challenges. The short-term dilemma for the governor of Plateau State is the perceived gray area between federal and state security responsibilities. If all security—military and police and intelligence—is a federal responsibility, then what remains for the governor to do? What is the role of the state's attorney general in prosecuting cases of murder committed within the context of postelection violence? With the full militarization of the short-term response in Plateau State, what is the role for state-level leadership and political initiatives?

Meanwhile, the grassroots neighborhoods in Jos have witnessed alarming levels of vigilante violence. Ethnoreligious cleansing of Jos, by gangs on both sides, has become the order of the day. The politicians' and policymakers' focus on the urban dimensions of this chaos, moreover, has meant that the herder-farmer challenge is being largely neglected. If

---

10   See "U.S. Warns of Attack by Muslim Sect in Nigeria's Capital," *New York Times*, November 7, 2011: "The unusually specific warning from American diplomats identified the Hilton, Nicon Luxury and Sheraton Hotels, whose guests include diplomats, politicians and Nigeria's business elite, as possible targets of the sect, known as Boko Haram. The embassy said its diplomats had been instructed to avoid the three hotels, but an embassy spokeswoman, Deb MacLean, would not provide any details about the threat or its source."

widespread ethnoreligious cleansing does spread to the rural areas, the national implications will be far reaching.

While the challenges posed by postelection violence, Boko Haram, and ethnoreligious cleansing in Plateau State certainly demand a short-term response, the longer-term responses of policymakers are the major concern of this monograph. These responses might include tackling political issues of power shift and federalism and constitutionalism; retooling the role of the military for domestic crises; enhancing human security in the realm of education, health, jobs, and infrastructure development; and directly addressing the socioreligious dimensions of the current crises.

If the political formula of power shift is to be revised by the dominant political party, the PDP, the full implications need to be negotiated and elaborated well before its implementation, abandonment, or replacement by another formula in the run-up to the 2014–15 political cycle. While this reassessment is essentially a political process, there does need to be some coordination between the political parties and the military-security planners and the federal think-tank policy planners. The federal character implications in such negotiations are fundamental to the process. The political unity of Nigeria is still at a stage where a one-sided power grab could destabilize the country. (The constitutional issues involved in applying federal character principles to power shift are considered separately below.)

Regarding military retooling for domestic engagements, the service chiefs in Abuja and the higher-level service training institutions (e.g., the Defence Academy in Kaduna) need to examine international precedents, as well as domestic political constituencies, to try to achieve the appropriate results. Changes need to be made not only in operational policies but also in training programs if the military presence is to stop being part of the problem and to start being part of the solution. The military's preoccupation with preventing regional coups and countercoups by rotating commanding officers needs to be tempered by a recognition that a domestic role for the military requires a more nuanced approach.

In addition, there is a need for a policy review of the relationship between police and military. While the military is quintessentially a federal institution (except for the future possibility of state national guard reserves), the police should not remain exclusively on the federal list. (The relationship between the police and military is discussed below, in the section on constitutionalism.)

Regarding longer-term perspectives on and responses to economic and human security challenges, there is a long laundry list of needs, from electric power to health and education. But from the perspective of *national unity*, three issues top that list. First, farmers need to be integrated into the "national grid" and/or into a "regional grid" via feeder roads and transportation links, enabling them to get their produce to market before it spoils and making them less dependent on small local markets. Among other advantages, this sense of connection will contribute to a sense of shared national interest. Second, even more than they need veterinarian expertise for their livestock and mobile education for their children, herders need measures to protect their own lives and those of their livestock. Some national strategy other than "resettlement" needs to be devised and implemented to allow safe passage during the transhumance seasons, and to recognize the herders' rights of land usage. Third, urban dwellers need a jobs program, including practical training. Among other benefits, such a program would go a long way toward giving urban youth a stake in society and engendering some sense of national loyalty.

The National Youth Service Corps (NYSC) program is a model of what can be done when political will exists. The NYSC was conceived as a way of encouraging university graduates to move around within the country, thereby promoting a sense of national unity. Unfortunately, the violence of the 2011 election, during which "Corpers" often assisted (and were targeted) at the polls, has meant that many parents no longer will allow their children to be assigned outside their own states—an attitude that, while understandable, undermines the purpose of the NYSC. Nonetheless, the fact that the NYSC was given its mandate by the government shows that government recognizes that the future of national unity rests in the hands of the next generation. This shows what can be done with political will. The urban youth gangs need something more that election cycles, during which they often provide "protection" to candidates, to give them hope and economic opportunity. There is a need for big-picture thinking on this matter. Urban violence always deters large-scale economic investment in cities, but such investment, including international investment, is crucial to job creation. If Nigeria is to provide its young people with work and develop an economy able to withstand increased foreign competition (especially from China), it needs to overcome the legacy of urban violence.

Long-term planning must also address the problems posed by socio-religious dynamics. NIREC operates at both the state and the national level, but the crises of 2011 have meant that representatives of those two levels rarely meet anymore. In Plateau State and Kaduna State, every effort should be made for the governors to revitalize these interfaith structures. In addition, as in the post–civil war periods in Liberia, Sierra Leone, and Côte d'Ivoire, churches and mosques should be used as venues for post-traumatic healing. Once killings have been contained, by whatever means, the post-traumatic stress disorder that often follows violence must be addressed to avoid further revenge retribution. How this can be organized should be a matter of strategic concern. The lessons of *The Imam and the Pastor,* such as the value of grassroots early warning, peace committees, and post-traumatic healing rituals, should be learned and transmitted across state and ethnoreligious lines.

Constitutional Challenges and Possible Responses

The Fourth Republic's Constitution is a 160-page document based on the 1979 Second Republic model. It was drawn up in the final days of the military regime under General Abdulsalami Abubakar, after the death of General Sani Abacha. It was ratified in May 1999, after the state and national elections of fall 1998 and spring 1999. The mood in the country, and among senior military leaders, was that a swift transition to civilian rule was imperative and that a new constitution should be adopted quickly and could be adjusted or amended subsequently, if experience indicated the need for changes. As mentioned previously, the underlying priority was to create a democratic framework for the unity of the country. A national political convention in 2005 organized by President Obasanjo did suggest a number of alterations to the Constitution, but the convention got bogged down over the issue of what percentage of oil revenues should accrue to the oil-producing states.

This section of the chapter reviews those elements of the Constitution that have a direct impact on postelection conflict management and national unity. The focus is not on the pros and cons of legal arguments or on legal precedents, but rather on the previously discussed political issues that have arisen from the respective clauses and topics.

The underlying goal of "national integration" is clearly stated in the Constitution (Sect. 15.2), as is freedom of movement (Sect. 41.). Even free and compulsory universal primary education is guaranteed as a right (Sect. 18.3). Other rights, structures, and processes include religious rights and guarantees; the three-tier federal formula; residency rights (i.e., for "settlers"); control of the security forces (police and military); multiple legal systems (including shari'a); immunity of selected officeholders (*not* members of the National Assembly!); the judiciary and election tribunals; and the amendment process. The following subsections examine in turn religious rights; federal structure; indigene/nonindigene issues; states of emergency; the relationship of the federal police to state governors; and electoral commission issues. The next section examines in greater depth the role of the police, military, and security services.

Religious Rights

Religious rights are guaranteed in the Constitution (e.g., freedom of thought and conscience [Sect. 35-38] and freedom to change religion). Freedom from discrimination is guaranteed (Sect. 42). A state religion is prohibited (Sect. 10), yet shari'a courts and appeals courts are well established (Sect. 244-260), including state shari'a courts of appeal (Sect. 275). In the mainstream judiciary, there are provisions for "appointment of persons learned in Islamic personal law and customary law" (Sect. 288).

Federal Structure

The three-tier federal formula is spelled out in detail, including the designation of the 36 states and 774 local government areas (LGAs), and their respective duties. The roles of state governments are delineated (Sect. 176-196), including the role of the state attorneys general (Sect. 195). The police are set up as a federal branch (Sect. 214-216), and the role of the armed forces is delineated (Sect. 217-220). The duties of the federal courts are clear (Sect. 230-267), as are the duties of other judicial branches (Sect. 286-296), including the establishment of election tribunals (Sect. 285). Federal character provisions are indicated throughout, including the "establishment of a body to ensure federal character of the armed forces" (Sect. 219).

Indigene/Nonindigene Issues

The Constitution contains several clauses relevant to the issue of indigenes vs. settlers—an issue that is central to this chapter. In June 2011, a group of citizens sued the federal government and thirteen states (including Plateau State) in the Federal High Court in Kaduna, claiming that the *interpretations* of the federal character principle in Section 147 (3) violated the "anti-discrimination" provision of the Constitution. They argued that "non-indigenes" were discriminated against in six fields: educational opportunities; employment opportunities; access to public and military service; property ownership; access to government infrastructure; and political participation and opportunities.[11] The case was still pending as of the writing of this chapter.

According to the anti-discrimination clause (Sect. 42 [1]): "A citizen of Nigeria of a particular community, ethnic group, place or origin, sex, religion or political opinion shall not, by reason only that he is such a person: a) be subjected either expressly by, or in the practical application of, any law in force in Nigeria or any such execution or administrative action of the government, to disabilities or restrictions to which citizens of Nigeria or other communities, ethnic groups, places of origin, sex, religious or political opinions are not subject to."

A related issue is federal character. According to Third Schedule, Part I, Federal Executive Bodies, C, "the Federal Character Commission, 8 (1) b, has as its purpose to: promote, monitor and enforce compliance with the principles of proportional sharing of all bureaucratic, economic, media, and political posts at all levels of government." The purpose of federal character provisions is to provide a framework for inclusiveness of all citizens.

States of Emergency

According to Section 305 (1):

> Subject to the provisions of this Constitution, the President may by instrument published in the Official-Gazette of the Government of the Federation issue a Proclamation of a state of emergency in the Federation or any part thereof; . . . (3) The President shall have power to issue a Proclamation of state of emergency only when: . . . (c) there is actual breakdown of public order and public safety in the federation or any part thereof to such extent as to require extraordinary measures to restore peace and security; (d) there is a clear and present danger of an actual breakdown of public order and public safety in the federation or any part thereof requiring extraordinary measures to avert such danger; . . . (f) there is any other public danger which clearly constitutes a threat to the existence of the Federation."

According to Subsection (6): "A Proclamation issued by the President under this section shall cease to have effect (c) after a period of six months has elapsed since it has been in force." It should be noted, how-

---

11   See the report by the Institute for Human Rights and Development in Africa, "Nigeria: Constitutional Challenges to Indigene-Settler Divide Still Awaits Judgement," June 17, 2011, http://www.ihrda.org/2011/06/nigeria-constitutional-challenge-to-indigene-settler-divide-still -awaits-judgement/.

ever, that the House of Assembly can extend the state of emergency for an additional six months.

The Relationship of the Federal Police to State Governors

According to Section 215 (4):

> The Governor of a state or such Commissioner of the Government state as he may authorize in that behalf, may give to the Commissioner of Police of that state such lawful directions with respect to the maintenance and security of public safety and public order within the state as he may consider necessary, and the Commissioner of Police shall comply with those directions or cause them to be complied with: Provided that before carrying out any such direction under the foregoing provision of this subsection the Commissioner of Police may request that the matter be referred to the President or such Minister of the Government of the Federation as may be authorized in that behalf by the President for his direction.

The wording of this subsection does seem to leave a gray area by failing to specify what should happen if the governor and the president have different opinions as to the situation requiring attention.

Electoral Commission Issues

The provisions for an Independent National Electoral Commission are spelled out in Third Schedule, Part I, Federal Executive Bodies, Section F, which constitutes the National Electoral Commission as the chair and twelve other members, who may delegate their powers to any (state) resident electoral commissioner. (The election tribunals set up in Section 285 are for the National Assembly and the state and local offices. The election tribunal for the presidential election consists of a panel of selected members of the Supreme Court.)

*   *   *

The larger question in all of these issues is who interprets the Constitution, and the possible influence of the executive branches on such determinations. The key to ensuring respect among all Nigeria's citizens for constitutional interpretations is to maintain the independence of the judiciary and enable the judiciary to follow the founders' intent, which in broad terms is to promote the national unity of the country while respecting democratic principles and individual rights. The killings in Plateau State hardly reflect this constitutional imperative of preserving national unity.

The Role of the Police, Military, and Security Services

The role of the police is spelled out in the Constitution (see above). So, too, is the role of the military. According to Section 217:

> (1) There shall be an armed force for the Federation which shall consist of an Army, a Navy, an Air Force and such other branches of the armed forces of the Federation as may be established by an Act of the National Assembly. (2) The Federation shall, subject to an Act of the National Assembly made in that behalf, equip and maintain the armed forces as may be considered effective for the purpose of (a) defending Nigeria from external aggression; (b) maintaining its territorial integrity and securing its borders from violation on land, sea, or air; (c) suppressing insurrection and acting in aid of civil authorities to restore order when called upon to do so by the President, but subject to such conditions as may be prescribed by an Act of the National Assembly; (d) performing such other functions as may be prescribed by an Act of the National Assembly. (3) The composition of the officer corps and other ranks of the armed forces shall reflect the federal character of Nigeria.

This constitutional role clearly subjects the armed forces to civilian control. But what has been the outcome when the armed forces have been called on to restore order during domestic crises, such as those described in this monograph? The following discussion examines in turn the current status of Nigeria's police force; the status of the military's readiness to manage domestic conflict; and the role of the national security adviser and State Security Service.

The Current Status of Nigeria's Police Forces

As of 2008, the Nigerian Police Force (NPF) consisted of 20,613 senior police officers, 28,175 police investigators, and 263,425 rank and file—a total of 312,213. By 2011, there were approximately 371,800 police at all levels, organized into seven commands and five directorates, all under the inspector-general of police. The directorates include criminal investigations, logistics, supplies, training, and operations. One branch of the NPF is the Port Security Police, with several thousand personnel. In addition, a Police Mobile Force (MOPOL) has been established as an antiriot unit to counter civil disturbances. (At present, there are twelve MOPOL commands, spread among the thirty-six state commands and FCT.) There are approximately thirteen hundred police stations nationwide. Police are not normally issued weapons except on special assignments. In 1989, General Babangida decided that a certain percentage of police officers would be assigned to their home areas to facilitate community relations, although, because of federal character rotations, meeting this percentage remains a challenge. A National Police Council (NPC) coordinates with all stakeholders, with the president serving as chairman. The NPC consists of all state governors, the minister of interior, the chairman of the Public Service Commission, and the inspector-general of police.[12] One of the major challenges facing the police force is reducing the high level of corruption within its ranks.[13]

So far during the Fourth Republic, there have been six inspectors-general of the NPF, reflecting most major areas of the country: Musiliu Smith, Mustafa Adebayo Balogun,[14] Sunday Ehindero, Mike Okiro, Ogbonna Okechukwu Onovo, and, since 2010, Hafiz Ringim, who comes from Jigawa in the Kano area. Even before the Boko Haram movement reached public attention, there were efforts to reform the police. As of 2011, the government had presented a white paper with seventy-nine recommendations for consideration by the National Assembly. The recommended reforms included increasing pay for police officers, dealing with police with criminal records, setting up a public complaints program, improving training for recruits, and upgrading the communications systems. Perhaps the most important of the recommendations was a call to prevent extrajudicial killings of the sort that targeted the leader of Boko Haram in 2009. The fact that Boko Haram regards the police as a prime target (and a prime source of weapons) compounds the challenge of dealing with such extremists—as does the fact that the general public clearly sees serious problems with the police and, in some areas of the country, is reluctant to communicate or cooperate with the police.

The Status of Military Readiness to Manage Domestic Conflict

The three services of the military have active-duty personnel totaling around 85,000 regular troops and 82,000 paramilitary troops. This num-

12   In practice, the NPC doesn't really function. A Police Service Commission exists and functions and is supposed to be independent, headed by its own chairman. See Sections L and M of the third schedule of the Constitution.

13   The need to tackle police corruption is also central to the strategies for dealing with Boko Haram, because it is one of the main points justifying the group's attacks on the "corrupted" state of Nigeria. As previously noted, there was a presidential committee on police reform that tried to address this issue referred to in the Human Rights Watch report on police reform in 2010 (http://www.hrw.org/reports/2010/08/17/everyone-s-game-0).

14   Balogun is from the southwest and was inspector-general of police during the years 2002–5. While in office, he was indicted for stealing $100 million. Corruption has been endemic in the police force. For example, even at the local level, "user fees" are often charged at checkpoints

ber is substantially lower than the 250,000 personnel who were on active duty in 1977 in the aftermath of the civil war. Many of the officers are sent to Pakistan for training (specifically, to the Staff College in Quetta and the National Defence University in Islamabad). Initial officer training is conducted at the Nigeria Defence Academy in Kaduna, the Armed Forces Command and Staff College in Jaji (near Kaduna), and the National War College in Abuja. The Air Force sponsors the Air Force Military School, which is located in Jos. The Navy (including the Coast Guard) has about 8,000 personnel, has operational commands in Lagos and Calabar, and conducts training in Lagos. As noted previously, the armed forces have served in numerous peacekeeping missions abroad.

Since the inception of the Fourth Republic in 1999, the eight chiefs of staff of the Nigerian Army have reflected the federal character principle, as shown in this list of names, region, and ethnicity: Victor Malu, north, Hausa-Tiv; Ishaya Bamiyi, north, Hausa-Zuru; Alexander Ogomudia, south-south, Edo; Martin Luther Agwai, north, Hausa-Kaje; Owoye Andrew Azazi, south-south, Ijaw; Luka Yusuf, north, Hausa-Kaje; Abdulrahman Bello Dambazau, north, Hausa; Onyabor Azubuike Ihejirika, southeast, Igbo.

In 2011, the overall chief of defence staff was Air Chief Marshal Oluseyi Petinrin, who is highly regarded as a strategic planner.[15] The minister of defence was initially Adetokunbo Kayode,[16] but in July he was replaced by Bello Haliru Mohammed (from Kebbi State).[17] Thus, in the immedi-

---

15 Oluseyi Petrinin was born January 19, 1955, in Ipetu-Ijesa in Ori-Ade Local Government Area of Osun State. He enlisted in the Nigerian Defence Academy in 1974 and was commissioned on January 3, 1977. From 1977 to 1978, he attended pilot training at Maxwell Air Force Base in Alabama, United States. He later attended the Air Command and Staff College at Maxwell Air Force Base. Petrinin has served with the Air Defence Group, Maiduguri; the Operations HQ Training Command, Kaduna; and, as director of national military strategy, at the National Defence College. He received a master's degree in strategic studies from the University of Ibadan. He was appointed chief of the Air Staff in August 2008.

16 Adetokunbo Kayode was born October 31, 1958, in Ondo State, and holds a Yoruba traditional title. He studied law at the University of Lagos and served as counsel to the Peoples Democratic Party. He was minister of culture and tourism and minister of labor and productivity before being appointed minister of defence in April 2010 by Acting President Jonathan.

17 According to Mohammed's profile at the Safer Africa Group website: "Dr. Bello Haliru Mohammed was born in Birnin Kebbi, capital of Kebbi state on 9 October 1945. . . . He attended the famous Government College (now Barewa College), Zaria. In 1966, he proceeded to Ahmadu Bello University (ABU) also in Zaria, where he studied veterinary medicine. He is a Fellow of the College of Veterinary Surgeons of Nigeria (FCVSN). Mohammed started work as a lecturer at Ahmadu Bello University, Zaria, but he was soon summoned to responsibilities beyond the ivory tower. In 1977, he was appointed Commissioner for Agriculture under the military government in the then Sokoto State (the state was later split into Sokoto and Kebbi States in 1995). He was subsequently redeployed as Commissioner for Education under the same government. In 1988, he was appointed, by the then military President, Gen. Ibrahim Babangida, to head the Nigerian Customs Service (NCS) as its Comptroller General. He held that post until 1994. . . . During Gen.

ate postelection environment, both Petinrin and Kayode were from the southwest; the chief of staff of the Nigerian Army, Ihejirika, was from the southeast; and the national security adviser, Azazi (discussed below), was from the south-south. The appointment of Bello Mohammed as defence minister will help redress this lack of zonal balance, but it will not dispel northern mistrust of the military's senior leadership.

By September 2011, the armed forces were, in effect, in charge of security in Borno State, Yobe State, Plateau State, and Abuja. (The military in Kaduna State was not as evident as in the other crisis states, but still exerted a strong presence.) The police have not had the capacity to control security in those situations.

The result of these postelection domestic crises has been an extremely heavy-handed use of military force, which in the cases of Maiduguri and Jos has led to citizen complaints of further casualties. According to *Christian Today*, for example:

> Members of the Nigerian military have been implicated in violence in Plateau State after military identification documents were allegedly recovered from the scene of an early morning August 15 attack. According to human rights agency Christian Solidarity Worldwide (CSW), four military identity documents were allegedly found after the attack on the community of Heipang, located close to Jos Airport, where nine people were killed. . . . There have been a number of troublesome reports regarding the conduct of members of the Joint Task Force (JTF) charged with maintaining peace in Plateau State. They range from lack of intervention in raids on villages to suspected collusion of soldiers in the violence. . . . On August 2, CSW reported that members of the JTF opened fire on a protest by hundreds of female farmers from Gyeri Village, seven kilometers from Bukuru in Plateau State, wounding three of them. The farmers had marched to the military outpost in protest at the lack of intervention during an attack by Fulani tribesmen armed with

---

Abacha's ill-fated transition programme from 1995-1998, Mohammed was a founding member of the Democratic Party of Nigeria. After Abacha's death and the dissolution of the DPN and other parties, he then became a founding member of the Peoples Democratic Party (PDP). . . . After the PDP's victory in the 1999 elections, President Olusegun Obasanjo in September of that year, appointed Mohammed as a Commissioner on the Revenue Mobilization Allocation and Fiscal Commissions (RMAFC). . . . Less than two years later, in June 2001, Obasanjo appointed him as Minister of Communications, a post he held till May 2003. Soon after he left the cabinet, Mohammed again returned to the party bureaucracy. In June 2004, he was elected National Vice Chairman of the PDP for the North West Zone. . . . In March 2008, he was elevated to the office of deputy National Chairman of the party. In January 2011, he emerged as the PDP's seventh National Chairman." See http://saferafricagroup.com/2011/07/12/profile-dr-bello-haliru-mohammed-minister-of-defence/

machetes on over 14 farms that had destroyed crops as they were ripening."[18]

In Maiduguri, the violence by military forces against homes suspected of harboring Boko Haram members has been even more dramatic, as noted in chapter 2. The public relations branch of the Army admitted via the news media in August 2011 that some troops have been "over-zealous." How the military can serve a more constructive role in crisis management is a matter of strategic concern, given the high stakes of national unity.

The pattern of overkill in domestic situations by troops not trained to handle such situations with minimal force is a major problem in Nigeria. Improvements in training and leadership are essential if this heavy-handedness is to be curbed, as is a commitment to the judicious interpretation of the federal character of the personnel deployed and a reassessment of the role of the military in domestic crises. While the Constitution may validate such involvement with presidential authorization, military interaction with grassroots communities has often exacerbated violence. The need for strategic thinking and planning in the political realm is evident.

The Role of the National Security Adviser

The national security adviser (NSA) and the State Security Service (SSS) are charged with securing the internal security of Nigeria. General Andrew Owoye Azazi was reappointed NSA to President Jonathan on May 30, 2011.[19] He is a career specialist in intelligence work and has been trained in both the United Kingdom and the United States. His close ethnogeographic relationship to Jonathan has been a matter of concern in the north. In the run-up to the 2011 elections, he was well known for urg-

---

18 See "Nigerian Military Implicated in Violent Attacks," August 20, 2011, *Christian Today*, http://www.christiantoday.com/article/nigerian.military.implicated.in.violent.attacks/28473.htm.

19 Andrew Azazi was born in present-day Bayelsa State on February 1, 1952. In 1972, he was admitted to the Nigerian Defence Academy in Kaduna. He has specialized in intelligence work. According to Safer Africa Group: "He attended Staff Intelligence and Security Course, School of Service Intelligence, Ashford, Kent, UK and the Combined Strategic Intelligence Training Programme at the Defence Intelligence College, Washington DC, United States. . . . He attended the Armed Forces Command and Staff College (AFCSC), Jaji, and the highly regarded National War College (now National Defence College) in Abuja. . . . He thereafter proceeded to the University of Ibadan, where he earned a Master of Science (MSc) degree in Strategic Studies. . . . He served as Assistant Defence Attache at the Nigerian Embassy in Washington DC, United States, for a period of three years. He later rose to become Director of Military Intelligence in 2003. . . . In January 2005, Azazi was appointed General Officer Commanding (GOC) 1 Division, Nigerian Army, Kaduna. He was subsequently appointed Chief of Army Staff (COAS) in June 2006 and Chief of Defence Staff in 2007. It was from that post that he retired from the army on 20 August 2008. He was appointed National Security Adviser by President Jonathan on 4 October 2010, following the resignation of retired General Aliyu Gusau in September 2010." See his profile at http://saferafricagroup.com/2011/05/31/profile-general-owoye-andrew-azazi.

ing a military presence at polling stations, despite the protestations of the INEC leaders, who felt it would intimidate voters.

In the postelection period, with its growing concerns about terrorist violence, Azazi has been proactive on a variety of fronts. According to one media account:

> The National Security Adviser, Gen. Andrew Azazi, and the Director-General of the State Security Service (SSS), Ita Ekpen-yong, yesterday called for an amendment to the Explosives Act. . . . Azazi, who was represented by Maj.-Gen. Babatunde Samuel, said: "As the National Security Adviser, I urge this gathering to play a key role in national security as security is everybody's business. You will agree with me that the Explosive Act of 1964 and Explosive Regulation of 1967 are all outdated, as they do not take into cognisance the present day realities. . . ." He asked the gathering to "make very cogent input to a bill to the National Assembly that will take into account today's realities on the issue of explosives. . . . In ensuring the realization of this objective, everything possible must be done to ensure that commercial explosives, which are indispensable tools for the exploitation of minerals, do not constitute any risk to national security."[20]

Maintaining internal security in a democracy is very much a matter of balancing the right to conduct legitimate civilian activities with the need to prevent or contain violence and instability. (This is a worldwide issue in democracies in the twenty-first century, given the nearubiquity of terrorist concerns.) If the perception arises in Nigeria that security revolves around the person and interests of the president, who deploys security forces to exact vengeance on political opponents, this perception can undermine democracy itself.

Which raises the issue of the SSS. According to *Wikipedia:*

> The State Security Service (SSS) . . . is the primary federal government law enforcement agency of Nigeria. It is primarily responsible for internal policing, and is one of three successor organizations to the National Security Organisation (NSO), dissolved in 1986. The SSS has come under repeated criticism from both within Nigeria and without charging it as an instrument of political repression, used by whatever government is then in power to harass and intimidate political opponents. SSS

---

20   See John Ofikhenua, "SSS, NSA Call for Amendment of Explosives Act," *Bob Tuskin Radio Show,* August 17, 2011, http://www.bobtuskin.com/2011/08/17/sss-nsa-call-for-amendment-of-expl.

officials maintain they act constitutionally, providing needed internal peace and security for the people of Nigeria. . . .

The mission of the SSS is to protect and defend the Federal Republic of Nigeria against domestic threats, to uphold and enforce the criminal laws of Nigeria, and to provide leadership and criminal justice services to both federal and state law-enforcement organs. The SSS is also charged with the protection of the President, Vice President, Senate President, Speaker of the House of Representatives, State Governors, their immediate families, other high ranking government officials, past Presidents and their spouses, certain candidates for the offices of President and Vice President, and visiting foreign heads of state and government. . . . Its present Director General is Mr. Ita Ekpeyong who took over from the exiting Director General Afakriya Gadzama in September 2010.[21]

What has the SSS done, especially with regard to the Boko Haram threat? Its two most public activities have been to arrest suspected members of Boko Haram and to monitor preaching in churches and mosques. In the case of people arrested, the decision whether to prosecute them seems to follow the directives of the president. Thus, for instance, *All Africa.com* reported on July 5, 2011:

The State Security Service (SSS) Monday said it had arrested over 100 suspected members of the Boko Haram sect but they would not be prosecuted—in line with President Goodluck Jonathan's decision to adopt a political solution to the problem. . . . SSS spokesperson Marilyn Ogar said the arrests were made in six states—Borno, Bauchi, Kaduna, Kano, Yobe, and Adamawa. All are in the North-east and North-west. Ogar explained that since Jonathan had decided to use the "carrot and stick" approach on suspects of Boko Haram, SSS would not go contrary to that strategy.[22]

Monitoring churches and mosques is a delicate matter. According to the media:

The officials of the State Security Service in Kogi State have kicked off their next assignment by monitoring preaching in Churches & Mosques throughout Kogi State. This is an effort to monitor ongoing religion crisis in the state. The state director of

---

21 See *Wikipedia*, s.v. "State Security Service," http://en.wikipedia.org/wiki/State_Security_Service.

22 See "Nigeria: State Security Services—Arrested Boko Haram Members Won't Face Trial," *All Africa.com*, July 5, 2011, http://allafrica.com/stories/201107050955.html.

SSS, Mike Fubara, told journalists in Lokoja on Wednesday that the organization had also been monitoring open air preaching and other religious events in different parts of the state. Fubara said that it was now mandatory for intending preachers from within and outside the state to undergo screening and get clearance from the SSS before preaching.[23]

The *Daily Times* adds:

> The SSS boss said that banks and corporate organizations operating in the state had been invited to meetings and given specific instructions to increase security in and around their premises. He said similar meetings had also been held with the leadership of transport unions, adding that operation of commercial motorcycles would come under new regulations as soon as Ramadan was over.[24]

The monitoring of churches and mosques involves a delicate balance between respecting constitutional guarantees and rights regarding freedom of religion, on the one hand, and the need to obtain information that might be security relevant, on the other hand. But who decides what constitutes a security threat? Are SSS officers sufficiently conversant with religious ideas to approve or disapprove of preaching, whether Christian or Muslim? The legacy of the National Security Organisation (NSO), which was abolished in 1986 because of its overreach into the lives of citizens, is a caution to the new role of its successor organization, the SSS—that is, even in times of postelection crises, limits must be placed on what can and should be allowed in the name of security. It is a short step from the militarization of security to a society in which all citizens are monitored by secret police.

The Special Response Group

At the end of December 2011, the Nigerian Army set up a "special squad to combat the menace of Boko Haram." As reported in *Punch:*

> The Chief of Army Staff, Lt. Gen. Azubuike Ihejirika, who spoke at a two-day security awareness workshop organized by the Nigerian army on Wednesday, said the suicide attacks carried out by Boko Haram had only indicated that the group did not have respect for human lives. Ihejirika said the Special

---

23   See "Nigerian SSS to Monitor Preaching in Churches & Mosques in Kogi State," *Naijan.com*, August 11, 2011, http://naijan.com/nigerian-sss-to-monitor-preaching-in-churches-mosques.

24   See "SSS Monitors Mosques, Churches in Kogi," *Daily Times*, August 11, 2011, http://dailytimes .com.ng/article/sss-monitors-mosques-churches-kogi.

Response Group would complement the efforts of the Joint Task Force and other security operatives in the battle to restore sanity in the society. Ihejirika said the decision was informed by the need to boost the capacity of his men to handle the challenge of Boko Haram. Ihejirika noted that security operatives had encountered difficulty in protecting potential victims of terror attacks because of the nature of the operations of those behind such attacks. He said, "The unpredictable and random nature of terrorist acts makes it difficult for security forces to protect all potential victims and targets, since they are faceless and have an unlimited number of potential targets." He stated that the lack of the expected degree of training played a major role in the way security operatives had handled the Boko Haram issue. The COAS said the leadership of the army would ensure that it came up with new strategies to handle such emergent threat to peace and security. Meanwhile, the Youth Wing of the Christian Association of Nigeria has said the continued attack on Nigerians by Boko Haram is a serious threat to the unity and corporate existence of Nigeria.[25]

Whatever training and strategic adjustments are made by the military and security forces in Nigeria, the question remains: What are the alternatives to such a military/security state approach to the challenges outlined in this chapter? Answers to this question can be found in the fields of conflict management and resolution and third-party mediation, and in such related fields as post-traumatic healing. While there are clear religious and socioeconomic factors in Nigerian conflicts, many of the underlying issues are political.

Conflict Management and Resolution

Death tolls from all three crises analyzed in this monograph have collectively reached the thousands. One policy issue is degrees of accountability.[26] Another is the challenge of post-traumatic healing. This latter is an area where both indigenous NGOs and university-based centers for peace studies (such as at the Usmanu Danfodiyo University, Sokoto) can play a role. There are many approaches to such healing, from truth and reconciliation commissions, to local cultural practices (such as *gacaca* in Rwanda), to psychiatric clinics and resources (as in Liberia), to international courts of justice. In most cases, the goal is to move beyond the

---

25   See "Army Establishes Special Squad to Combat Boko Haram," *Punch,* December 22, 2011.

26   Human Rights Watch realizes that arresting people implicated in violence can exacerbate tensions but argues that the failure to hold perpetrators accountable also fuels the cycle of violence.

trauma of killings and mutilations, and provide people some hope that the future will be more just than the past.

In this process, politicians can be either part of the problem or part of the solution. The experiment of civilian rule in Nigeria is always cautioned by the realization that, for most of the years since independence, senior military officers have not only ruled the country but also held it together. Whether the younger generation of Western-educated technocrats at the helm of the Fourth Republic can preserve national unity remains to be seen.

The issue of *political will* goes to the heart of the reforms suggested in this monograph. Clearly, Nigerian democracy is messy, but if it is unable to meet existential challenges to national unity, it may be doomed. Whether it is possible to achieve constitutional adjustments and security reforms remains to be seen. But politically motivated denial of the problems does Nigeria no service—hence the need to step back and take a more analytical view of the 2011 crises in Nigeria.

Conclusions

At a fundamental level, all political systems must reach a consensus on matters of *community* and matters of *authority* if they are to achieve stability or remain stable. Community issues include the external boundaries of the system, as well as the internal designations. Authority issues revolve around two elements: power and legitimacy. This relationship can be expressed as a formula, A = P + L, where *power* is the ability to produce intended effects, and *legitimacy* is the approval or acceptance of the basis of decision-making leadership by the broader population. One extreme variation is power without legitimacy, as in a harsh military regime or an autocracy. Another extreme is legitimacy—for instance, via elections—without power, which often produces a "strong man" backlash in an attempt to create stability.

Challenges to the nature of community may take the form of separatist movements and/or attempts to change the foundational vision of the political union, such as moving from a religious base to a secular base, or vice versa. Challenges to authority may take constitutional forms or extraconstitutional forms.

In Nigeria, the inherited external community boundaries of the former colonial state have served as the basic vision of national unity. The internal boundaries of Nigeria have shifted from an initial two-tier/ three-state federal system to the present three-tier/36-state union with its 774 local government authorities designated in the Constitution. The advantage of a *federal* framework over a unitary framework is that conflict can often be contained at the state or local levels, rather than rising to the national level, as is often the case in many smaller nonfederal African countries. The disadvantage of a federal system is that when conflict does rise to the national level, it can destabilize the entire system, and the components of the federation serve as ready-made units for secession.

This monograph has argued that the central trauma of community and authority in Nigeria since independence in 1960 has been the civil war of 1967–70. The attempt to break up the country, plus the subsequent reign of military rulers—interspersed briefly with successive civilian regimes— has focused the attention of successive generations of Nigerians around the need to "keep Nigeria one" (the official slogan that came out of the civil war era). This monograph, too, has focused on this subject and has argued that the way in which *conflict is managed* may well determine the future of community and authority in Nigeria. The civil war experience also serves as a reminder that challenges to the political system are usually driven not by a single grievance or ambition but by a mixture of factors, including religion, ethnicity, regionalism, economics, and politics.

The irony of national elections in Africa has been that combinations of these factors may come to the surface during the electoral process despite the good intentions of democratic reformers. In situations where external boundaries are weak, porous, or virtually nonexistent, there is the ever-present chance that whole segments of society may wish to detach in some way from the larger polity. As the twenty-first century unfolds, this may increasingly take an extremist form of *religious* secession and/or recombination, whether of the radical Muslim variety (e.g., al Qaeda in the Islamic Maghreb) or the extremist Christian variety (e.g., the Lord's Resistance Army in Uganda and neighboring countries). The common response by governments to such situations has been increasing *militarization* of conflicts, in which the state (whatever its basis of legitimacy) turns to military power (both internal and external) to manage the conflict. If such military power does not have some basis in *legitimacy*, militarization of a conflict can simply add fuel to the flames.

This monograph has argued that the Nigerian presidential election of 2011 turned into a potential tipping point, as to both the nature of conflict and the means of managing conflict. While it is too early to assess the longer-term consequences of violence, the policy remedies and political accommodations necessary to strengthen national unity require both *short-term tactics* and *long-term strategic assessment*. System instability in Nigeria is a matter of concern both internally, for vulnerable populations, and externally, for the international community, especially when officials and private elements also become the targets of antiestablishment violence.

This concluding chapter will focus on five elements of conflict analysis and resolution that are germane to Nigeria in the post-2011 era: an assessment of analytical factors fueling conflicts; confidence-building measures in the remediation of conflicts; short- and longer-term policies to mitigate violent system-threatening conflict (plus scenarios of alternative futures); the challenges of implementing such policies; and a summary assessment of conflict management and resolution in northern Nigeria and nationally.

Analytical Factors in Conflict Management

Throughout this monograph, reference has been made to community identity factors such as religion, ethnicity, political allegiance, and region-alisms (including zonal). References to *identity politics* usually revolve around some combination of these factors: not just Muslim vs. Christian, for instance, but also Hausa-Fulani vs. Yoruba vs. Igbo vs. minorities, PDP vs. others, northern vs. southern, and so forth. Often, these identity factors are intentionally disguised by various mechanisms, such as using state of origin, or geocultural zones as surrogate identities. Nor are these identities written in stone, since *situational identities* are often far more salient. As noted in chapter 3, identities are dynamic, not static, and the challenge in national terms is to foster a sense of Nigerian identity to go along with the various combinations of subnational identities.

Yet, there are two other types of identities salient to conflict analysis in Nigeria that need emphasizing here: generational identities and socio-economic status (SES) identities. There may be combinations of these, such as references to "junior officers vs. senior officers," in which generation is reinforced by SES. But there is an emerging sense in Nigeria of tension among all generations.

Nigeria's "first generation" of leaders was born between 1937 and 1949, and thus today its members are in their sixties and seventies. A "second generation" of leaders or potential leaders was born between 1950 and 1960, and today its members are in their fifties. A "third generation," just beginning to assume leadership positions, was born between 1961 and 1975, and thus its members are their midthirties and forties. A "fourth generation" (not yet at the leadership level) increasingly frustrated by lack of jobs and other opportunities, was born after 1976 and includes those characterized as "youth" by anxious Nigerian commentators. Youth cohorts, whether in politics or religion or economics, have begun to assert their independence. Youth gangs in urban areas are one manifestation of this phenomenon, and such groups do not look to elders for guidance as they may have in the past.

While the tensions between generations are mitigated to some extent by family or religious brotherhood ties, those ties are beginning to erode under the impact of urban migration and other agents of social change.

Within the political economy at the elite level, the most obvious tensions are between the older generation of power brokers (often with military backgrounds) and those in the upcoming middle generations, who are eager to take over the reins of power. Those members of the middle generations who have managed to already achieve power tend to disregard the advice of their elders, whom they see as out of touch with the modern world. As these educated technocrats take over from the elders, Nigeria is coming increasingly under the control of a generational cohort less attuned than its predecessor to the dangers and early indicators of national disunity.

What about the relationship of youth to older generations? Historically, in northern Nigeria the Islamic reform movements, especially during the founding of the Sokoto Caliphate, were led by young men. If the movements pressed successfully for reforms, the youth became the leadership cadre, and hence the "establishment." Within the Nigerian *ummah* (community), at least in the Sokoto caliphal areas, the Muslim establishment has usually made every effort to incorporate the next generation, which then loses its "youth" status and becomes part of the establishment. In the Hausa language, there is a range of terms for age groups, from "youth" through "elders."

What has happened since the 1990s is that certain Muslim "youth" movements have refused to be co-opted into the establishment. Thus, the so-called Shi'ites have explicitly rejected overtures to be part of the National Supreme Council of Islamic Affairs (NSCIA) umbrella organization. More recently, the Boko Haram movement has refused to accept the authority (i.e., the legitimacy) of the sultan of Sokoto or even of the traditional emirs. (Part of this may be the Borno heritage, but part is a rejection of the "corruption" of the mainstream establishment.)

Counterintuitively, within the political realm generational dynamics go a long way to accounting for the appeal of Muhammadu Buhari to the "youth," because he reached over the heads of the first, second, and even third generations and became the folk hero for the fourth generation. Table 5 makes this clear.

Regarding identities based on socioeconomic status, as mentioned in the discussion of Borno in chapter 2, there is a range of terms in Hausa for different socioeconomic groups, ranging from "common people" (*talakawa*) to "big men" (*manya manya*). During the First Republic, in the north the major opposition political party—the Northern Elements Progressive Union (NEPU), led by Aminu Kano—appealed directly to the common people. At the same time, the dominant northern party was based in part on links between a wide range of northern elites—traditional and modern—who in turn brought their respective constituencies under the umbrella of the Northern People's Congress (NPC), led by Ahmadu Bello. Some of these same contrasting SES profiles exist at

Table 5. Four Generations of Northern and National Leaders: Selected Examples

Name	Born	State	Ethnicity*	Occupation	Religion	Party (2011)	Highest Office
First Generation: 1937–49							
Olusegun Obasanjo	1937	Ogun	Y	military	Christian	PDP	President
Ibrahim Babangida	1941	Niger	G	military	Muslim	PDP	Head of state
Muhammadu Buhari	1942	Katsina	HF	military	Muslim	CPC	Head of state
Jonah Jang	1944	Plateau	B	military	Christian	PDP	Gov. Plateau
Atiku Abubakar	1946	Adamawa	HF	business	Muslim	PDP	Vice President
David Mark	1948	Benue	Id	military	Christian	PDP	Senate President
Patrick Yakowa	1948	Kaduna	M	civil service	Christian	PDP	Gov. Kaduna
Second Generation: 1950–60							
Umaru Musa Yar'Adua	1951	Katsina	HF	education	Muslim	PDP	President
Andrew Azazi	1952	Bayelsa	Ij	military	Christian	--	NSA
Attahiru Bafarawa	1954	Sokoto	HF	local govt.	Muslim	ACN	Gov. Sokoto
Namadi Sambo	1954	Kaduna	HF	architect	Muslim	PDP	Vice President
Ibrahim Shekarau	1955	Kano	HF	education	Muslim	ANPP	Gov. Kano
Sa'ad Abubakar III	1956	Sokoto	HF	military	Muslim	--	Sultan
Goodluck Jonathan	1957	Bayelsa	Ij	education	Christian	PDP	President
Attahiru Jega	1957	Kebbi	HF	education	Muslim	--	Chair INEC
Tijjani Bande	1957	Kebbi	HF	education	Muslim	--	Dir. NIPSS
Nuhu Ribadu	1960	Adamawa	HF	law/police	Muslim	ACN	Chair EFCC
Nasir el-Rufai	1960	Katsina	HF	surveyor	Muslim	CPC	Min. FCT
Third Generation: 1961–75							
Kashim Shettima	1966	Borno	K	economics	Muslim	ANPP	Gov. Borno
Fourth Generation: 1976–2011							
No-one yet in leadership positions							

Ethnicity Key: Y = Yoruba, G = Gwari, HF = Hausa-Fulani, B = Berom, Id = Idoma, M = Minority, Ij = Ijaw, K = Kanuri

present between the CPC, which draws support from the common people, and the PDP, which draws its support from the elites.

The disparity in income in the north—and indeed in Nigeria as a whole—does not in itself translate into "classes" in the Western sense. Even the standard ways of measuring income disparities tend to founder on the shoals of redistributive cultural mechanisms.[1] The oil-driven economy does provide opportunities for business entrepreneurs—including the famous "Hausa traders"—and persons of professional talent to rise through social mobility. Furthermore, the concept of SES uses as one of its key indicators *educational level*, which in a highly mobile society can cast a broad social net. (In addition, the technology-driven social media are now available to almost everyone.)

The most obvious variation in "class theory" is that Hausa culture favors a quintessential *patron-client* society, in which the big men have an elaborate network of "clients" who provide loyalty (and services) in return for loyalty. Thus, whether one is looking at political, economic, or religious leaders, the pattern is for wealthy or powerful men to "retain" clients, even at the grassroots level, who are part of a loyalty network. Before 2009 and the killing of Muhammad Yusuf, the Boko Haram movement in Borno was clearly linked to some big men.

Patron-client relationships, which historically characterized the mainstream political parties in the north, fueled sometimes by money and sometimes by loyalty networks, may have broken down during the 2011 election. In part, this was due to the impact of Buhari, who, in the tradition of Aminu Kano, spoke directly to the "common man."

In places such as Jos, where these historic big-man patterns never really existed, the NEPU pattern of speaking directly to the masses by religious and political leaders (now facilitated by social media) touches the grassroots levels without intermediation. The Hausa-speaking urban

---

1   The standard way of measuring income disparity is via the Gini index. According to the World Bank's website, "Gini index measures the extent to which the distribution of income (or, in some cases, consumption expenditure) among individuals or households within an economy deviates from a perfectly equal distribution. A Lorenz curve plots the cumulative percentages of total income received against the cumulative number of recipients, starting with the poorest individual or household. The Gini index measures the area between the Lorenz curve and a hypothetical line of absolute equality, expressed as a percentage of the maximum area under the line. Thus a Gini index of 0 represents perfect equality, while an index of 100 implies perfect inequality." See "GINI Index," http://data.worldbank.org/indicator/SI.POV.GINI. Nigerian distribution of family income on the Gini index was 43.7 in 2003, although subnational data are not available publicly. Hence, there is no way of retrieving subnational variations in the north without access to the raw data, which is provided to international organizations by the Nigerian government.

gangs thus echo parts of the classic patterns but also represent a new phenomenon in terms of rootlessness and social alienation. The Berom-speaking youth have always had a cultural predisposition toward a chief-less culture, despite the colonial creation of a Berom "chief."

In Plateau State, the cattle herders, who were historically not involved in election voting, still have strong cultural ties to their local-level chiefs (*ardo*), but have weaker cultural ties to the urban Fulani than before. This is problematic in terms of how government efforts work with Fulfulde-speaking pastoralists. It is unlikely that the enforced settlement of such transhumance citizens would reinforce the same sort of identity loyalties associated either with their SES cohorts in the farming (*kauye*) or urban (*birni*) communities or with their non-Fulfulde-speaking ethnic cohorts.

Thus, the pressures of rapid social change, born of the oil boom, have had a profound impact on generational interaction patterns and on historic SES identities, although echoes of the politics of the First Republic are still evident. The other major identity factors—ethnicity, religion, and regionalism (including "zones" and "city state" affiliation)—intertwine to create a rich mix of potentially situational identity combinations relevant to the various patterns and types of cooperation and/or violent conflict.

What are some of the types of violent conflict in the Nigerian political domain? The academic definition of conflict as incompatible values is transformed when such conflict involves violence toward persons or properties. What form violence takes—and it can range from the symbolic burning of buildings to ethnic cleansing and targeted assassinations—depends on the capacity and the will of those who employ violence. When violence takes on a life of its own, it can reach the level of irredentist movements, civil war, and even genocide.[2]

Systematic analysis of violent conflict by social scientists includes the multiple-methods approach. In addition, there are the more focused commission-of-inquiry methods of the policymakers and other decision makers, plus the simulation scenarios of long-term strategists. Think tanks deal with all of the above.

---

2   For a discussion of types of violent conflict in Africa and methods of measuring violence, see
     Donald Morrison, Robert Mitchell, and John Paden, *Black Africa: A Comparative Handbook*
     (New York: Paragon, 1989), which systematically compares violent conflict over time in thirty-
     two African countries and correlates "dependent variables," such as violence, with several hun-
     dred social, economic, and political "independent variables."

Confidence-Building Measures
in Conflict Mitigation

As the case of contemporary Nigeria clearly demonstrates, one of the major challenges in conflict mitigation is the inevitable range of *unintended consequences* of policies. For instance, when police try to break up urban demonstrations, the police become the targets of violence, and they in turn target those who are targeting them. Military forces try to dislodge cells of potential terrorists but end up destroying sections of towns, which alienates citizens and leads to more violence. Security services try to crack down on suspects ("culprits") and/or their sponsors and end up violating democratic norms. Conflict resolvers who intervene in other people's conflicts may reinforce their own cultural values and may appear to have a partisan bias. State governors, trying to devise policies to mitigate violence, may overreach and end up alienating some of the stakeholders. Amnesty for regional troublemakers may backfire and encourage the development of protection rackets by youth, who calculate that they have nothing to lose and everything to gain by kidnapping and creating turmoil.

In addition, the relations between federal, state, and local government authorities during the Fourth Republic on matters of security may result in a paralysis of will and/or a power grab by one level over another. In 1980, during the dispute between federal and state officials regarding the Maitatsine extremist violence in Kano (mentioned in chapter 2), each level of government produced its own commission of inquiry, which largely blamed each other. During the Second Republic, the state governor in Kano was from one political party and the president was in the other party. Many of the approximately ten thousand deaths this Maitatsine confrontation caused resulted from the failure of the police to stem the movement and the subsequent use of heavy military artillery to wipe out a whole section of Kano City.

Yet, while inaction is not an option by government officials of whatever level, some state governors, especially those with military backgrounds, may be inclined to quickly seize one or another policy option without first assessing its unintended consequences or contemplating a longer-term, comprehensive program of mitigation. Officials who prefer to set up commissions of inquiry may end up with a fuller grasp of the problem, but it may take them at least several months to do so, during which time the problem will likely worsen.

In the short term, the introduction of *confidence-building measures* can often be the first step in getting at the roots of conflict. The key is to do no harm. Whatever the merits of various policy approaches, the early stages of response can either help or hurt the longer-term prospects for conflict mitigation. The opposite of a "to do" list, is a "don't do" list. For example, if the problem confronting a policymaker is postelection violence, it is usually not productive to blame or investigate (or worse, incarcerate) the losing candidate, unless there is immediate evidence of malfeasance. If the police are holding a suspect in custody as part of an effort to reduce violence, it is counterproductive to kill that suspect (especially on Al Jazeera television, as in the case of Muhammad Yusuf). So, too, is trying to imprison an imam who is leading Eid prayers when violence occurs. So, too, is setting up tribunals that are not seen to be free from executive interference. Even using a former head of state to mediate a conflict (e.g., recruiting Obasanjo to mediate in Jos) can be counterproductive if policymakers fail to recognize that the public sees that figure as biased.

Confidence-building measures are often a matter of political wisdom and leadership. Thus, if a state polity (or indeed the entire country) is split along partisan lines, the wise leader will seek to reach out and build bridges to the other side. The use of leadership symbols, often magnified in the media, can be positive if handled well. The use of intermediaries, if seen to be balanced and fair, can be productive. (The use of retired leaders who are known to be social bridge builders is often a wise step.) In short, leaders must step up to the crisis and exert leadership in a broad sense.

The attempt in fall 2011 to set up a "rainbow coalition" of stakeholders in Plateau State by Governor Jang was a step in the right direction. Sometimes, the use of international observers and/or mediators can be positive, because it draws attention to the fact that the international community is watching events unfold. Clear and legitimate civilian control of the police and military is also a crucial step in calming, rather than inflaming, situations. Indeed, it is a top priority in strategic policy thinking to ensure that the police and military leadership are seen to be professional and neutral.

All of these confidence-building measures are a means of allowing time for longer-term policies and strategies to emerge that can get at root causes of disaffection and try to build national unity in a proactive way. Obviously, given the history of violent conflict in Nigeria, it would be helpful if such contingency options were developed prior to the outbreak of turmoil. Even more important is to anticipate the structural barriers to action, especially those at the constitutional level and try to resolve these matters in a forward-looking, preemptive manner.

Longer-Term Policies and Strategies for Conflict Mitigation

Medium-term conflict mitigation policies in Nigeria should aim to extend over the next four or five years, that is, up to and beyond the general election in April 2015. Longer-term policies should extend over the next nine or ten years and beyond, that is, up to the "Vision 20/20" target of the PDP to move Nigeria into the ranks of the top twenty global economies by 2020. For economic targets to be met, including providing electric power throughout the federation, violent conflict must be reduced in a way that reinforces national unity.

To contextualize the longer-term policies, it is useful to note that most strategic thinking is based on scenario planning. The intention of strategic planners is not to predict but to anticipate the range of possibilities so that decision makers can develop lateral vision and anticipate events. Usually, such possibilities may be couched in lay terms such as "the good, the bad, and the ugly."

In the context of Nigeria's current conflicts and enduring quest for national unity, it might be useful to sketch a few such scenarios in reverse order: the ugly ("The Road to Juba"),[3] the bad ("The Long Goodbye"),[4] and the good ("Muddling Through"). In all cases, external as well as internal factors are in play. The key to scenario planning is to identify factors, create a plausible narrative, and use "imagination and discipline." It is beyond the scope of this monograph to develop such scenarios, but a few possibilities might concentrate the thinking of strategic planners.

An Ugly Scenario: The Road to Juba

It is 2014 and the north-south split is widening in the run-up to the 2015 elections. The president has managed to get a constitutional amendment passed that allows for a seven-year presidential term, and although he has promised not to run again, there is widespread speculation that he will do so. The north and southeast both want the top slot. The price of oil has recovered, and the Excess Crude Account, depleted during the 2011 elections, is once again full. Money is flowing throughout the system (mainly

---

3   The Shell Oil worst-case scenario for Nigeria was called "The Road to Kinshasa," referring to a failed, but not a split, state. See Vincent Cable, *Nigerian Scenarios, 1996–2010* (Abuja: Shell Oil, 1996). Changing the reference to Sudan would emphasize the thirty-year war, the final split, and the continuing disputes over oil-producing areas.

4   This title is taken from one of the scenarios in Daniel Yergin and Thane Gustafson, *Russia 2010: And What It Means for the World* (Cambridge Energy Research Associates, 1995).

Conclusions 143

at the top), although there is still no electricity and the roads are deteriorating. Grassroots expectations go up temporarily, then fall precipitously.[5]

Meanwhile, the educated/professional class in the north is saying that enough is enough, and is no longer fully committed to "the Nigeria project." Southern voices are calling for a Sovereign National Conference, although the Movement for the Actualization of the Sovereign State of Biafra (MASSOB) wants a separate state of Biafra, the Movement for the Emancipation of the Niger Delta (MEND) wants an Ijaw state, and the Oodua (Oduduwa) People's Congress (OPC) wants a Yoruba state. The minorities in the Middle Belt want to break from the north, and Borno wants to reclaim its sovereignty. Kano and Sokoto begin to refer to the precolonial civil war of the 1890s when the commercial capital rejected the leadership of the Caliphate. Each of the thirty-six states begins to make contingency plans for its own survival in case of a breakup of the federation. Zamfara rejects ties with Sokoto. Jigawa rejects ties with Kano. Yobe rejects ties with Borno. In the Delta, there is fierce fighting between youth from Ijaw, Ogoni, and Itsekiri factions, each of which is trying to pre-position itself for access to oil in case of a breakup.

But the usual ethnoregional factors turn out to be less important than the grassroots uprising during the "Nigerian Spring" in the fall of 2014. This insurrection does not impact Abuja, which becomes an enclave of comparative calm thanks to its protection by the military, but the Nigerian Spring does impact the state capitals throughout the federation. Jos is in turmoil. Boko Haram has gained widespread legitimacy because of its opposition to corrupt elites, and has taken over Maiduguri. Kaduna has become a no-go zone of gang warfare. Kano is taken over by a new Islamic faction calling for a Greater Sudanic Caliphate, based in Kano. A grassroots movement demanding a Jukun state gathers steam in the northeast. In the southwest, Lagos and Ibadan merge into a single conurbation along what comes to be called "the Jesus Highway." The southeast, caught up in its Biafran fervor, cannot agree on leadership, and local youth gangs take to kidnapping what remains of the wealthy elite, although by this time most southern flight capital has gone to the United States and northern flight capital has gone to Dubai.

The international community has lost interest in Nigeria because of an intense inward-looking predisposition stemming from the continuing economic recession. Greece has defaulted and the Eurozone is in disar-

---

5   For a classic discussion of rebellion caused by dashed expectations, see Ted Robert Gurr, *Why Men Rebel* (Princeton, NJ: Princeton University Press, 1970).

ray. The budget cuts in Britain have failed to revive the economy and all concessionary aid has been cut. New oil sand deposits in Canada come on stream in 2014 and free North America from its dependence on Nigerian oil. Russian gas is now supplying Europe.

The Nigerian military steps in, but internal factions begin to erupt, especially after some targeted assassinations of key military leaders, in failed attempted coups. Finally, the military leaders decide to split the country along north-south lines. Thus begins the thirty-year civil war in Nigeria over who gets what in terms of land and resources. Grassroots factions reject all of the previous leaders, many of whom flee the country. The NIPSS report, which had tried to look for ways of holding the country together, came out in 2013 but never made it into the public domain.[6]

A Bad Scenario: The Long Goodbye

The Sovereign National Conference of June 2014 breaks up in disarray over the question of sovereignty regarding subsoil minerals (including oil). The newly formed Niger Delta People's Congress (NDPC) declares the independence of the new sovereign state of "Niger Delta" on October 1, 2014. There is little resistance from the rest of the country, which is unwilling or unable to use force to curtail the separation. The southwest is doing well on its own. The north has had enough of the failed Nigeria project and has been promised development aid by the Saudis. The military and federal civil servants begin to return to their home states. There is no large-scale or overt violence, just a long goodbye, as each section of the country turns inward and struggles to survive in the new environment.

The international community recognizes Niger Delta. Commercial interests begin to invest heavily. The Chinese build a first-rate transpor-

---

6   In 2005, there were reports in the Nigerian media that the U.S. government had predicted the collapse of Nigeria by 2015. Given the instability during 2011 (and thereafter) in Nigeria, the U.S. ambassador felt compelled to deny that such a prediction was made by the U.S. government. See "U.S. Govt Never Said Nigeria Will Break Up by 2015—Envoy," *Vanguard*, February 2, 2012: "Ambassador of the United States of America to Nigeria, Mr. Terence McCulley has said his country never predicted that Nigeria would break up by 2015 as earlier reported. The envoy who was in Ibadan Thursday explained further that the prediction was done by a private agency that carried out a survey and not the US government as claimed by the report. He said the US government considered Nigeria as a strategic partner in Africa adding that the role that Nigeria plays in peace keeping operations in the continent was very vital. Describing the violent activities of Boko Haram sect as unfortunate, he said he was optimistic that it would soon be resolved by the combined efforts of both Christian and Muslim youth to solve the problem. To him, the issue of the Boko Haram menace could be attributed to political rivalry between the north and the south stating that his country was playing a major role in checking the excesses of the sect, noting further that with the sending of bomb technicians to Nigeria, it was indicative of the robust relationship between the two countries. . . . He continued saying 'Nigeria is also a country of diverse faiths, and Nigeria also draws its strength from this diversity. In spite of this—perhaps because of it—some people seek to exploit religious differences in Nigeria.'"

tation infrastructure in the state. The major oil companies negotiate new deals for offshore drilling rights. At the grassroots level, life goes on as usual, with occasional demands for a bigger share of the oil wealth. The north begins to retrogress on all the standard measures of development, including GDP per capita.

A Good Scenario: Muddling Through

Despite the challenges, wiser heads prevail and the unity of the country is preserved. Conflict mitigation approaches are developed and grievances are dealt with in a politically sensitive manner. The Army and police are retrained to be part of the solution. The SSS, broken up and reformed as the "Federal Bureau of Investigation," becomes a model of effectiveness admired throughout the developing world. Local government spearheads the development of local communities, replacing the previous model of top-down, trickle-down development. The international community is impressed and provides increased concessionary aid, especially in rural development, urban jobs programs, and universal primary education. Political elections are regulated by the new INEC reforms. The NIPSS report, which came out in 2013, was fully implemented.

Most important, the gravity of the challenges encountered in 2011 has impelled the government to undertake the hard choices that had long been put off:

- INEC reforms have been undertaken in the areas of campaign reforms and appointment of resident electoral commissioners

- The gap between grassroots citizens and the upper levels of the political economy has been addressed through devolution of more responsibilities to the local authority governments

- Job creation and youth employment have been given a high priority through the introduction of training programs and a strategic decision to refocus investment capital

- Educational reforms have included the implementation of universal primary education using indigenous languages where possible, with transitions to English at higher levels

- Links to the Koranic schools have been established by schools of education in all major northern federal universities

- Religious knowledge courses have been established in all K-12 schools, with local parental input welcomed

- The education of herders has been enhanced, and the herders themselves have been given due consideration regarding grazing trails

- The interfaith councils at all levels have been given full political support
- The role of traditional rulers has been recognized, especially in the realm of conflict mitigation
- The security forces have been completely overhauled to allow more local input
- The National Youth Service Corps (NYSC) has been given a renewed mandate and new leadership, with better cross-cultural training and full guarantees of personal security in cross-state assignments
- The indigene-nonindigene issue has been resolved quickly by the Supreme Court, with specified state residential codes replacing the former ethnic codes for indigene status
- Panels of highly respected individuals have been set up to deal with root causes of intercommunal violence in hot spots
- The most egregious aspects of governmental entitlement spending and other leadership perks have been brought under control
- Civic education courses have been introduced at all K-12 levels and have been designed to promote a realistic commitment to democratic federalism and national unity

The Challenges of Implementation

The chief recommendations offered in this monograph should by now be clear: engage grassroots communities in development and participation; develop conflict mitigation practices at all levels; manage religious and political dissent in a sensitive manner; train and deploy police and military resources in domestic crisis management; focus on youth education and employment; create a truly independent judiciary; regulate campaign finances; and strengthen leadership capabilities at all levels.

We are, however, left with one central question: How to implement such long-term policies, given the realities of contemporary Nigerian political and economic life?

The democratic system in Nigeria presents a rigorous challenge to creating and implementing policies. The National Assembly is cumbersome at best, even with executive prodding, as seen in the national election law reforms of 2010. The need for approval from the National Assembly and other constitutional checks and balances are intended to slow things down so that full deliberation may occur. Yet, they are not well suited to crisis situations, where executive leadership is imperative.

Many of the recommendations offered in this monograph do require legislative approval, and some may require constitutional interpretation. As noted previously, the president has recommended *direct funding* from the federal government to local government authorities, but this reform is tied up with constitutional amendments regarding extending presidential terms. The larger question is how to strengthen local government in a three-tier federation without creating total dependency on the center.

An issue of pressing concern is the role of the NYSC. This is a prime example of a mechanism intended to foster national unity and enable students to give back to the nation. The program is in jeopardy at present because of concerns that participants may be exposed to violence and conflict. This program should be reinvented to meet its original goals, and extend such goals into the domain of conflict mitigation. Appropriate reinvention will require executive and legislative attention.

The president set up the Lemu panel to examine postelection violence and the Galtimari committee to focus on Boko Haram. But if the recommendations of reports issued by such groups are to be implemented, the president must take the lead. He must ensure that reports received by the executive are digested, that the government then produces white papers outlining implementation, and that implementation actually occurs. The question is whether the president can "govern"[7] in the sense of producing constructive outcomes.

The judiciary will play a key role in unlocking the standoff on two key issues tackled in this monograph: governors' roles in public security in their states; and rights of mobility, residence, and "indigene" lands. The judiciary also plays a pivotal role in adjudicating election petitions. The crucial issues of the 2011 election appeals process have been settled by the Supreme Court. Yet, how the federal government, INEC, Muhammadu Buhari, and the CPC will respond to this process will be crucial to the stability of Nigeria.

Civil society organizations (CSOs) also have a role to play in national unity. Often, they have been single-issue organizations (focusing, for instance, on electoral practices). Such organizations are usually located in the south or in Abuja. The extension of such organizations to the north, or the creation of partnerships between such organizations and potential northern counterparts, would add to the pressure for reforms and boost their chances of being implemented. The paradigm of The Imam and

---

7   Prior to the 2011 election, a southern presidential candidate representing a small party is reported to have said: "The president can win, but can he govern?"

the Pastor and other conflict resolution CSOs should be evaluated and extended to other areas of the country.

The role of quasi-governmental institutions such as NIREC should be revisited at both the national and state levels. The roles of the sultan and other religious leaders need to be strengthened to withstand grass-roots challenges in the religious domains. The management of religious symbols is extremely important and will need the full cooperation of the religious establishment on both sides of the Muslim-Christian divide.

The role of NIPSS needs to be reassessed to allow it to conduct more than midcareer training, although such training is crucial to the national endeavor. NIPSS's focus on pluralism and national unity, drawing on Nigerian and other national experiences, could be expanded into an ongoing research and consultancy effort and facilitation of conflict mediation processes.

These institutional changes are likely to prove helpful, but the central issue of implementation is political will at the highest levels. If issues of implementation are handed off to the military, even if the military has been well trained for such challenges, then other options may be closed off. Civilian control of the military is essential if the issues highlighted in this monograph are to be engaged by a broader spectrum of actors.

The role of the international community in implementation is important, both at the government-to-government level (such as the U.S.-Nigeria Binational Commission) and through NGOs. The international community is evidently interested in spurring Nigeria's economic development, but international actors need to devote more attention to conflict management, which has become the necessary (but not sufficient) condition for economic growth. The role of international observers during election periods should be increased to cover a longer period, stretching from pre-election campaigning to election day and through to postelection processes.

The question of British and U.S. security and military assistance and training for Nigeria is sensitive, but it is also a matter of public record and will be closely watched by all sides in Nigeria. According to one account:

> The Nigerian government has worked to counter militant threats by stepping up coordination with foreign intelligence agencies. British ambassador Andrew Lloyd was in Nigeria on Sept. 20 to follow up on an earlier discussion between British Prime Minister David Cameron and Nigerian officials on the creation of an intelligence fusion center in the country. Addi-

tionally, the United States is providing training and material to set up a 200-strong Nigerian special operations unit designated for counterterrorism purposes. Western governments are concerned about Boko Haram's growing aggressiveness as well as reports about possible exchanges between the Islamist sect and al Qaeda in the Islamic Magreb and al Shabaab, an Islamist military organization based in Somalia. Apart from a few Nigerian radicals who have traveled to cities in the Sahel, however, there has been no evidence to substantiate these reports.[8]

While U.S. counterinsurgency training normally occurs in Italy, not in Nigeria, if such training develops more fully in 2012, it will certainly be more obvious to the Nigerian media. How the United States manages the symbolism of cooperation with the Nigerian military, especially given the regional security provisions of the Binational Commission and the larger policy mandate to reach out to the hearts and minds of the international Muslim community, remains to be seen.

What was clear at the end of 2011 was that the level of organized violence in the northeast (and other parts of the country) had increased dramatically. This is reflected in the rising level of attention shown by the international media. In November 2011, for instance, Al Jazeera ran half-hour segments on Boko Haram, and the *New York Times* ran daily back-page stories after the early November bombings. The level of sophistication of the bombings and their devastating effect has prompted expressions of concern from the secretary general of the United Nations, not to mention security services worldwide. The international aspects of Nigeria's relations with its West African neighbors have also captured some international attention since the collapse of the Gaddafi regime and the possibility that Libyan weapons might pour into West Africa.[9]

Yet, the international community must not allow its concerns about al Qaeda in the Islamic Maghreb and/or al Shabab to dominate its relations with Nigeria. The political blowback from elements of the Nigerian polity against the Jonathan administration may be inevitable as military

8 See "Nigeria: Boko Haram's Unlikely Threat," *Stratfor*, September 27, 2011, at the *Stratfor* website, www.stratfor.com.

9 See "Boko Haram: FG Worried over Inflow of Libyan Weapons," *Thisday*, November 30, 2011: "Federal Government has expressed concern over lack of Nigerian military presence near its border with Republic of Niger alleged to be the major route through which groups like Boko Haram smuggle Libyan weapons into the country." The defense minister, Haliru Mohammed Bello, responded, saying that the federal government was planning "defence pacts and cooperation with neighbouring states of Niger, Mali, Mauritania and Central African Republic to stop the proliferation of Libyan weapons in their countries." Bello also announced the establishment of a Nigerian defense attaché for Niger Republic.

cooperation with Western countries becomes more visible. According to a December 2011 blog by Tondu Aonduna, entitled "Boko Haram and America's Offer of 'Military Cooperation' with Nigeria":[10]

> At the best of times, media reports attesting to the presence of foreign military units in a national jurisdiction ought to raise great concern and even dismay. The alleged recommendation of "military assistance" (to the Jonathan regime) about a week ago by a committee of America's House of Representatives, allegedly to help it fight the Boko Haram terrorist threat, should be scrutinized openly and not shrouded in secrecy.
>
> Overwhelmed by the daunting challenges that the nation is confronted with, President Jonathan and his lackluster regime are increasingly relying on repressive and other actions that are bound to cause further strife and alienation amongst the long-suffering people of our country. . . . The country must now grapple with a potentially destabilizing action as indicated in the disturbing report (by Sahara Reporters, among other news organizations), about three weeks ago that American "special forces," on the orders of the increasingly unpopular Obama administration, have been deployed in northern Nigeria, supposedly to fight the Islamic sect bearing the curious sobriquet of Boko Haram. The American embassy in Nigeria has offered a tepid and unconvincing denial that their country's so-called special forces have been sent to this country. Interestingly, the Jonathan regime has apparently not made any statement denying the alleged deployment.[11]

The author of the above article, who clearly has a northern perspective, goes on to criticize Jonathan for

> the infantile but dangerous decision to have more American mercenaries on Nigerian soil at this point in our history. It is bewildering that despite the bombs that MEND has so far exploded (from the Niger-Delta to Lagos and Abuja), . . . Jonathan persists in vainly trying to absolve the self-styled military group. With Boko Haram, he is at his primordial and revanchist best. The president has effectively refused serious dialogue as an option to handle the Boko Haram imbroglio. . . . What makes Jonathan believe that Nigerians in the affected areas will roll out

---

10   See Tondu Aonduna, "Boko Haram and America's Offer of 'Military Cooperation' with Nigeria," *Gamji.com*, December 12, 2011, http://www.gamji.com/article9000/NEWS9544.htm.

11   Ibid.

the red carpet for American mercenaries and their political masters with a human rights track record that is chillingly dismal?[12]

(The above sentiments became more pronounced in January 2012,
when the Binational Commission met to discuss regional security in the
north. Even prominent Nigerian politicians joined in the criticism of the
government or at least raised questions as to why the Nigerian government was so weak as to need such outside help.)

In short, the unintended consequences of U.S. security engagement
in Nigeria may put the United States directly in the middle of Nigerian
politics—in the middle, indeed, of the impassioned debate about whether
the most dangerous of the existential threats to the country comes from
extremists in the far north or from extremists in the south-south. This
development may well cause serious headaches for the professional diplomats in Abuja. Warnings about U.S. involvement are even coming from
widely respected U.S. academics such as Jean Herskovits.[13]

The U.S. Commission on International Religious Freedom (USCIRF)
has set an example of how religious freedom and religious tensions can be
monitored and, it is to be hoped, ameliorated, through cooperation with
Nigerian counterparts. The danger of U.S. involvement on the religious
front, however, is the possibility that extraneous religious influences will
intrude on and distort USCIRF's efforts to adopt a neutral approach to
Muslim-Christian relations in Nigeria.

---

12   Ibid.

13   See Jean Herskovits, "Boko Haram Is Not the Problem," *Sahara Reporters,* January 3, 2012: "The
     United States must not be drawn into a Nigerian 'war on terror'—rhetorical or real—that would
     make us appear biased toward a Christian president. Getting involved in an escalating sectar-
     ian conflict that threatens the country's unity could turn Nigerian Muslims against America
     without addressing any of the underlying problems that are fueling instability and sectarian
     strife in Nigeria. . . . In late November, a subcommittee of the House Committee on Homeland
     Security issued a report with the provocative title: 'Boko Haram: Emerging Threat to the U.S.
     Homeland.' The report makes no such case, but nevertheless proposed that the organization
     be added to America's list of foreign terrorist organizations. The State Department's Africa Bu-
     reau disagrees, but pressure from Congress and several government agencies is mounting. . . .
     Many Nigerians already believe that the United States unconditionally supports Mr. Jonathan's
     government, despite its failings. They believe this because Washington praised the April elec-
     tions that international observers found credible, but that many Nigerians, especially in the
     north, did not. Likewise, Washington's financial support for Nigeria's security forces, despite
     their documented human rights abuses, further inflames Muslim Nigerians in the north. . . .
     The United States should not allow itself to be drawn into this quicksand by focusing on Boko
     Haram alone. Washington is already seen by many northern Muslims—including a large num-
     ber of longtime admirers of America—as biased toward a Christian president from the south.
     The United States must work to avoid a self-fulfilling prophecy that makes us into their enemy.
     Placing Boko Haram on the foreign terrorist list would cement such views and make more Ni-
     gerians fear and distrust America."

Full-strength diplomacy by the United States and other major play-
ers on the international stage is the path to sensible policy alternatives.
Such diplomacy includes making sure that all professional positions are
filled with qualified persons, and that in a country as large and diverse as
Nigeria, there is a U.S. regional presence throughout the country. There
is a critical need for professional capacity building, including language
skills in Hausa (and Arabic). Like Nigerians, international actors should
aim to do no harm.[14] Yet, lacking the capacity to reach out to the far
north—due to limited resources, minimal consular presence, and security restrictions—the international community is flying blind. The same
disconnect that characterizes the Nigerian polity in its relationships
with the grassroots communities also characterizes, for the most part,
the international community.

Conflict Resolution and National Unity in Nigeria

Managing or mitigating the conflicts currently disrupting Nigeria will
be a long-term challenge. Whatever short-term fixes are adopted to curb
the violence (fixes that are often implemented with policies and tools ill
equipped for the task), the more pressing issue is how to remediate such
violence without provoking greater political or religious backlash. The
ultimate challenge is how to ensure the unity of Nigeria. The "Nigeria
project" is an underlying priority for its citizens and for the world. Accom-
plishing that project will take the combined efforts of Nigerians and all
who wish Nigeria well. The long-term experience of university scholars,
think tanks, and former diplomats focusing on conflict resolution methods and processes are valuable resources that should not only be brought
to the mediation table but also injected into strategic planning. There are
many deadly worst-case scenarios waiting to happen, but there is also a
range of brighter alternatives.

There is a Hausa proverb that can be loosely rendered as "God helps
those who help themselves" (*Allah ya ce, "Tashi in taimakeka"*).[15] It applies
to the destinies not only of individuals but also of nations. Nigeria's destiny as a strong, unified, democratic country in the community of nations,
capable of handling the inevitable challenges of political elections and
religious diversity, is a narrative waiting to be written.

---

14   For example, while placing Boko Haram on a U.S. terrorist watch list might send a symbolic
      message of support to the Nigerian government, it could also have the unintended effect of
      reinforcing the group's "martyr" status at the grassroots level.

15   Literally, "God says, 'Get up and I will help you.'"

Appendices

Appendix A: Maps

These eight maps illustrate the religious, cultural, geographic, and political contexts for this monograph. They include the Islamic patterns in Africa and northern Nigeria, the unification of Northern and Southern Nigeria in 1914, ethnic distribution patterns, the contemporary thirty-six-state federation, the twelve shari'a states in the far north (all of which voted for Buhari), and the Lake Chad Basin, which is the original location for the Boko Haram movement and the area where Nigerian borders were closed by state of emergency in December 2011.

1. Islam in Africa
2. The Sokoto Caliphate, Mid-nineteenth Century
3. Unification of Nigeria, 1914
4. Ethnic Distribution in Nigeria
5. Contemporary Nigeria: Thirty-six States
6. Nigerian States with Shari'a Law, 2000
7. Presidential Election Results, 2011
8. Lake Chad Basin

Sources

Maps 1–6 are from John N. Paden, *Muslim Civic Cultures and Conflict Resolution: The Challenge of Democratic Federalism in Nigeria* (Washington, DC: Brookings Institution Press, 2005). Map 7 is based on table 3 in chapter 1 of this monograph. Map 8 is from Tijjani Muhammad-Bande, "Multilateral Water Organisations and Nigeria's National Interest: Lake Chad Basin Commission and Niger Basin Authority," in Attahiru M. Jega and Jacqueline W. Farris, eds., *Nigeria at Fifty: Contributions to Peace, Democracy and Development* (Abuja: Shehu Musa Yar'Adua Foundation, 2010).

Map 1. Islam in Africa

lap 2. The Sokoto Caliphate, Mid-nineteenth Century

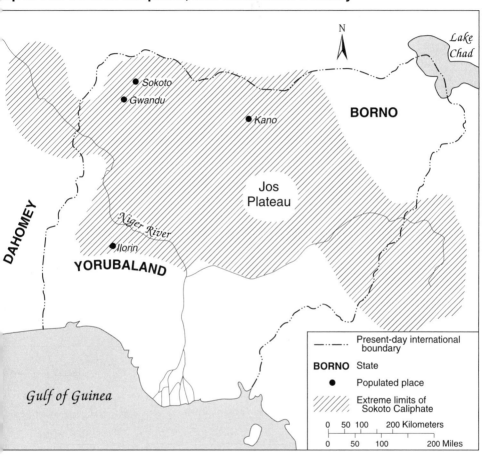

Map 3. Unification of Nigeria, 1914

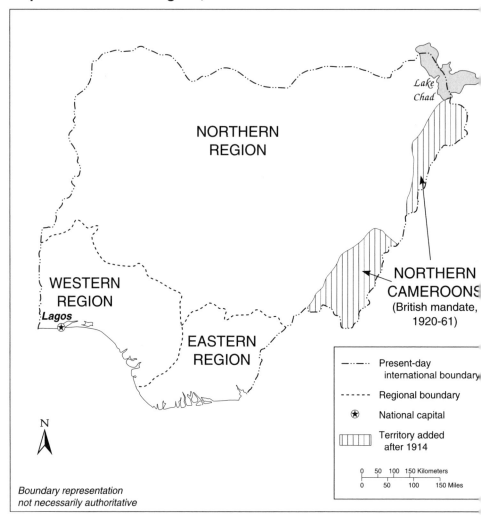

NORTHERN
REGION

*Lake
Chad*

NORTHERN
CAMEROONS
(British mandate,
1920-61)

WESTERN
REGION

Lagos

EASTERN
REGION

N

—··—·· Present-day
          international boundary

------ Regional boundary

⊛ National capital

Territory added
after 1914

0   50   100 150 Kilometers
0   50   100   150 Miles

*Boundary representation
not necessarily authoritative*

Map 4. Ethnic Distribution in Nigeria

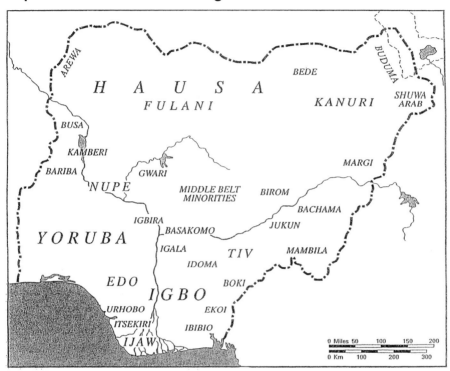

Map 5. Contemporary Nigeria: Thirty-six States

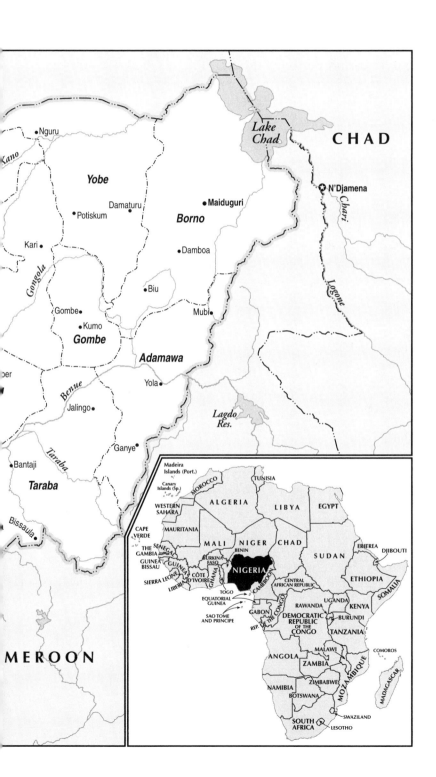

Map 6. Nigerian States with Sharia' Law, 2000–Present

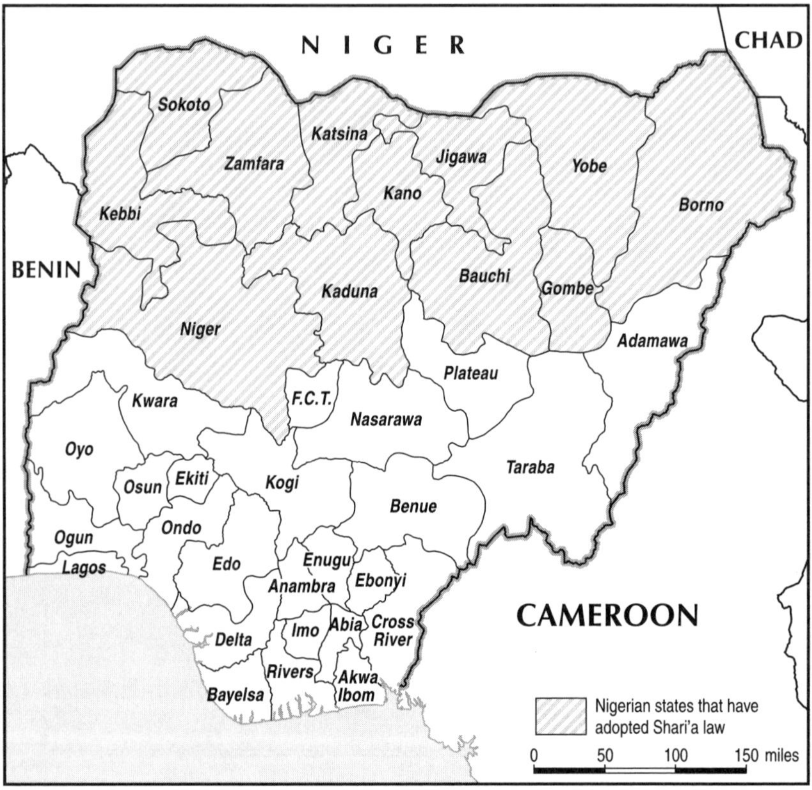

Map 7. Presidential Election Results, 2011

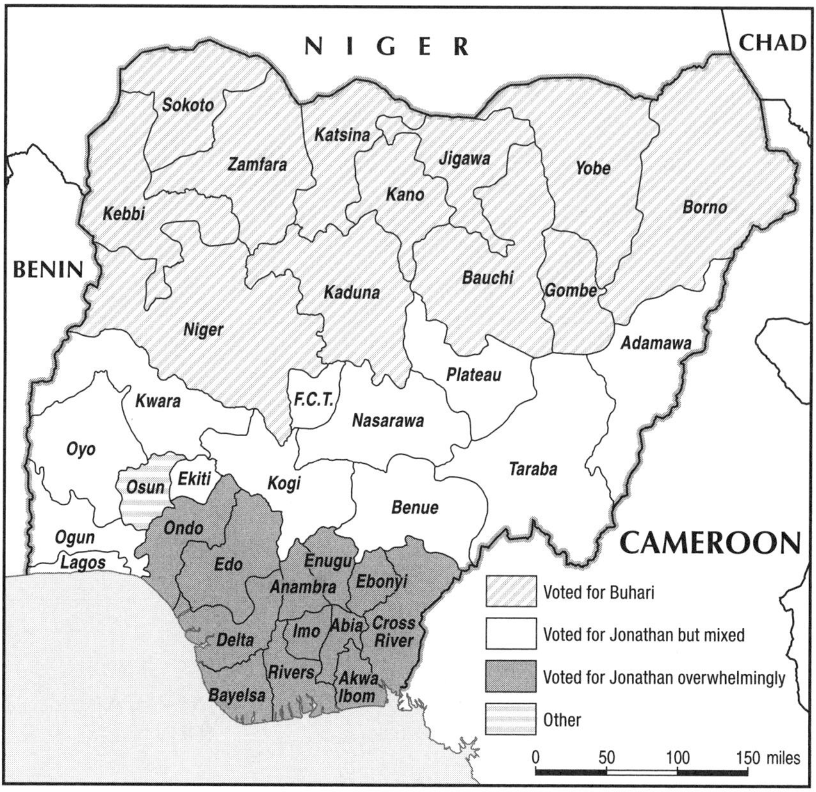

Map showing Nigerian states with election results legend:
- Voted for Buhari
- Voted for Jonathan but mixed
- Voted for Jonathan overwhelmingly
- Other

Scale: 0   50   100   150 miles

Map 8. Lake Chad Basin

Appendix B: Federal Character Patterns (November 2011)

Section 14 of the 1999 Constitution states: "The composition of the Government of the Federation or any of its agencies and the conduct of its affairs shall be carried out in such a manner as to reflect the federal character of Nigeria and the need to promote national unity, and also to command national loyalty, thereby ensuring that there shall be no pre-dominance of persons from a few ethnic or other sectional groups in that Government or in any of its agencies."

The five tables below suggest that this constitutional provision is being observed. Not all appointments are of equal political weight, of course, and not all states are of equal population weight. Nonetheless, overall, there is a clear indication of intent to follow the federal character guidelines. (Further analysis would need to focus on the power ministries, rather than just the number of cabinet ministers, which gives equal weight to the secondary ministries.)

A rank ordering of *zones* would need to be corrected for the fact that the southeast has five states and the northwest has seven. Even so, the rank order of zones is illustrative of the strength of the south-south and the relative weakness of the northeast in terms of representation: northwest, 16; south-south, 16; north central, 14; southeast, 13; southwest, 12; and northeast, 8.

B.1. Federal Legislative and Judicial Leaders

Zone	State	Position	Name
Southeast	(3)		
	Enugu	Deputy Senate President	Senator Ike Ekweremadu
	Imo	Deputy Speaker, House	Chief Emeka Ihedioha
	Ebonyi	Secretary, Federal Government	Senator Anyim Pius Anyim
South-South	(1)		
	Cross River	Senate Majority Leader	Senator Victor Ndoma-Egba
Southwest	(1)		
	Oyo	House Majority Leader	Hon. Mulikat Adeola Akande
North Central	(2)		
	Benue	Senate President	Senator David Mark
	Niger	President, Court of Appeal	Justice Dalhatu Adamu
Northeast	(0)		
Northwest	(2)		
	Jigawa	Chief Justice	Justice Dahiru Musdapher
	Sokoto	Speaker, House of Representatives	Alhaji Aminu Tambuwal

Total: 9 major legislative and judicial positions

B.2. Federal Ministers

Zone	State	Ministry	Name
Southeast	(4)		
	Abia	Labour	Barrister Emeka Wogu
	Anambra	Aviation	Mrs. Stella Oduah-Ogiemwonyi
	Ebonyi	Health	Professor Onyebuchi Chukwu
	Enugu	Power	Professor Barth Nnaji
South-South	(7)		
	Akwa Ibom	Science & Technology	Professor Ita Okon Basse Ewa
	Bayelsa	Petroleum	Mrs. Diezani Alison-Madueke
	Delta	Niger Delta Affairs	Elder Godsday Orubebe
	Edo	Works	Arch. Mike Onolememen
	Delta	Finance & Economy	Dr. Ngozi Okonjo-Oweala
	Cross-River	Culture & Tourism	Edem Duke
	Rivers	Lands & Housing	Ama Pepple
Southwest	(5)		
	Ekiti	Police Affairs	Navy Capt. Caleb Olubolade (ret.)
	Lagos	Trade & Investment	Mr. Olusegun O. Aganga
	Ogun	Foreign Affairs	Amb. Olugbenga Ashiru
	Ondo	Communication Tech.	Omobola Johnson Olubusola
	Ogun	Agriculture & Natural Resources	Akinwunmi Ayo Adesina
North Central	(5)		
	Benue	Interior	Comrade Abba Moro
	Kogi	Attorney General Federation/Justice	Mr. Mohammed B. Adoke
	Kwara	Youth Development	Mal. Bolaji Abdullahi
	Nasarawa	Information & Communication	Mr. Labaran Maku
	Plateau	Water Resources	Sarah Reng Ochekpe
Northeast	(3)		
	Adamawa	Women Affairs	Hajia Zainab Maina
	Bauchi	Federal Capital Territory	Senator Bala Mohammed
	Gombe	Transport	Senator Idris A. Umar
Northwest	(6)		
	Sokoto	Sports	Alhaji Yusuf Suleiman*
	Jigawa	Education	Professor Ruqayatu Rufai
	Kaduna	Environment	Hadiza Ibrahim Mailafia
	Kano	National Planning	Dr. Shamsudeen Usman
	Katsina	Mines & Steel Development	Arch. Mohammed Musa Sada
	Kebbi	Defence	Dr. Bello Mohammed

Total: 30 federal ministers

* Subsequently resigned

B.3. Federal Ministers of State

Zone	State	Ministry	Name
Southeast			
	Imo	Foreign Affairs	Professor Viola Onwuliri
South-South			
	Rivers	Education	Nyesom Wike
Southwest			
	Osun	Defence	Erelu Olusola Obada
	Oyo	Federal Capital Territory	Mrs. Olajumoke Akinjide
North Central			
	Niger	Niger Delta Affairs	Hajia Zainab Ibrahim Kuchi
	Benue	Trade & Investment	Dr. Samuel Ioraer Ortom
Northeast			
	Borno	Agriculture & Natural Resources	Alhaji Bukar Tijani
	Yobe	Finance	Dr. Yerima Lawal Ngama
	Bauchi	Health	Dr. Mohammed Pate
Northwest			
	Zamfara	Works	Ambassador Bashir Yuguda
	Jigawa	Foreign Affairs	Nurudeen Mohammed
Total: 11 ministers of state			

166   Appendix B

B.4. Other Top Federal Executive Positions

Zone	State	Position	Name
Southeast	(5)		
	Abia	Chief of Army Staff	Lt. General Onyeabo Azubuike Ihejirika
	Abia	Controller General, Immigration	Mrs. Rosemary Chinyere Uzoma
	Enugu	Secretary, PPPRA	Engineer Goody Chike Egbuji
	?	Chair RMAFC	Mr. Elias N. Mbam
	?	Director, General BPP	Engineer Emeka Eze
South-South	(7)		
	Cross River	Director General , SSS	Mr. Ita Ekpenyong
	Bayelsa	National Security Advisor	General Andrew Azazi
	Delta	Director, DPR	Andrew Obaji
	Edo	Chair, NPA	Chief Anthony Anenih
	Rivers	Chair, ICPC	Mr. Francis Elechi
	Delta	Vice-Chair. NCC	Dr. Eugene Juwah
	Delta	Chair, FIRS	Mrs. Ifueko Omoigui-Okauru
Southwest	(4)		
	Osun	Chief Defence Staff	Air Chief Oluseyi Petinrin
	Ogun	Controller General, Prisons	Mr. Olusola Ogundipe
	Ogun	Secretary, PEF	Mrs. Adefunke Kasali
	Ogun	Director General, BPE	Mrs. Bolande Onagoruwa
North Central	(5)		
	Kwara	Director General, NDLEA	Femi Ajayi
	Kwara	Chief Naval Staff	Vice-Admiral Ola Ibrahim
	Kogi	Managing Director, NNPC	Mr. Austen Oniwon
	Benue	Auditor-General	Mr. Samuel Orkura
	Benue	Chair, EFCC	Mrs. Farida Waziri*
Northeast	(2)		
	Adamawa	Head of Service	Alhaji Isa Bello Sali
	Bauchi	Chair, NAPEP	Alhaji Muktar Tafawa-Balewa
Northwest	(6)		
	Kano	Chief of Air Staff	Air Marshall Mohammed Dikko Umar
	Jigawa	Inspector General Police	Hafiz Abubakar Ringim*
	Katsina	Commandant General, Customs	Alhaji Abdullahi Inde
	Kano	Governor, CBN	Sanusi Lamido Sanusi
	Kano	Secretary, PTDF	Mr. Rabe Darma
	Kebbi	Chair. INEC	Professor Attahiru Jega

Total: 29 top federal executive positions

*Subsequently resigned

B.5. Summary of State Representation at Federal Level*

Zone	State	Legis./ Judicial	Ministers	Ministers of State	Other Top Positions	Total
Southeast		(3)	(4)	(1)	(3+2)	(13)
	1. Abia		1		2	3
	2. Anambra		1			1
	3. Ebonyi	1	1			2
	4. Enugu	1	1		1	3
	5. Imo	1		1		2
South-South		(1)	(7)	(1)	(7)	(16)
	6. Akwa Ibom		1			1
	7. Bayelsa		1		1	2
	8. Cross River	1	1		1	3
	9. Delta		2		3	4
	10. Edo		1		1	2
	11. Rivers		1	1	1	3
Southwest		(1)	(5)	(2)	(4)	(12)
	12. Ekiti		1			1
	13. Lagos		1			1
	14. Ogun		2		2	3
	15. Ondo		1			1
	16. Osun			1	2	3
	17. Oyo	1		1		2
North Central		(2)	(5)	(2)	(5)	(14)
	18. Benue	1	1	1	2	5
	19. Kogi				1	1
	20. Kwara		1		2	3
	21. Nasarawa		1			1
	22. Niger	1	1	1		3
	23. Plateau		1			1
Northeast		(0)	(3)	(3)	(2)	(8)
	24. Adamawa		1		1	2
	25. Bauchi		1	1	1	3
	26. Borno			1		1
	27. Gombe		1			1
	28. Taraba**					0
	29. Yobe			1		1
Northwest		(2)	(6)	(2)	(6)	(16)
	30. Jigawa	1	1	1	1	4
	31. Kaduna		1			1
	32. Kano		1		3	4
	33. Katsina		1		1	2
	34. Kebbi		1		1	2
	35. Sokoto	1	1			2
	36. Zamfara			1		1

* President Jonathan (Bayelsa) and Vice President Sambo (Kaduna) are not included because they were not appointed by the executive branch, even though they are intended to reflect a federal character balance between the north and the south.
** Taraba is the only state not represented. The northeast as a whole has the smallest number of federal character appointees. Borno has only one appointee and Yobe has only one.

Appendix C: Memorandum of Understanding, 2011—NIPSS and GMU

The following is an abbreviated version of a memorandum of understanding signed in 2011 by George Mason University and the National Institute for Policy and Strategic Studies. This agreement establishes the intention to work in cooperation on matters of mutual concern regarding conflict analysis and resolution in Nigeria.

The addendum is an abbreviated version of the original legislative act that established NIPSS in 1979. The framers' intent was to set up a national think tank and training center to address issues of national concern.

A Memorandum of Understanding Concerning the Establishment of Academic Cooperation between National Institute for Policy and Strategic Studies and George Mason University

This Memorandum of Understanding ("MOU"), dated this 14th day of September, 2011, is made by and between National Institute for Policy and Strategic Studies ("NIPSS"), located at P.M.B. 2024 Bukuru, Plateau State, Nigeria, and George Mason University, an educational institution and agency of the Commonwealth of Virginia, located at 4400 University Drive, Fairfax, Virginia, 22030-4444 ("George Mason") (together, the "Parties").

In order to realize a higher level of understanding between the United States and Nigeria, NIPSS and George Mason hereby agree to initiate academic cooperation between the two Parties.

1. **Purpose:** The Purpose of this MOU is to stimulate and to support educational intercultural activities and projects between the United States and Nigeria.

2. **Scope:** NIPSS and the School for Conflict Analysis and Resolution at George Mason agree to explore the possibility of collaborative endeavors in the following areas:

   a) Research and publications
   b) General exchange of information and reports on the ground
   c) Joint task force for seeking funding pertinent to the relationship

d) Exchange of personnel, including, where possible supporting capacity building

3. **Implementation:** Specific collaborations shall be the subject of a separately negotiated agreement . . .

4. **Future Cooperation:** Both Parties expect to continue discussions concerning possible future phases of their work together. This MOU is entirely independent of future cooperation on subsequent phases, which will be separately evaluated and require separate agreements.

5. **Approval:** . . . This and any supplemental agreements must comply with all George Mason University policies, as well as those of relevant accrediting agencies or governmental bodies.

6. **Term and Termination:** This MOU shall continue for three (3) years, at which time the Parties may negotiate a renewal. This MOU may be terminated by either Party without cause upon providing written notice to the other Party no later than six (6) months prior to the date of termination.

7. **Intellectual Property:** The parties will ensure that the intellectual property rights are fully addressed and agreed upon consistent with the existing laws and regulations, prior to the initiation of each academic collaborative activity.

Signed:

Peter N. Stearns, Provost, George Mason University

Andrea Bartoli, Dean, School for Conflict Analysis and Resolution, George Mason University

Tijjani Muhammad-Bande, Acting Director General, National Institute for Policy and Strategic Studies

Addendum

National Institute for Policy and Strategic Studies Act, 1979, Chapter 262, No. 20

"An Act to establish the National Institute for Policy and Strategic Studies to serve as a centre where representatives from all walks of the Nigerian national life could come together by way of workshops, seminars and other action oriented courses, studies and conferences to analyze and exchange views as to long-term national goals . . .

3.   Objectives and functions of the Institute:

(1) The Institute shall serve as a high level centre of reflection, research, and dialogue where academics of intellectual excellence, policy initiators and executors and other citizens with high level of practical experience and wisdom drawn from different sectors of national life in Nigeria would meet to reflect and exchange ideas on the great issues of society, particularly as they relate to Nigeria and Africa, in the context of the dynamics of a constantly changing world.

(2) For purposes of subsection (1) of this section, the Institute is hereby empowered —

(a) to conduct courses for top level policy makers and executors drawn from different sectors of the national policy with a view to expanding their outlook and perspective and stretching their conceptual capacity and qualities of discernment and analysis and thereby helping to improve their overall performance in their different fields of action;

(b) to award certificates of attendance to those who participate in a sufficient and satisfactory manner in any of its courses;

(c) to conduct seminars, workshops and other action-oriented programmes whether on a continuing or ad hoc basis for leaders in the public services (including the armed forces and other disciplined forces), the private sector, political organizations, professional and other groups with a view to promoting and defining, and enhancing appreciation for, long range national plans and objectives;

(d) to identify, encourage, stimulate, assemble, organize and help deploy to the best national advantage the country's intellectual talents and experienced policy analysts who are likely to make positive contributions to the treatment of complex policy problems;

(e) to organize and carry out, on an inter-disciplinary basis in intellectual support of those charges with making and implementing policy for Nigeria, research in depth into the social, economic, political, security, scientific, cultural and other problems facing the country, and to formulate and present, in useable form, the available options of their solution;

(f) to disseminate by way of publication of books, records, reports or otherwise, information about any part of its activities, to the extent deemed justified by the Board in the interest of the nation, and generally as a contribution towards knowledge and for better national and international understanding; and

(g) to promote or undertake any other activity that in the opinion of the Board is calculated to help achieve the purposes of the Institute.

(3) The Institute shall carry out its tasks and responsibilities in an objective, non-partisan manner, independently of any group in the body politic.

(4) The Institute shall establish and maintain a library comprising such books, records, reports and other publications as may be directed by the Board for the advancement of knowledge in the areas of work undertaken by it, for research purposes and for other purposes connected with the functions conferred on the Institute by or pursuant of this Act."

Index

Page numbers in *italic* refer to figures, tables, and maps; page numbers in **bold** refer to biographical profiles.

and Binational Commission, 31
and U.S. military cooperation, 149–151
appointed president, 14
appointed vice president, 14
as "accidental president," 30
death threat from Boko Haram, 43n3
incumbent candidate, 17
postelection personal security of, 115
public image of, 63
state of emergency address, 4–5
Jos. *See* Plateau State, Jos
Judicial Commission of Inquiry report
    on 2011 disturbances in Kaduna,
    23n22
judicial process
    and political elite system, 26
    legitimacy of, 32–36, 39, 111
Junaid, Muhammad, 59
Justice, Development and Peace/Caritas
    Nigeria (JDPC), and election
    monitoring, 25

Kaduna State
    inquiry into 2011 election violence, 23
    Kaduna City, 80n9, 88, 95, 95n50
Kanemi, Abubakar ibn Umar Garbai, el-
    shehu of Borno, **48n13**
Kanemi, Mustafa Amin, el-
    shehu of Borno, **48n14**
Kano State
    Kano City, 80, 80n11, 140
    Maitatsine, 140
Kano, Aminu, 136, 138
Katsina, and predominantly Muslim
    population, 109
Kayode, Adetokunbo, **125n16**, 125–126,
Kukah, Mathew (bishop of Sokoto), on
    national unity, 8

Labour Party, 82
leadership, national, reform, 61–65
legal system
    national civil code, 54
    national criminal code, 54
    shari'a law, 54
    traditional civil code, 54

Lemu panel, 8n13, 21–23, 36–38, 62, 109,
    111, 115, 147

Lemu, Ahmed (Sheikh), **23n2**, 121
local government
    reform, 51–52, 72
    strengthening of, 147
local government areas, 51
Long Goodbye (planning scenario), 144–45

Maiduguri, military buildup in, 41–42
Malu, Victor, 125
Mark, David, **37n49**, 37
    death threat from Boko Haram, 43n3
MASSOB (Movement for the Actualization
    of the Sovereign State of Biafra), in
    planning scenario, 143
media in Nigeria, 20, 32, 43
    and clothing worn by political
    leaders, 63
MEND (Movement for the Emancipation
    of the Niger Delta), 66n41, 143, 150
    in planning scenario, 143
Middle Belt
    and the north, 75
    military officers from, 76, 87
militarization of conflict, 134
military
    and identity politics, 116
    and the Constitution, 123
    assistance, international, 148–52
    force, used in domestic crises, 126–27
    power and legitimacy, 134
    readiness, to manage domestic conflict,
        124–127
    reform, 65–68, 73
    role of, in conflict management, 108
    strategy, 65–68
    training, 117, 125
military-grassroots relationship, 67
military-police relationship, and long-
    term policymaking, 117
"mistake of 1914." *See* north-south amalga-
    mation (1914)
Mohammed, Bello Haliru, **125–26n17**,
    125–26
Momoh, Tony, 34
morality, and political legitimacy, 63
Movement for Sunnah and Jihad. *See* Boko
    Haram
Muddling Through (planning scenario),
    145–46

Muslims. *See also* Christian-Muslim relations
marginalization of, 6–7
younger generation, 78

Nasir el-Rufai, Malam, **36n44**, 34, 36, *137*
National Assembly, 43–44, 44n4
and policy implementation, 146–47
and relations between military and traditional leaders, 68
and security forces legislation, 122–23
elections, 19
National Defence University (Pakistan), 125
national identity and subnational identities, 135
National Institute for Policy and Strategic Studies (NIPSS), 45, 69–71, 69n45, 73
in planning scenario, 144, 145
national integration, and long-term policymaking, 119
national leadership
politics of, 62
reform of, 61–65
National Party of Nigeria (NPN), 109–110
National Police Council (NPC), role of, 124
National Republican Convention (NRC), 110
National Security Adviser (NSA), 127–30. *See also individual NSAs*
national security budget, 6
National Security Organization, precurser of SSS, 128, 130
National Supreme Council of Islamic Affairs (NSCIA), and youth movements, 136
National Television Authority, 25
national unity, 107–132
and economic policy, 142
and generational leadership, 136
and military strategy, 65
as a political goal, 7, 8, 10
based on democratic means, 107
strategic planning, 141
strengthening of, 134
National War College, 125
National Youth Service Corps (NYSC), 146, 147
and long-term policymaking, 118
as targets for election violence, 27
in planning scenario, 146
Native Authority system, police force, 55
Niger Delta
and international business interests, 31
and Jonathan administration, 114
and military strategy, 66
Niger Delta People's Congress, 144
Nigerian Bar Association, and election monitoring, 25
Nigerian Defence Academy, 71, 125
Nigerian Inter-Religious Council (NIREC), 53, 62
and interfaith conflict resolution, 20
and long-term policymaking, 118
and policy implementation, 148
Nigerian Peoples Party (NPP), 110
Nigerian Police Force (NPF). *See* police
Nigerian Supreme Council for Islamic Affairs (NSCIA), 28
nongovernmental organizations, 80, 148
postelection violence research, 24
role in conflict resolution, 38–39, 131
north-south amalgamation (1914), 13, *156*
exploitation by Boko Haram, 112
north-south relations, 43, 64, 107. *See also* Christian-Muslim relations
and military strategy, 66
at grassroots level, 28
Northern Elements Progressive Union (NEPU), 76, 136, 138
Northern Peoples' Congress (NPC), 76, 136
Nothern Governors' Forum, 71

Obama, Barack, on 2011 election, 21
Obasanjo, Olesegun, 14, 14n3, 19n11, 30, 56, 81n11, 125–26n17
and conflict mediation, 94, 94n46, 103
and constitutional reform, 119
and power shift principle, 110
and state of emergency in Plateau State, 83–84
and states of emergency, 71
influence on Jonathan, 30
Ogomudia, Alexander, 125
oil and gas industry, 7, 138–39
Ojukwu, C. Odumegwu, death of, 9–10n22, 65n40

state elections, 82

state government. *See also* governors
  and identity politics, 113
  and violence mitigation policy, 140–41
  budgets, 82
  in Plateau State, 141

state governments
  and the Constitution, 120

State Security Service (SSS)
  and political repression, 128–29, 129–130
  in planning scenario, 145
  monitoring churches and mosques, 129–130

state-federal government relations. *See* intergovernmental relations

states of emergency, and the Constitution, 121–22

strategic planning, reform capacities for, 68–74

Supreme Court, and 2011 election review, 4, 36

teacher training, 59–60

three-tier federal structure, 53, 120

Tinubu, Bola
  and political deal-making, 19–20
  on rule of law, 32–33

Track II diplomacy, 29, 39, 53

traditional leaders, 68
  and ethnoreligious violence, 113
  and grassroots communities, 53
  and political reform, 52–54
  as conflict resolvers, 45, 53
  authority of, 53, 115
  role of, in political reform, 72

Transition Monitoring Group, 25

transportation networks
  and long-term policymaking, 118
  postelection security measures for, 115

U.S. Commission on International Religious Freedom (USCIRF), report on interfaith conflict, 20

U.S.-Nigeria Binational Commission. *See* Binational Commission

UN building (Abuja), bombing of, 42

unemployment, 58

unification of Nigeria. *See* north-south amalgamation (1914)

United States
  and counterinsurgency training, 116
  and election monitoring, 39
  and full-strength diplomacy, 152
  and Nigerian politics, 30–31
  and political symbolism, 63–64
  foreign policy toward Nigeria, 7–8, 67
  in planning scenario, 143–44
  military cooperation with Nigeria, 31, 148–52

Unity Party of Nigeria (UPN), 109–110

universities
  establishment of, 59
  role in conflict resolution, 38

Usman Dan Fodio, 78

Usmanu Danfodio University, 59

Uwais Committee on Electoral Reform, 33n39

Vindication of Rights Group, 80

violence. *See specific types of violence*

violent conflict
  government response to, 107
  organized, 149
  types of, 139

voting behavior, and religious affiliation, 18

Western education, 58, 60

Wuye, James, 79–80n9, 104n64

Yakowa, Patrick, and political symbolism, 64

Yar'adua Foundation, 71

Yar'adua, Umaru, 14–15n6, 31, 36n34, 87, 137

youth gangs. *See* gangs

Yusuf, Luka, 125

Yusuf, Muhammad, killing of, 41, 46, 50, 138, 141

Yusufiyya (cult), in north, 50

About the Author

Dr. John N. Paden is Clarence Robinson Professor of International Studies at George Mason University (GMU), where he reports directly to the provost. He has served on numerous GMU doctoral committees in the School for Conflict Analysis and Resolution (S-CAR), the School of Public Policy (SPP), the Department of Economics, and the Department of Public and International Affairs. He also teaches in the undergraduate Honors College and holds senior synthesis seminars in political science, focusing on globalization and global patterns of political leadership. He was a philosophy major at Occidental College and a Rhodes Scholar at Oxford in philosophy, politics, and economics. He completed a doctorate in politics at Harvard.

Dr. Paden has served as Norman Dwight Harris Professor of International Studies and Director of African Studies at Northwestern University, Professor of Public Administration at Ahmadu Bello University in Zaria, Nigeria, and was the Founding Dean, Faculty of Social and Management Sciences, at Bayero University in Kano, Nigeria. He has worked in the Hausa-speaking Muslim areas of northern Nigeria over the past forty years, and was part of a team that helped plan the new Nigerian federal "unity" capital in Abuja. He has served as an international observer during the Nigerian presidential elections of 1999 (Kaduna), 2003 (Kano), and 2007 (Katsina).

Some of his Nigeria-related books include *Religion and Political Culture in Kano* (winner of the Herskovits Prize); *Ahmadu Bello, Sardauna of Sokoto: Values and Leadership in Nigeria*; *Muslim Civic Cultures and Conflict Resolution: The Challenge of Democratic Federalism in Nigeria*; and *Faith and Politics in Nigeria: Nigeria as a Pivotal State in the Muslim World*. Other African-related books include *The African Experience* (four volumes); *Values, Identities, and National Integration: Empirical Research in Africa*; *Black Africa: A Comparative Handbook*; and *Understanding Black Africa: Data and Analysis of Social Change and Nation Building*.

Dr. Paden served for fifteen years on the executive committee of a Ford Foundation U.S.-China scholars exchange program to help set up African studies in China. He has served on review panels at the United States Institute of Peace and participated in Nigeria working groups at the Council on Foreign Relations and the Center for Strategic and International Studies. Between 2002 and 2006, he was a member of the Brookings Institution task force on U.S. policy toward the Islamic world.

Dr. Paden has worked closely with colleagues at the Usmanu Dan-fodiyo University, Sokoto (Nigeria), especially at the Center for Peace Studies. In 2009, he received an honorary doctorate in humane letters from Occidental College for his contributions to the development of Africa. He lives with his wife in northern Virginia.

About the School for
Conflict Analysis and Resolution

George Mason University is part of the Commonwealth of Virginia higher education system. In forty years, it has grown to 33,320 students, and serves students from 141 nations. Located on Northern Virginia campuses close to Washington, D.C., Mason is widely recognized for its forward-thinking academic programs and is uniquely positioned, institutionally and geographically, to provide rich, wide-reaching access to the nation's professional, intellectual, and cultural treasures within the context of a robust academic experience.

Mason's School for Conflict Analysis and Resolution (S-CAR) was the first program in conflict analysis and resolution in the United States. It is now the largest U.S. conflict resolution program and the only one offering a full complement of academic degrees, including a Bachelor of Arts, Bachelor of Science, Master of Science, Doctor of Philosophy, and five professional development Graduate Certificates. S-CAR operates as the central hub of a global network of programs and projects that align with its mission to expand and integrate the theory, research, and practice of conflict resolution for the promotion of international cooperation and peace.

The School's community includes a worldwide network of scholars, graduate and undergraduate students, alumni, practitioners, and organizations dedicated to advancing the field of conflict resolution and peace work. Many of S-CAR's graduates have become faculty at conflict resolution and peace studies programs at universities across the nation and internationally. Others hold positions of leadership in grassroots and local nongovernmental organizations, as well as in a variety of national government agencies and international organizations such as USAID, OXFAM, CARE, and the World Bank. S-CAR's pioneering faculty continues to develop foundational theoretical frameworks and research methodologies that are referred to widely across the field and in other academic programs.